BIBLE HANDBOOK

BIBLE HANDBOOK

THOMAS NELSON PUBLISHERS
Nashville

© 1993 by Thomas Nelson, Inc.

Published in Nashville, Tennessee, by Thomas Nelson, Inc.

Adapted from *The Layman's Overview of the Bible,* George W. Knight and James R. Edwards, General Editors (Thomas Nelson, 1987), incorporating material from *The New Open Bible* (Thomas Nelson, 1990, 1985, 1983) and the section on the Apocrypha by Thomas G. Oey, Ph.D.

Unless otherwise indicated, Scripture quotations are from the New King James Version of the Bible, © 1979, 1980, 1982, Thomas Nelson, Inc., Publishers, and from the New Revised Standard Version, © 1989, the Division of Christian Education of the National Council of Churches of Christ in the United States of America. Used by permission.

Library of Congress Cataloging-in-Publication Data

Nelson's quick-reference Bible handbook.
    Rev. and enl. ed. of: The layman's overview of the Bible / George W. Knight and James R. Edwards. © 1987.
    ISBN 0-8407-6904-0
    1. Bible—Handbooks, manuals, etc.   I. Knight, George W. (George Wendell), 1940–   Layman's overview of the Bible.
II. Thomas Nelson Publishers.   III. Title: Bible handbook.
BS417.N45   1993
220.6'1—dc20   92–47032
                                                CIP

Printed in the United States of America
1 2 3 4 5 6 7 8 — 00 99 98 97 96 95 94 93

CONTENTS

♦

PART TWO
THE NEW TESTAMENT

PART THREE
THE APOCRYPHA

PART FOUR
EXPLORING THE BIBLE

PREFACE

◆

> *Philip ran to him, and heard him reading the*
> *prophet Isaiah, and said, "Do you understand*
> *what you are reading?"*
> *And he said, "How can I, unless someone*
> *guides me?"*
>
> *—Acts 8:30–31*

MANY people would read the Bible more regularly and profitably if they, like the Ethiopian court official Philip encountered, had someone to guide them. *Nelson's Quick-Reference*™ *Bible Handbook* offers you the undivided attention of a personal guide—in a small book. It is a brief, to-the-point, hand-sized guide to your own reading tour of the Bible. Like the ideal tour guide, it provides just enough background information, along with a generous sprinkling of clues and cues, to make sure that you don't overlook the most important features. Then it backs out of the way so that you experience your reading journey firsthand, without a lot of noisy commentary overloading you with everybody else's opinions.

You can use *Nelson's Quick-Reference*™ *Bible Handbook* any way you want to. One way would be to read the section for the book of the Bible you want to read first. Note the "Keys to" feature, which gives you the briefest overview of the book. It alone orients you regarding what to expect from the book. The timeline* and "Historical Setting" help you imagine a bit of the when and why of the book's writing. "Theological Contribution" and "Special Considerations" point out crucial insights that believers have valued for centuries. The "Survey" corresponds with the full-page chart of the book. Together with the detailed outline, these help you see the main parts of the book and how they fit together into a whole.

When you've read the *Handbook* section, you're oriented with a practical map for your own exploration of the Bible book. As you read through the book, keep the *Handbook* close by. The book chart and outline will continue to guide you.

Besides this full treatment of the Bible's sixty-six books, the *Handbook* also surveys the books of the Apocrypha more briefly in Part Three. And Part Four offers four different plans for group or class study of the Bible using the *Handbook*.

However you want to read the Bible—singly or in a group—*Nelson's Quick-Reference*™ *Bible Handbook* will help get you on your way and keep you on track. We pray that your exploration of the Bible, guided by the *Handbook* and the Holy Spirit, will lead to your ever increasing understanding of God's revelation in Scripture.

*Timelines sometimes use approximate dates and are not always drawn to scale in order to include key dates that help readers place events in a larger perspective.

INTRODUCTION

♦

The Thrilling Story of the Book of Books

The sacred book known as the Holy Bible is accepted by the church as uniquely inspired by God, and thus authoritative, providing guidelines for belief and behavior.

Major Divisions

The Bible contains two major sections known as the Old Testament and the New Testament. The Old Testament tells of the preparation that was made for Christ's coming. The New Testament tells of Christ's coming, His life and ministry, and the growth of the early church.

The English word *testament* normally refers to a person's will, the document which bequeaths property to those who will inherit it after the owner's death. But the meaning of testament from both the Hebrew and the Greek languages is "settlement," "treaty," or "covenant." Of these three English words, "covenant" best captures the meaning of the word *testament*. Thus, the two collections that make up the Bible can best be described as the books of the old covenant and the books of the new covenant.

The old covenant is the covenant sealed at Mount Sinai in the days of Moses. By this covenant, the living and true God, who had delivered the Israelites from slavery in Egypt, promised to bless them as His special people. They were also to worship Him alone as their God and to accept His law as their rule for life (Ex. 19:3–6; 24:3–8).

The new covenant was announced by Jesus as he spoke to His disciples in the upper room in Jerusalem the night before His death. When He gave them a cup of wine to drink, Jesus declared that this symbolized "the new covenant in My blood" (Luke 22:20; 1 Cor. 11:25).

While these two covenants, the old and the new, launched great spiritual movements, Christians believe these movements are actually two phases of one great act through which God has revealed His will to His people and called for their positive response. The second covenant is the fulfillment of what was promised in the first.

Authority of the Bible

The authority of the Bible is implied by its title, "the Word of God." It is the written record of the Word of God which came to prophets, apostles, and other spokesmen, and which "became flesh" in Jesus Christ. Christians believe Jesus Christ was the Word of God in a unique sense. Through Jesus, God communicated the perfect revelation of Himself to humankind. For Christians the authority of the Bible is related to the authority of Christ. The Old Testament was the Bible that Jesus used—the authority to which He made constant appeal and whose teachings He accepted and followed.

Revelation and Response

According to the Bible, God has made Himself known in a variety of ways. "The heavens declare the glory of God" (Ps. 19:1). While God is revealed in His creation and also through the inner voice of human conscience, the primary means by which He has made Himself known is through the Bible and through Jesus Christ, His Living Word.

God has revealed Himself through His mighty acts and in the words of His messengers, or spokesmen. Either of these ways is incomplete without the other. In the Old Testament record, none of the mighty acts of God is emphasized more than the Exodus—God's deliverance of the Israelites from Egyptian bondage. As He delivered His people, God repeatedly identified Himself as their redeemer God. "I am the Lord your God, who brought you out of the land of Egypt, out of the house of bondage. You shall have no other gods before Me" (Ex. 20:2–3).

If they had been delivered with no explanation, the nation of Israel would have learned little about the God who redeemed His people. The Israelites might have guessed that in such events as the plagues of Egypt and the parting of the waters of the Red Sea, some supernatural power was at work on their behalf. But they would not have known the nature of this power or God's purpose for them as a people.

God also communicated with His people, the nation of Israel, through Moses, to whom He had already made Himself known in the vision of the burning bush. God instructed Moses to tell the Israelites what had been revealed to him. This was no impersonal force at work, but the God of their ancestors, Abraham, Isaac, and Jacob. In fulfillment of His promises to them, God was acting now on behalf of their descendants.

In communicating with His people, God revealed both His identity and His purpose. His purpose was to make the Israelites a nation dedicated to His service alone. This message, conveyed to the Israelites through Moses, would have been ineffective if God had not delivered them personally. On the other hand, His deliverance would have been meaningless without the message. Together both constituted the Word of God to the Israelites—the saving message of the God who both speaks and acts.

In addition to God's revelation of Himself through the Bible, God's Word also records the *response* of those to whom the revelation was given. Too often the response was unbelief and disobedience. But at other times, people responded in faith and obedience. The Psalms especially proclaim the grateful response of men and women who experienced the grace and righteousness of God.

In the New Testament writings, revelation and response came together in the person of Jesus Christ. On the one hand, Jesus was God's perfect revelation of Himself—He was the divine Word in human form. His works of mercy and power portrayed God in actions, especially His supreme act of sacrifice to bring about "the redemption that is in Christ Jesus" (Rom. 3:24). His teaching expressed the mind of God.

The words and acts of Jesus also proclaimed the meaning and purpose of His works. For example, His act of casting out demons "with the finger of God" (Luke 11:20) was a token that the kingdom of God had arrived. He also declared that His death, which He interpreted as the fulfillment of prophetic Scripture (Mark 14:49), was "a ransom for many" (Mark 10:45).

In His life and ministry, Jesus also illustrated the perfect human response of faith and obedience to God. Jesus was "the Apostle [God's Messenger to us] and High Priest [our Representative with God] of our confession" (Heb. 3:1). Thus, Jesus performed the mighty acts of God and He spoke authoritatively as God's Messenger and Prophet.

Perservation of the Bible

The Bible is a written, authoritative record by which any teaching or theory may be judged. But behind the writing lay periods of time when these messages may have circulated in spoken form. The stories of the patriarchs (Abraham, Isaac, Jacob, and Jacob's twelve sons) may have been passed from generation to generation by word of mouth before they were written. The messages of the prophets were delivered orally before they were fixed in writing. Narratives of the life and ministry of Christ were probably repeated orally for two or more decades before they were given literary form. But the Bible owes its preservation to the fact that all these oral narratives were eventually written. Just as God originally inspired the Bible, He has used this means to preserve His Word for future generations.

None of the original biblical documents—referred to by scholars as the "original autographs"—has survived. No scrap of parchment or papyrus bearing the handwriting of any of the biblical authors has been discovered. But before the original documents disappeared, they were copied. These copies of the original writings are the texts on which current translations of the Bible are based.

The process of copying and recopying the Bible has continued to our time. Until the middle of the fifteenth century A.D., all the copying was done by hand. Then, with the invention of printing in Europe, copies could be made in greater quantities by using this new process. Each copy of the Bible had to be produced slowly by hand with the old system, but now the printing press could produce thousands of copies in a short time. This made the Scriptures available to many people, rather than just the few who could afford handmade copies.

The Canon of the Bible

The word *canon* means a "rod"—specifically, a rod with graduated marks used for measuring length. Since the fourth century A.D. the word has come to be used for the collection of books officially recognized by the church as the Holy Bible. Every book in the canon was considered authoritative but not every authoritative book was in the canon. Christians recognized the entire Old Testament as their Bible from the earliest of times. Roman Catholic Christianity sees the canon as an important source of authority along with the tradition of the church. Protestant and evangelical Christianity views the canon as the sole authority.

Differences still exist in the order and content of the Old Testament. Both Catholic and Protestant Bibles follow the order of the Vulgate, a Latin translation of the Bible produced about A.D. 400. However, the actual number of books in the Protestant Bible follows the Hebrew Bible, while the Bible used by the Roman Catholic, Greek, and Russian Orthodox Churches follows the Vulgate's content by including the "extra books" known as the Apocrypha/Deuterocanon.

The "Bible" which Jesus used was the Hebrew Old Testament. He left no instructions about forming a new collection of authoritative writings to stand beside the books which He and His disciples accepted as God's Word. The Old Testament was also the Bible of the early church, but it was the Old Testament as fulfilled by Jesus. Early Christians interpreted the Old Testament in the light of His person and work. This new perspective controlled the early church's interpretation to such a degree that, while Jews and Christians shared the same Bible, they understood it so differently that they might almost have been using two different Bibles.

Quite early in its history, the church felt a need for a written account of the teachings of Jesus. His teachings did provide the basis for the new Christian way of life. But the church grew so large that many converts were unable to rely on the instructions of those who had heard and memorized the teachings of Jesus. From about A.D. 50 onward, probably more than one written collection of sayings of Jesus circulated in the churches. The earliest written gospel appears to have been the Gospel of Mark, written in the 60's.

Early Christians continued to accept the Old Testament as authoritative. But they could interpret the Old Testament in the light of Jesus' deeds and words only if they had a reliable record of them. So, alongside Moses and the prophets, they had these early writings about Jesus and letters from the apostles, who had known Jesus in the flesh.

When officials of the early church sought to make a list of books about Jesus and the early church which they considered authoritative, they kept the Old Testament, on the authority of Jesus and His apostles. Along with these books they recognized as authoritative the writings of the new age—four Gospels, or biographies, on the life and ministry of Jesus; the thirteen letters of Paul; and letters of other apostles and their companions. The gospel collection and the apostolic collection were joined together by the Book of Acts, which served as a sequel to the gospel story as well as a narrative background for the earlier epistles.

The primary standard applied to a book was that it must have been written either by an apostle or by someone close to the apostles. This guaranteed that their writing about Jesus and the early church would have the authenticity of an eyewitness account. As in the earlier phase of the church's existence, "the apostles' doctrine" (Acts 2:42) was the basis of its life and thought. The apostolic writings formed the charter, or foundation documents, of the church.

English Translations of the Bible

Shortly after James VI of Scotland ascended the throne of England as James I (1603), he convened a conference to settle matters under dispute in the Church of England. The only important result of this conference was an approval to begin work on the King James Version of the English Bible (KJV).

A group of forty-seven scholars, divided into six teams, was appointed to undertake the work of preparing the new version. Three teams worked on the Old Testament; two were responsible for the New Testament; and one worked on the Apocrypha. They used the 1602 edition of the Bishops' Bible as the basis of their revision, but they had access to many other versions and helps, as well as the texts in the original biblical languages. When the six groups had completed their task, the final draft was reviewed by a committee of twelve. The King James Version was published in 1611.

The new version won wide acceptance among the people of the English-speaking world. Nonsectarian in tone and approach, it did not favor one shade of theological or ecclesiastical opinion over another. The translators had an almost instinctive sense of good English style; the prose rhythm of the version gave it a secure place in the popular memory. Never before had an English version of the Bible been more admirably suited for reading aloud in public.

Although there was some resistance to the King James Version at first, it quickly made a place for itself. For more than three centuries, it has remained "The Bible" throughout the English-speaking world.

During the last fifty years the Authorized, or King James, Version had been joined by a host of other English translations—all designed to communicate God's Word clearly and concisely to a modern age. These include the Revised Standard Version (1946–1952), the New American Bible (1970), the New American Standard Bible (1971), the Good News Bible (1976), the New International Version (1978), the New King James Version (1982), and the New Revised Standard Version (1989).

Behind the Bible is a thrilling story of how God revealed Himself and His will to human spokesmen and then acted throughout history to preserve His Word and pass it along to future generations. The processes of canonization, preservation, and translation show that God is still involved in speaking His prophetic truth and calling His people to faith and obedience. In the words of the prophet Isaiah, "The grass withers, the flower fades, but the word of our God stands forever" (Is. 40:8).

BIBLE
HANDBOOK

PART ONE

◆

THE OLD TESTAMENT

THE title "Old Testament" apparently came from the writings of the apostle Paul, who declared, "For until this day the same veil remains unlifted in the reading of the Old Testament, because the veil is taken away in Christ" (2 Cor. 3:14).

The word *testament* is best translated "covenant." God called a people, the nation of Israel, to live in covenant with Him. The Old Testament begins with God's creation of the universe and continues by describing the mighty acts of God in and through His people. It closes about 400 years before the coming of Jesus Christ.

The thirty-nine books of the Old Testament were written over a period of several centuries in the Hebrew language, except for a few selected passages, which were written in Aramaic.

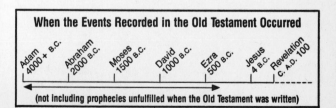

When the Events Recorded in the Old Testament Occurred

Adam 4000+ B.C.　Abraham 2000 B.C.　Moses 1500 B.C.　David 1000 B.C.　Ezra 500 B.C.　Jesus 4 B.C.　Revelation C. A.D. 100

(not including prophecies unfulfilled when the Old Testament was written)

ONE

BOOKS OF THE LAW

THE first five books of the Old Testament are called the Books of the Law or the Pentateuch, a Greek term meaning "five volumed." The Hebrew word for this collection is Torah, meaning "instruction, teaching, or doctrine."

BOOKS OF THE LAW

BOOK	SUMMARY
Genesis	Creation and the establishment of the covenant relationship
Exodus	Deliverance of the people of Israel from slavery in Egypt
Leviticus	The ceremonial law
Numbers	Wandering of God's people in the wilderness
Deuteronomy	The second giving of the law by Moses before the people occupy the Promised Land

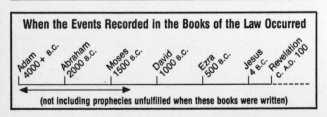

When the Events Recorded in the Books of the Law Occurred

Adam 4000 + B.C.   Abraham 2000 B.C.   Moses 1500 B.C.   David 1000 B.C.   Ezra 500 B.C.   Jesus 4 B.C.   Revelation c. A.D. 100

(not including prophecies unfulfilled when these books were written)

The Book of Genesis

◆

KEYS TO GENESIS

Key Word: *Beginnings*

Genesis gives the beginning of almost everything, including the beginning of the universe, life, humanity, sabbath, death, marriage, sin, redemption, family, literature, cities, art, language, and sacrifice.

Key Verses: *Genesis 3:15; 12:3*

Key Chapter: *Genesis 15*

Central to all of Scripture is the Abrahamic Covenant, which is given in 12:1–3 and ratified in 15:1–21. Israel receives three specific promises: (1) *the promise of a great land*—"from the river of Egypt to the great river, the River Euphrates" (15:18); (2) *the promise of a great nation*—"and I will make your descendants as the dust of the earth" (13:16); and (3) *the promise of a great blessing*—"I will bless you and make your name great; and you shall be a blessing" (12:2).

◆

Authorship and Date

The Book of Genesis gives no notice about its author. The early church, however, held to the conviction that Moses wrote the book, as did the Jerusalem Talmud and the first-century Jewish historian Josephus. In spite of the number of modern scholars who reject the Mosaic authorship of Genesis, the traditional view has much to commend it. Both the Old Testament and the New Testament contain frequent testimony to the Mosaic authorship of the entire Pentateuch (Lev. 1:1–2; Neh. 13:1; Matt. 8:4; Acts 26:22).

Historical Setting

Moses may have finished writing the Book of Genesis not long before his death on Mount Nebo (Deut. 34). During this time the children of Israel, now led by Joshua, were camped east of the Jordan River, poised for the invasion of Canaan.

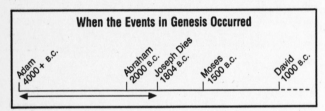

When the Events in Genesis Occurred

Adam 4000+ B.C.　　Abraham 2000 B.C.　Joseph Dies 1804 B.C.　　Moses 1500 B.C.　　　David 1000 B.C.

Theological Contribution

The Book of Genesis is a primary source for several basic doctrines of the Bible. The book focuses on God primarily in two areas: He is the Creator of the universe, and He is the one who initiates covenant with His people. Genesis ties creation and covenant together in a stunning manner: the God who initiates covenant is the same God who has created the entire universe. The eternal God and almighty Creator enters into covenant with His people (Gen. 1:1; John 1:1).

God's covenant with Abraham is the basic plot of the Scripture: to accomplish His plan for the nations of the world through His people Israel, the descendants of Abraham. That covenant (Gen. 12:1–3; 15:1–21) contains a number of personal blessings on the father of the faith. But the climax of the text is in the words of worldwide import: "And in you all the families of the earth shall be blessed" (Gen. 12:3). This promise was realized in the person of the Lord Jesus Christ, the Seed of Abraham, through whom peoples of all nations and families may enter into the joy of knowing the God of Abraham.

Special Consideration

The Book of Genesis takes the reader to the moment when the Creator spoke into being the sun, moon, stars, planets, galaxies, plants, moving creatures, and humankind. The student who expects to find in Genesis a scientific account of how the world came into existence, with all questions concerning primitive life answered in technical language, will be disappointed. Genesis is not an attempt to answer such technical questions.

Survey of Genesis

The Four Great Events

Chapters 1—11 lay the foundation upon which the whole Bible is built and center on four key events. **(1)** *Creation:* God is the sovereign Creator of matter, energy, space, and time. Humankind is the pinnacle of the Creation. **(2)** *Fall:* Creation is followed by corruption. In the first sin humankind is separated from God (Adam from God), and in the second sin, human is separated from human (Cain from Abel). In spite of the devastating curse of the Fall, God promises hope of redemption through the seed of the woman (3:15). **(3)** *Flood:* As humankind multiplies, sin also multiplies until God is compelled to destroy humanity with the exception of Noah and his family. **(4)** *Nations:* Genesis teaches the unity of the human race: we are all children of Adam through Noah, but because of rebellion at the Tower of Babel, God fragments the single culture and language of the post-Flood world and scatters people over the face of the earth.

The Book of Genesis

FOCUS	Four Events				Four People			
REFERENCE	1:1 ——	3:1 ——	6:1 ——	10:1 ——	12:1 ——	25:19 ——	27:19 ——	37:1 —— 50:26
DIVISION	Creation	Fall	Flood	Nations	Abraham	Isaac	Jacob	Joseph
TOPIC	Human Race				Hebrew Race			
	Historical				Biographical			
LOCATION	Fertile Crescent (Eden-Haran)				Canaan (Haran-Canaan)			Egypt (Canaan-Egypt)
TIME	c. 2000 Years c. 4000+–c. 2166 B.C.				281 Years c. 2166–1885 B.C.			81 Years (1885–1804 B.C.)

The Four Great People

Once the nations are scattered, God focuses on one man and his descendants through whom He will bless all nations (12—50). **(1)** *Abraham:* The calling of Abraham (12) is the pivotal point of the book. The three covenant promises God makes to Abraham (land, descendants, and blessing) are foundational to His program of bringing salvation upon the earth. **(2)** *Isaac:* God establishes His covenant with Isaac as the spiritual link with Abraham. **(3)** *Jacob:* God transforms this man from selfishness to servanthood and changes his name to Israel, the father of the twelve tribes. **(4)** *Joseph:* Jacob's favorite son suffers at the hands of his brothers and becomes a slave in Egypt. After his dramatic rise to the rulership of Egypt, Joseph delivers his family from famine and brings them out of Canaan to Goshen.

Genesis ends on a note of impending bondage with the death of Joseph. There is great need for the redemption that is to follow in the Book of Exodus.

Outline of Genesis

Part One: Primeval History (1:1—11:9)

The Book of Exodus

Authorship and Date

Exodus is one of the first five books of the Old Testament—books that have traditionally been assigned to Moses as author. The disciples (John 1:45), Paul (Rom. 10:5) and Jesus (Mark 7:10; 12:26; Luke 20:37; John 5:46, 47; 7:19, 22, 23) testified to Mosaic authorship as well. It must be dated some time before his death about 1400 B.C.

◆

KEYS TO EXODUS

Key Word: *Redemption*

Central to the Book of Exodus is the concept of redemption. Israel was redeemed *from* bondage in Egypt and *into* a covenant relationship with God.

Key Verses: *Exodus 6:6; 19:5, 6*

Key Chapters: *Exodus 12—14*

The climax of the entire Old Testament is recorded in chapters 12—14: the salvation of Israel through blood (the Passover) and through power (the Red Sea).

◆

Historical Setting

Exodus covers a crucial period in Israel's early history as a nation. Most conservative scholars believe the Hebrews left Egypt about 1440 B.C. Some believe it took place much later, around 1280 B.C. About two-thirds of the book describes Israel's experiences during the two years after this date. This was the period when Israel traveled through the wilderness toward Mount Sinai and received instructions from God through Moses as he met with God on the mountain.

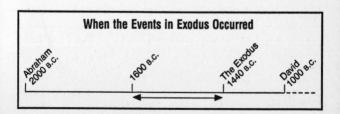

When the Events in Exodus Occurred

Abraham 2000 B.C. — 1600 B.C. — The Exodus 1440 B.C. — David 1000 B.C.

Theological Contribution

The Book of Exodus has exercised much influence over the faith of Israel, as well as Christian theology. The Bible's entire message of redemption grows out of the covenant relationship between God and His people first described in this book. In addition, several themes in the book can be clearly traced in the life and ministry of Jesus. Moses received the Law on Mount Sinai; Jesus delivered the Sermon on the Mount. Moses lifted up the serpent in the wilderness to give life to the people; Jesus was lifted up on the cross to bring eternal life to all who trust in Him. The Passover served as the base on which Jesus developed the Last Supper as a lasting memorial for His followers.

Special Consideration

The crossing of the Red Sea is one of the most dramatic events in all of the Bible; the biblical writers repeatedly refer to it as the most significant sign of God's love for Israel. A helpless slave people had been delivered from their enemies by their powerful Redeemer God.

Survey of Exodus

Redemption from Egypt (1—18)

Exodus begins where the Book of Genesis leaves off. For many years the descendants of Joseph have grown and prospered with the blessings of the Egyptian ruler. But with a new king over Egypt, the Hebrews have been reduced to the status of slaves and put to work on the Pharaoh's building projects. When the Israelites finally turn to God for deliverance from their bondage, God quickly responds by redeeming them "with an outstretched arm and with great judgments" (6:6).

Some of the major events covered by this rapidly moving book include God's call to Moses through the burning bush to lead His people out of bondage (3:1—4:17); the series of

The Book of Exodus

FOCUS	Redemption from Egypt			Revelation from God		
REFERENCE	1:1 ———	2:1 ———	5:1 ———	15:22 ———	19:1 ———	32:1 ——— 40:38
DIVISION	The Need for Redemption	The Preparation for Redemption	The Redemption of Israel	The Preservation of Israel	The Revelation of the Covenant	The Response of Israel to the Covenant
TOPIC	Narration				Legislation	
	Subjection		Redemption		Instruction	
LOCATION	Egypt			Wilderness	Mount Sinai	
TIME	430 Years			2 Months	10 Months	

plagues sent upon the Egyptians because of Pharaoh's stubbornness (7:1—12:30); the release of the captives and their miraculous crossing of the Red Sea, followed by the destruction of Pharaoh's army (15:1–31); God's provision for the people in the wilderness through bread, quail, and water (16:1–17:7).

Revelation from God (19—40)

The emphasis moves from narration in chapters 1—18 to legislation in chapters 19—40. On Mount Sinai, Moses receives God's moral, civil, and ceremonial laws, as well as the pattern for the tabernacle to be built in the wilderness. After God judges the people for their worship of the golden calf, the tabernacle is constructed and consecrated.

Outline of Exodus

The Book of Leviticus

Authorship and Date

Most conservative Bible students acknowledge Moses as the author of the Book of Leviticus, probably about 1440 B.C. But some scholars insist the book was pulled together from many different sources by an unknown editor several centuries after Moses' death. This theory overlooks the dozens of instances in Leviticus where God spoke directly to Moses and Moses wrote down His instructions to be passed along to the people (4:1; 6:1; 8:1; 11:1).

◆

KEYS TO LEVITICUS

Key Word: *Holiness*

Leviticus centers around the concept of the holiness of God, and how an unholy people can acceptably approach Him and then remain in continued fellowship.

Key Verses: *Leviticus 17:11; 20:7, 8*

Key Chapter: *Leviticus 16*

The Day of Atonement *("Yom Kippur")* was the most important single day in the Hebrew calendar as it was the only day the high priests entered into the Holy of Holies to "make atonement for you, to cleanse you, *that* you may be clean from all your sins before the LORD" (16:30).

◆

Historical Setting

The Book of Leviticus belongs to the period in Israel's history when the people were encamped at Mount Sinai following their miraculous deliverance from slavery in Egypt.

Theological Contribution

The Book of Leviticus is important because of its clear teachings on three vital spiritual truths: atonement, sacrifice, and holiness. Without the background of these concepts in Leviticus, we could not understand their later fulfillment in the life and ministry of Jesus.

Chapter 16 of Leviticus contains God's instructions for observing the Day of Atonement. New Testament writers later compared this familiar picture to the sacrifice of Jesus on our behalf. But unlike a human priest, Jesus did not have to offer sacrifices, "first for His own sins and then for the people's, for this He did once for all when He offered up Himself" (Heb. 7:27).

The Book of Leviticus instructs the covenant people as to the blood offering—presenting the blood of a sacrificed animal to God—a symbol of the worshiper offering his own life to God. Again, this familiar teaching assumed deeper meaning in the New Testament when applied to Jesus. He gave His life on our behalf when He shed His blood to take away our sins.

The basic meaning of *holiness* as presented in the Book of Leviticus is that God demands absolute obedience of His people. The root meaning of the word is "separation." God's people were to be separate from, and different than, the surrounding pagan peoples.

Special Consideration

The blood of bulls and goats so prominent in Leviticus had no power to take away sin. But each of these rituals was "a shadow of the good things to come" (Heb. 10:1). They pointed forward to God's ultimate sacrifice, given freely on our behalf: "So Christ was offered once to bear the sins of many" (Heb. 9:28).

Survey of Leviticus

Sacrifice (1—17)

This section teaches that God must be approached by the sacrificial offerings (1—7), by the mediation of the priesthood (8—10), by the purification of the nation from uncleanness (11—15), and by the provision for national cleansing and fellowship (16, 17). The blood sacrifices remind the worshipers that because of sin the holy God requires the costly gift of life (17:11). The blood of the innocent sacrificial animal be-

The Book of Leviticus

FOCUS	Sacrifice				Sanctification			
REFERENCE	1:1 ———	8:1 ———	11:1 ———	16:1 ———	18:1 ———	21:1 ———	23:1 ———	25:1 ——— 27:1—27:34
DIVISION	The Laws of Sacrifice				The Laws of Sanctification			
	The Offerings	Consecration of the Priests	Consecration of the People	National Atonement	For the People	For the Priests	In Worship	In the Land of Canaan	Through Vows
TOPIC	The Way to God				The Walk with God			
	The Laws of Acceptable Approach to God				The Laws of Continued Fellowship with God			
LOCATION	Mount Sinai							
TIME	c. 1 Month							

comes the substitute for the life of the guilty offerer: "without shedding of blood there is no remission" (Heb. 9:22).

Sanctification (18—27)

The Israelites serve a holy God who requires them to be holy as well. To be holy means to be "set apart" or "separated." They are to be separated *from* other nations *unto* God. In Leviticus the idea of holiness appears eighty-seven times, sometimes indicating ceremonial holiness (ritual requirements), and at other times moral holiness (purity of life). This sanctification extends to the people of Israel (18—20), the priesthood (21 and 22), their worship (23 and 24), their life in Canaan (25 and 26), and their special vows (27).

Outline of Leviticus

The Book of Numbers

Authorship and Date

Numbers is one of the first five books of the Old Testament—books that have traditionally been assigned to Moses as author. He is the central personality of the book, and the book itself contains references to his writing (33:2). He must have written Numbers some time just before his death as the Hebrew people prepared to enter the land, about 1400 B.C.

◆

KEYS TO NUMBERS

Key Word: *Wanderings*

Numbers records the failure of Israel to believe in the promise of God and the resulting judgment of wandering in the wilderness for forty years.

Key Verses: *Numbers 14:22, 23; 20:12*

Key Chapter: *Numbers 14*

The critical turning point of Numbers may be seen in Numbers 14 when Israel rejects God by refusing to go up and conquer the Promised Land.

◆

Historical Setting

The events in the Book of Numbers cover a span of about 39 or 40 years in Israel's history—from 1440 B.C., when they left their encampment at Mount Sinai, to 1400 B.C., when they entered the land of Canaan by crossing the Jordan River near Jericho.

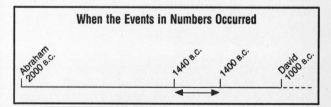

When the Events in Numbers Occurred

Abraham 2000 B.C.   1440 B.C.   1400 B.C.   David 1000 B.C.

Theological Contribution

The Book of Numbers presents the concept of God's correcting wrath upon His own disobedient people. Through their rebellion, the Hebrews had broken the covenant. Even Moses was not exempt from God's wrath when he disobeyed God. But God did not give up on His people. While He might punish them in the present, He was still determined to bless them and bring them ultimately into a land of their own.

Special Consideration

The Israelite warriors counted in the two censuses in the Book of Numbers have been a puzzle to Bible scholars (see chaps. 1 and 26). In each case, they add up to an army of more than 600,000. If this is correct, then the total Israelite population must have been more than 2,000,000 people. Such a figure seems out of line for this period of ancient history when most nations were small.

One possible explanation is that the word translated *thousands* in English could have meant something like units, tents, or clans in the Hebrew language. If so, a much smaller number was in mind. But other scholars believe there is no reason to question the numbers, since the Israelites did increase dramatically during their years of enslavement in Egypt (Ex. 1:7–12).

Survey of Numbers

The Old Generation (1:1—10:10)

The generation that witnessed God's miraculous acts of deliverance and preservation receives further direction from God while they are still at the foot of Mount Sinai (1:1—10:10). God's instructions are very explicit, reaching every aspect of their lives. He is the author of order, not confusion; and this is seen in the way He organizes the people around the tabernacle. Turning from the outward conditions of the camp (1—4) to the inward conditions (5—10), Numbers describes the spiritual preparation of the people.

The Book of Numbers

FOCUS	The Old Generation		The Tragic Transition				The New Generation		
REFERENCE	1:1 ———————— 5:1 ————————		10:11 —— 13:1 —— 15:1 —— 20:1 ——				26:1 —— 28:1 —————— 31:1 ———— 36:13		
DIVISION	Organization of Israel	Sanctification of Israel	To Kadesh	At Kadesh	In Wilderness	To Moab	Reorganization of Israel	Regulations of Offerings and Vows	Conquest and Division of Israel
TOPIC	Order		Disorder				Reorder		
	Preparation		Postponement				Preparation		
LOCATION	Mount Sinai		Wilderness				Plains of Moab		
TIME	20 Days		30 Years 3 Months and 10 Days				c. 5 Months		

The Tragic Transition (10:11—25:18)

Israel follows God step by step until Canaan is in sight. Then in the crucial moment at Kadesh they draw back in unbelief. Their murmurings had already become incessant, but their unbelief after sending out the twelve spies at Kadesh Barnea is something God will not tolerate. Their rebellion at Kadesh marks the pivotal point of the book. The generation of the Exodus will not be the generation of the conquest.

Unbelief brings discipline and hinders God's blessing. The old generation is doomed to kill time literally for forty years of wilderness wanderings—one year for every day spent by the twelve spies in inspecting the land. Only Joshua and Caleb, the two spies who believed God, enter Canaan. Almost nothing is recorded about these transitional years.

The New Generation (26—36)

When the transition to the new generation is complete, the people move to the plains of Moab, directly east of the Promised Land (22:1). Before they can enter the land they must wait until all is ready. Here they receive new instructions, a new census is taken, Joshua is appointed as Moses' successor, and some of the people settle in the Transjordan. God's people can move forward only as they trust and depend on Him.

Outline of Numbers

The Book of Deuteronomy

Authorship and Date

Conservative Bible students are united in their conviction that Moses wrote this book, but many liberal scholars theorize that Deuteronomy was written several centuries later. This theory unfortunately overlooks the statement of the book itself that Moses wrote Deuteronomy (31:9–13) and the use of the first-person pronoun throughout the book. Chapter 34, about his death, probably was added by his successor Joshua as a tribute to Moses. The date of the writing must have been some time around 1400 B.C.

◆

KEYS TO DEUTERONOMY

Key Word: *Covenant*

The primary theme of the entire Book of Deuteronomy is the renewal of the covenant.

Key Verses: *Deuteronomy 10:12, 13; 30:19, 20*

Key Chapter: *Deuteronomy 27*

The formal ratification of the covenant occurs in Deuteronomy 27, as Moses, the priests, the Levites, and all of Israel "take heed and listen, O Israel: This day you have become the people of the LORD your God" (27:9).

◆

Historical Setting

The Book of Deuteronomy marks a turning point in the history of God's chosen people. Because of their rebellion and unfaithfulness, they had wandered aimlessly in the desert for two generations. Now they are camped on the eastern border of Canaan, the land which God had promised as their homeland.

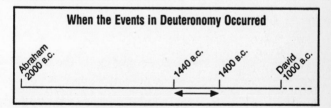

When the Events in Deuteronomy Occurred

Abraham 2000 B.C. — 1440 B.C. — 1400 B.C. — David 1000 B.C.

Theological Contribution

The New Testament contains more than 80 quotations from Deuteronomy; Jesus Himself often quoted from Deuteronomy. During His temptation, He answered Satan with four quotations from Scripture. Three of these came from this key Old Testament book (Matt. 4:4, Luke 4:4—Deut. 8:3; Matt. 4:7, Luke 4:12—Deut. 6:16; Matt. 4:10, Luke 4:8—Deut. 6:13). When Jesus was asked to name the most important commandment in the law, He responded with the familiar call from Deuteronomy: "You shall love the Lord your God with all your heart, with all your soul, and with all your mind" (Matt. 22:37; Deut. 6:5; Mark 12:30; Luke 10:27).

Special Consideration

Some people look upon the laws of God in the Old Testament as burdensome and restrictive. The Book of Deuteronomy, however, teaches that God's laws are given for our own good to help us stay close to Him in our attitudes and behavior.

Survey of Deuteronomy

Moses' First Sermon (1:1—4:43)

Moses reaches into the past to remind the people of two undeniable facts in their history: (1) the moral judgment of God upon Israel's unbelief, and (2) the deliverance and provision of God during times of obedience.

Moses' Second Sermon (4:44—26:19)

These chapters review the three categories of the Law: (1) *The testimonies (5—11)*. These are the moral duties—a restatement and expansion of the Ten Commandments plus an exhortation not to forget God's gracious deliverance. (3) *The statutes (12:1—16:17)*. These are the ceremonial duties—sacrifices, tithes, and feasts. (3) *The ordinances (16:18—26:19)*. These are the civil (16:18—20:20) and social (21—26) duties—the system of justice, criminal laws, laws of warfare,

The Book of Deuteronomy

FOCUS	First Sermon	Second Sermon					Third Sermon	
REFERENCE	1:1 ——— 4:44 ———	12:1 ———	16:18 —	21:1 —	27:1 ———	29:1 ———	31:1 ———	34:12
DIVISION	Review of God's Acts for Israel	Exposition of the Decalogue	Ceremonial Laws	Civil Laws	Social Laws	Ratification of Covenant	Palestinian Covenant	Transition of Covenant Mediator
TOPIC	What God Has Done	What God Expected of Israel					What God Will Do	
TOPIC	Historical	Legal					Prophetical	
LOCATION	Plains of Moab							
TIME	c. 1 Month							

rules of property, personal and family morality, and social justice.

Moses' Third Sermon (27—34)

In these chapters Moses writes history in advance. He predicts what will befall Israel in the near future (blessings and cursings) and in the distant future (dispersion among the nations and eventual return). Moses lists the terms of the covenant soon to be ratified by the people. Because Moses will not be allowed to enter the land, he appoints Joshua as his successor and delivers a farewell address to the multitude. God Himself buries Moses in an unknown place.

Outline of Deuteronomy

TWO

BOOKS OF HISTORY

♦

THE story of the nation of Israel continues in the twelve historical books—the second major division of the Old Testament. These books contain descriptions of the settlement of God's covenant people in the Promised Land after their escape from Egypt and the years of wandering in the wilderness; the transition from rule by judges to rule by kings; the division of the nation into northern and southern factions; the destruction of the Northern Kingdom; and the captivity and return of the Southern Kingdom. The time period represented by these books covers about 700 years.

BOOKS OF HISTORY	
BOOK	SUMMARY
Joshua	The capture and settlement of the Promised Land
Judges	The nation of Israel is rescued by a series of judges, or military leaders
Ruth	A beautiful story of God's love
1 and 2 Samuel	The early history of Israel, including the reigns of Saul and David
1 and 2 Kings	A political history of Israel, focusing on the reigns of selected kings from the time of Solomon to the captivity of the Jewish people by Babylon

1 and 2 Chronicles	A religious history of Israel, covering the same period of time as 2 Samuel and 1 and 2 Kings
Ezra	The return of the Jewish people from captivity in Babylon
Nehemiah	The rebuilding of the walls of Jerusalem after Babylonian captivity
Esther	God's care for His people under Gentile rule

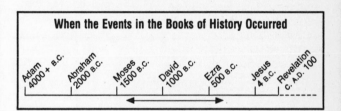

When the Events in the Books of History Occurred

Adam 4000+ B.C. — Abraham 2000 B.C. — Moses 1500 B.C. — David 1000 B.C. — Ezra 500 B.C. — Jesus 4 B.C. — Revelation C. A.D. 100

The Book of Joshua

Authorship and Date

Early Jewish tradition credited Joshua with writing this book; this is disputed by many modern scholars. But sections of the book strongly suggest that they were written by Joshua, and some of the battle narratives are written with such vivid description and minute detail that they suggest an author on the scene, Joshua himself (chaps. 6—8). A commonly accepted date for the death of Joshua is about 1375 B.C., so the book must have been completed shortly after this date.

KEYS TO JOSHUA

Key Word: *Conquest*

The entire Book of Joshua describes the entering, conquering, and occupying of the land of Canaan.

Key Verses: *Joshua 1:8; 11:23*

Key Chapter: *Joshua 24*

Joshua reviews for the people God's fulfillment of His promises and then challenges them to review their commitment to the covenant (24:24, 25), which is the foundation for all successful national life.

Historical Setting

The Book of Joshua covers about 25 years in one of the most important periods of Israel's history—their conquest and final settlement of the land which God had promised to Abraham and his descendants many centuries earlier. The specific years for this occupation must have been from about 1400 to 1375 B.C.

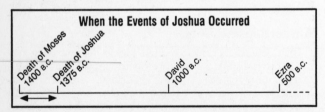

When the Events of Joshua Occurred

Death of Moses 1400 B.C.
Death of Joshua 1375 B.C.
David 1000 B.C.
Ezra 500 B.C.

Theological Contribution

One important message of the Book of Joshua is that true and false religions do not mix. Again and again throughout their history, the Hebrew people departed from worship of the one true God. This tendency toward false worship was the main reason for Joshua's moving farewell speech. He warned the people against worshiping these false gods and challenged them to remain faithful to their great deliverer Jehovah.

Special Consideration

Some people have difficulty with God commanding Joshua to destroy the Canaanites. But behind this commandment lay God's concern for his covenant people. He wanted to remove the Canaanites' idolatrous worship practices so they would not be a temptation to the Israelites. This command to Joshua also represented God's judgment against sin and immorality. God used Israel as an instrument of His judgment against a pagan nation.

Survey of Joshua

Conquest (1:1—13:7)

The first five chapters record the spiritual, moral, physical, and military preparation of Joshua and the people for the impending conquest of Canaan. Joshua is given a charge by God to complete the task begun by Moses (1:2). After being encouraged by God, Joshua sends out two spies who come back with a favorable report (in contrast to the spies of the previous generation). Obedience and faith are united in the miraculous crossing of the Jordan River (3:1—4:24).

Joshua's campaign in central Canaan (6:1—8:35) places a strategic wedge between the northern and southern cities preventing a massive Canaanite alliance against Israel. The Lord teaches the people that success in battle will always be by His power and not their own might or cleverness. Sin must be dealt with at once because it brings severe consequences and defeat at Ai (7:1—26).

The southern and northern campaigns (9:1—13:7) are also

The Book of Joshua

FOCUS	Conquest of Canaan		Settlement in Canaan			
REFERENCE	1:1	6:1	13:8	14:1	20:1	22:1 ——— 24:33
DIVISION	Preparation of Israel	Conquest of Canaan	Settlement of East Jordan	Settlement of West Jordan	Settlement of Religious Community	Conditions for Continued Settlement
TOPIC	Entering Canaan	Conquering Canaan	Dividing Canaan			
	Preparation	Subjection	Possession			
LOCATION	Jordan River	Canaan	Two and a Half Tribes—East Jordan Nine and a Half Tribes—West Jordan			
TIME	c. 1 Month	c. 7 Years	c. 8 Years			

successful, but an unwise oath made to the deceptive Gibeonites forces Israel to protect them and to disobey God's command to eliminate the Canaanites.

Settlement (13:8—24:33)

Joshua is growing old, and God tells him to divide the land among the twelve tribes. Much remains to be won, and the tribes are to continue the conquest by faith after Joshua's death. Chapters 13:8—21:45 describe the allocations of the land to the various tribes as well as the inheritances of Caleb (14 and 15) and the Levites (21).

The last chapters (22:1—24:33) record the conditions for continued successful settlement in Canaan. Realizing that blessing comes from God only as Israel obeys His covenant, Joshua preaches a moving sermon, climaxed by Israel's renewal of her allegiance to the covenant.

Outline of Joshua

The Book of Judges

Authorship and Date

Like the authors of several other historical books of the Old Testament, the author of Judges is unknown. But internal evidence indicates that the book was written after the events described in Judges, probably during the days of King Saul or King David, about 1050 to 1000 B.C.

Historical Setting

Israel's entry into the Promised Land under Joshua was not so much a total conquest as an occupation. Even after the

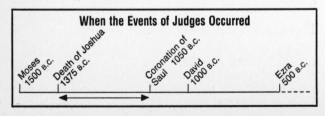

When the Events of Judges Occurred

Moses 1500 B.C. | Death of Joshua 1375 B.C. | Coronation of Saul 1050 B.C. | David 1000 B.C. | Ezra 500 B.C.

◆

KEYS TO JUDGES

Key Word: *Cycles*

The Book of Judges is written primarily on a thematic rather than a chronological basis (16—21 actually precede 3—15). The author uses the accounts of the various judges to prove the utter failure of living out the closing verse of Judges: "Everyone did *what was* right in his own eyes." To accomplish this, the author uses a five-point cycle to recount the repeated spiral of disobedience, destruction, and defeat. The five parts are: (1) sin, (2) servitude, (3) supplication, (4) salvation, and (5) silence.

Key Verses: *Judges 2:20, 21; 21:25*

Key Chapter: *Judges 2*

The second chapter of Judges is a miniature of the whole book as it records the transition of the godly to the ungodly generation, the format of the cycles, and the purpose of God in not destroying the Canaanites.

◆

land was divided among Israel's twelve tribes, the Israelites continued to face the possibility of domination by the warlike Canaanites during the 300-year period of the judges, from about 1375 to 1050 B.C.

Theological Contribution

Judges speaks of humanity's need for an eternal deliverer or a savior. The deliverance of the human judges was always temporary, partial, and imperfect. The book points forward to Jesus Christ, the great Judge (Ps. 110:6), who is King and Savior of His people.

Special Consideration

Many readers are troubled by the rash vow of the judge Jephthah in the Book of Judges. He promised God that if he were victorious in battle, he would offer as a sacrifice the first thing to come out of his house to greet him on his return. The Lord did give Jephthah victory. On his return, his daughter came out of the house to greet him, and he was forced to carry out his terrible vow (11:29–40).

Human sacrifice was never sanctioned by the nation of Israel. Indeed, God condemned it as an evil of the surrounding nations. The point the author of Judges made in recording this deed is the same he had in mind as he recorded the sins and excesses of Samson. The period of the judges was a time of such religious and political chaos that even the best of God's servants were seriously flawed.

Survey of Judges

Cycle of Unfaithfulness: Deterioration (1:1—3:4)

Judges begins with short-lived military successes after Joshua's death, but quickly turns to the repeated failure of all the tribes to drive out their enemies. The people feel the lack of a unified central leader, but the primary reasons for their failure are a lack of faith in God and a lack of obedience to Him (2:1–3). Compromise leads to conflict and chaos. Israel does not drive out the inhabitants (1:21, 27, 29, 30).

Deliverances (3:5—16:31)

This section describes seven apostasies (fallings away from God), seven servitudes, and seven deliverances. Each of the seven cycles has five steps: sin, servitude, supplication, salvation, and silence. These also can be described by the words *rebellion, retribution, repentance, restoration,* and *rest*. The monotony of Israel's sins can be contrasted with the creativity of God's deliverers, among them, Deborah, Gideon, and Samson.

The Book of Judges

FOCUS	Deterioration		Deliverance					Depravity			
REFERENCE	1:1 —————— 2:1	—— 3:5	4:1 ——	6:1 ——	10:6 ——	12:8 ——	13:1 ——	17:1 —	19:1 —	20:1-21:25
DIVISION	Israel Fails to Complete Conquest	God Judges Israel	Southern Campaign	Northern Campaign (1st)	Central Campaign	Eastern Campaign	Northern Campaign (2nd)	Western Campaign	Sin of Idolatry	Sin of Immorality	Sin of Civil War
TOPIC	Causes of the Cycles		Curse of the Cycles						Conditions During the Cycles		
	Living with the Canaanites		War with the Canaanites						Living Like the Canaanites		
LOCATION	Canaan										
TIME	c. 350 Years										

Depravity (17:1—21:25)

These chapters illustrate (1) religious apostasy (17 and 18) and (2) social and moral depravity (19—21) during the period of the judges. Chapters 19—21 contain one of the worst tales of degradation in the Bible. Judges closes with a key to understanding the period: "everyone did *what was* right in his own eyes" (21:25).

Outline of Judges

The Book of Ruth

◆

KEYS TO RUTH

Key Word: *Kinsman-Redeemer*

The Hebrew word for kinsman *(goel)* appears thirteen times in Ruth and basically means "one who redeems."

Key Verses: *Ruth 1:16; 3:11*

Key Chapter: *Ruth 4*

In twenty-two short verses, Ruth moves from widowhood and poverty to marriage and wealth (2:1). As kinsman-redeemer, Boaz brings a Moabite woman into the family line of David and eventually of Jesus Christ.

◆

Authorship and Date

The author of Ruth is unknown, although some scholars credit it to the prophet Samuel. The book had to be written some time after the birth of David, the last entry in the genealogy.

Historical Setting

The events in the book occurred at a dark time in Israel's history—"in the days when the judges ruled" (1:1), according to the historical introduction. This was a period of unrelieved chaos, when the nation lapsed again and again into worship of false gods.

Theological Contribution

Ruth's life gives us a beautiful example of the providence of God. He brings Ruth to precisely the right field where she

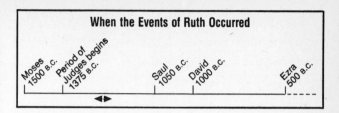

When the Events of Ruth Occurred

Moses 1500 B.C. | Period of Judges begins 1375 B.C. | Saul 1050 B.C. | David 1000 B.C. | Ezra 500 B.C.

can meet Boaz, who will be her kinsman-redeemer. God is also portrayed in the book as the model of loyal and abiding love (2:20).

Survey of Ruth

Ruth's Love Is Demonstrated (chaps. 1 and 2)

The story begins with a famine in Israel, a sign of disobedience and apostasy (Deut. 28—30). An Israelite named Elimelech ("My God Is King") in a desperate act moves from Bethlehem ("House of Bread"—note the irony) to Moab. Although he seeks life in that land, he and his two sons Mahlon ("Sick") and Chilion ("Pining") find only death. The deceased sons leave two Moabite widows, Orpah ("Stubbornness") and Ruth ("Friendship"). Elimelech's widow, Naomi, hears that the famine in Israel is over and decides to return, no longer as Naomi ("Pleasant") but as Mara ("Bitter"). She tells her daughters-in-law to remain in Moab and remarry. Orpah chooses to leave Naomi and is never mentioned again. Ruth, on the other hand, resolves to cling to Naomi and follow Yahweh, the God of Israel. She therefore gives up her culture, people, and language because of her love.

In Israel Naomi must let Ruth glean at the edge of a field. God's providential care brings her to the field of Boaz, Naomi's kinsman. Boaz ("In Him Is Strength") begins to love, protect, and provide for her.

The Book of Ruth

FOCUS	Ruth's Love Demonstrated		Ruth's Love Rewarded	
REFERENCE	1:1 ——————— 1:19 ———	——— 3:1 ————	——— 4:1 ———————	— 4:22
DIVISION	Ruth's Decision to Stay with Naomi	Ruth's Devotion to Care for Naomi	Ruth's Request for Redemption by Boaz	Ruth's Reward of Redemption by Boaz
TOPIC	Ruth and Naomi		Ruth and Boaz	
	Death of Family	Ruth Cares for Naomi	Boaz Cares for Ruth	Birth of Family
LOCATION	Moab	Fields of Bethlehem	Threshing Floor of Bethlehem	Bethlehem
TIME	c. 12 Years			

Ruth's Love Is Rewarded (chaps. 3 and 4)

Boaz takes no further steps toward marriage, so Naomi follows the accepted customs of the day and requests that Boaz exercise his right as kinsman-redeemer. In 3:10–13, Boaz reveals why he has taken no action; nevertheless, God rewards Ruth's devotion by giving her Boaz as a husband and by providing her with a son, Obed, the grandfather of David.

Outline of Ruth

The Book of First Samuel

◆

KEYS TO FIRST SAMUEL

Key Word: *Transition*

First Samuel records the critical transition in Israel from the rule of God through the judges to His rule through the kings.

Key Verses: *First Samuel 13:14; 15:22*

Key Chapter: *First Samuel 15*

First Samuel 15 records the tragic transition of king-ship from Saul to David.

◆

Authorship and Date

Since the name of the great prophet Samuel is associated with these books, it is logical to assume that he wrote both 1 and 2 Samuel. The Book of First Chronicles refers to "the book of Samuel the seer" (1 Chr. 29:29). However, all of 2 Samuel and a major portion of 1 Samuel deal with events that happened after Samuel's death. Many scholars believe that Abiathar the priest, who may have had access to royal records, wrote those parts of these two books that deal with the court life of David.

Historical Setting

The Books of First and Second Samuel describe a turning point in Israel's history, when the people insisted on a united kingdom under the ruling authority of a king. Saul was anointed by Samuel about 1050 B.C. and ruled for 40 years; David also ruled 40 years from 1010 to 971 B.C.

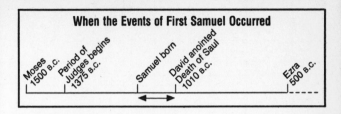

When the Events of First Samuel Occurred

Moses 1500 B.C. | Period of Judges begins 1375 B.C. | Samuel born | David anointed Death of Saul 1010 B.C. | Ezra 500 B.C.

Theological Contribution

The major contribution of 1 and 2 Samuel is the negative and positive views of the kingship which they present. In calling for a king the people were rejecting God's rule, but the throne that God established with David would be established forever in the person of Jesus Christ the Messiah.

Special Consideration

The story of David and Goliath (1 Sam. 17) points up the contrast between David and Saul. Saul demonstrated both his folly and his inability to rule, but David demonstrated his wisdom and faith, proving that he was God's man for the throne of Israel.

Survey of First Samuel

Samuel (1—7)

Samuel's story begins late in the turbulent time of the judges when Eli is the judge-priest of Israel. He is confirmed as a prophet when the "word of the LORD was rare" (chaps. 1—3). Corruption at Shiloh by Eli's notoriously wicked sons leads to Israel's defeat and the loss of the ark of the covenant in the crucial battle with the Philistines (4:1–11). The glory of God departs from the tabernacle. With the death of Eli Samuel begins to function as the last of the judges. His prophetic ministry (7:3–17) leads to a revival in Israel, the return of the ark, and the defeat of the Philistines.

The First Book of Samuel

FOCUS	Samuel		Saul		
REFERENCE	1:1 ————	4:1 ———— 8:1 ————	13:1 ————	15:10 ————	31:13
DIVISION	First Transition of Leadership Eli–Samuel	Judgeship of Samuel	Second Transition of Leadership Samuel–Saul	Reign of Saul	Third Transition of Leadership Saul–David
TOPIC	Decline of Judges		Rise of Kings		
	Eli	Samuel	Saul		David
LOCATION	Canaan				
TIME	c. 94 Years				

Saul (8—15)

In their impatient demand for a king, Israel's motive (8:5)
and criteria (9:2) are wrong. Saul begins well (9—11), but his
good characteristics soon degenerate. In spite of Samuel's solemn prophetic warning (12), Saul and the people begin to act
wickedly. Saul presumptuously assumes the role of a priest
and offers up sacrifices (13). He makes a foolish vow (14) and
disobeys God's command to destroy the Amalekites (15).

Saul and David (16—31)

When God rejects Saul, He commissions Samuel to anoint
David as Israel's next king. God's king-elect serves in Saul's
court (16:14—23:29) and defeats the Philistine Goliath (17).
Jonathan's devotion to David leads him to sacrifice the
throne (20:30, 31) in acknowledgment of David's divine
right to it (18). David becomes a growing threat to the in-
sanely jealous Saul; but he is protected from Saul's wrath by
Jonathan, Michal, and Samuel (19, 20). The future king flees
to a Philistine city where he feigns insanity (21), and flees
again to Adullam where a band of men forms around him
(22).

On two occasions David spares Saul's life when he has the
opportunity to take it (24—26). David again seeks refuge
among the Philistines, but is not allowed to fight on their
side against Israel. Saul, afraid of impending battle against the
Philistines, foolishly consults a medium at En Dor to hear the
deceased Samuel's advice (28). The Lord rebukes Saul and
pronounces his doom; Saul falls on his own sword as the battle goes to the Philistines on Mount Gilboa (31).

Outline of First Samuel

The Book of Second Samuel

Background and general themes of 2 Samuel are discussed under 1 Samuel (pp. 46–47).

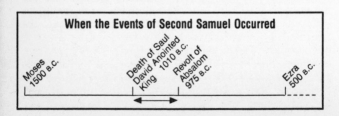

When the Events of Second Samuel Occurred

Moses 1500 B.C. — Death of Saul / David Anointed King 1010 B.C. — Revolt of Absalom 975 B.C. — Ezra 500 B.C.

◆

KEYS TO SECOND SAMUEL

Key Word: *David*

The central character of Second Samuel is David, around whom the entire book is written.

Key Verses: *Second Samuel 7:12, 13; 22:21*

Key Chapter: *Second Samuel 11*

The eleventh chapter of 2 Samuel is pivotal for the entire book. This chapter records the tragic sins of David regarding Bathsheba and her husband Uriah. All of the widespread blessings on David's family and his kingdom are quickly removed as God chastises His anointed one.

◆

Survey of Second Samuel

The Triumphs of David (1—10)

Chapters 1—4 record the seven-year reign of David over the territory of Judah. Even though Saul is David's murderous pursuer, David does not rejoice in his death because he recognizes that Saul had been divinely anointed as king. Saul's son Ishbosheth is installed by Abner as a puppet king over the northern tribes of Israel. David's allies led by Joab defeat Abner and Israel (2:17; 3:1). Abner defects and arranges to unite Israel and Judah under David, but Joab kills Abner in revenge. The powerless Ishbosheth is murdered by his own men, and David is made king of Israel (5:3). David soon captures and fortifies Jerusalem and makes it the civil and religious center of the now united kingdom. Under David's rule the nation prospers politically, spiritually, and militarily. David brings the ark to Jerusalem and seeks to build a house

The Second Book of Samuel

FOCUS	David's Triumphs			David's Transgressions		David's Troubles	
REFERENCE	1:1 ——————— 6:1 ——————— 8:1 ——————— 11:1 ——————— 12:1 ——————— 13:37 ——————— 24:25						
DIVISION	Political Triumphs	Spiritual Triumphs	Military Triumphs	Sins of Adultery and Murder		Troubles in David's House	Troubles in the Kingdom
TOPIC	Success			Sin		Failure	
	Obedience			Disobedience		Judgment	
LOCATION	David in Hebron	David in Jerusalem					
TIME	7½ Years	33 Years					

for God (7). His obedience in placing the Lord at the center of his rule leads to great national blessing (8—10).

The Transgressions of David (11)

David's crimes of adultery and murder mark the pivotal point of the book. Because of these transgressions, David's victories and successes are changed to the personal, family, and national troubles.

The Troubles of David (12—24)

The disobedience of the king produces chastisement and confusion at every level. David's glory and fame fade, never to be the same again. Nevertheless, David confesses his guilt when confronted by Nathan the prophet and is restored by God. A sword remains in David's house as a consequence of the sin: the baby born to David and Bathsheba dies, his son Amnon commits incest, and his son Absalom murders Amnon.

The consequences continue with Absalom's rebellion against his father. David is forced to flee from Jerusalem, and Absalom sets himself up as king. David would have been ruined, but God keeps Absalom from pursuing him until David has time to regroup his forces. Absalom's army is defeated by David's, and Joab kills Absalom in disobedience of David's orders to have him spared.

David seeks to amalgamate the kingdom, but conflict breaks out between the ten northern tribes of Israel and the two southern tribes of Judah and Benjamin. The closing chapters, actually an appendix, show how intimately the affairs of the people as a whole are tied to the spiritual and moral condition of the king.

Outline of Second Samuel

The Book of First Kings

◆

KEYS TO FIRST KINGS

Key Word: *Division of the Kingdom*

The theme of 1 Kings centers on the fact that the welfare of Israel and Judah depends upon the faithfulness of the people and their king to the covenant. The two books of Kings trace the monarchy from the point of its greatest prosperity under Solomon to its demise and destruction in the Assyrian and Babylonian captives. Observance of God's law produces blessing, but apostasy is rewarded by judgment.

Key Verses: *First Kings 9:4, 5; 11:11*

Key Chapter: *First Kings 12*

The critical turning point in 1 Kings occurs in chapter 12, when the united kingdom becomes the divided kingdom upon the death of Solomon.

◆

Authorship and Date

Early tradition credited the prophet Jeremiah with the writing of these two books, but most scholars today no longer hold to the Jeremiah theory. Evidence points to an unknown prophet who worked at the same time as Jeremiah to compile this history, some time after the Babylonians overran Jerusalem in 587 B.C.

Historical Setting

The four centuries covered by 1 and 2 Kings were times of change and political upheaval in the ancient world as the balance of power shifted. The Assyrian threat was particularly strong during the last 50 years of the northern kingdom. Under Tiglath-Pileser III, this conquering nation launched three devastating campaigns against Israel in 734, 733, and 732 B.C. The nation fell to Assyrian forces 10 years later in 722 B.C.

While Syria and Assyria were threats to Judah at various times, their worst enemy turned out to be the nation of Babylon. The Babylonians took captives and goods from Jerusalem in three campaigns—in 605 and 597 B.C. and in a two-year siege beginning in 588 B.C. in which Jerusalem finally fell in 587 B.C. The Temple was destroyed, and thousands of Judah's leading citizens were carried into captivity in Babylon.

When the Events of First Kings Occurred

Moses 1500 B.C. — Solomon 971 B.C. — Divided Kingdom 931 B.C. — Elijah/Elisha — Ezra 500 B.C.

Theological Contribution

The Books of First and Second Kings present an interesting contrast between King David of Judah and King Jeroboam I, the first king of the northern kingdom of Israel. Jeroboam established a legacy of idol worship by mixing false religion with worship of the one true God, and each succeeding king of Israel was measured against the standard of Jeroboam's idolatry. But King David was used as a standard of righteousness and justice.

Special Consideration

The Books of First and Second Kings describe several miracles wrought by God through the prophets Elijah and Elisha.

In addition to proving God's power, these miracles are also direct attacks on the pagan worship practices of the followers of Baal. Elijah's encounter with the prophets of Baal on Mount Carmel, for example, was a test of the power of Baal. Baal was silent, but God responded as Elijah had predicted.

Survey of First Kings

United Kingdom (chaps. 1—11)

Solomon's half-brother Adonijah attempts to take the throne as David's death is nearing, but Nathan the prophet alerts David who quickly directs the coronation of Solomon as coregent (chap. 1). Soon the kingdom "established in the hand of Solomon" (2:46). Solomon's ungodly marriages (cf. 3:1) eventually turn his heart from the Lord, but he begins well with a genuine love for God and a desire for wisdom. This wisdom leads to the expansion of Israel to the zenith of her power. Solomon's empire stretches from the border of Egypt to the border of Babylonia, and peace prevails.

From a theocratic perspective, Solomon's greatest achievement is the building of the Temple. The ark is placed in this exquisite building, which is filled with the glory of God, and Solomon offers a magnificent prayer of dedication. However, Solomon's wealth becomes a source of trouble when he begins to purchase forbidden items and his many foreign wives lead him into idolatry. God pronounces judgment and foretells that Solomon's son will rule only a fraction of the kingdom (Judah).

Divided Kingdom (chaps. 12—22)

Upon Solomon's death, his son Rehoboam chooses the foolish course of promising more severe taxation. Jeroboam, an officer in Solomon's army, leads the ten northern tribes in revolt. They make him their king, leaving only Judah and Benjamin in the south under Rehoboam. This begins a chaotic period with two nations and two sets of kings. Continual

The First Book of the Kings

FOCUS	United Kingdom			Divided Kingdom		
REFERENCE	1:1 ——— 3:1 ———		9:1 ——— 12:1 ———	15:1 ———	16:29 ———	22:53
DIVISION	Establishment of Solomon	Rise of Solomon	Decline of Solomon	Division of the Kingdom	Reigns of Various Kings	Reign of Ahab with Elijah
TOPIC	Solomon			Many Kings		
	Kingdom in Tranquility			Kingdoms in Turmoil		
LOCATION	Jerusalem: Capital of United Kingdom			Samaria: Capital of Israel Jerusalem: Capital of Judah		
TIME	c. 40 Years			c. 90 Years		

enmity and strife exists between the northern and southern kingdoms. The north is plagued by apostasy and the south by idolatry. Of all the northern and southern kings listed in this book, only Asa (15:9–24) and Jehoshaphat (22:41–50) do "what was right in the eyes of the LORD" (15:11; 22:43).

Ahab brings a measure of cooperation between the northern and southern kingdoms, but he reaches new depths of wickedness as a king. He introduces Jezebel's Baal worship to Israel. The prophet Elijah ministers during this low period in Israel's history, providing a witness of the word and power of God. Ahab's treachery in the matter of Naboth's vineyard causes a prophetic rebuke from Elijah (21). Ahab repents but later dies in battle because of his refusal to heed the words of Micaiah, another prophet of God.

Outline of First Kings

The Book of Second Kings

Background and general themes of 2 Kings are discussed under 1 Kings (pp. 55–57).

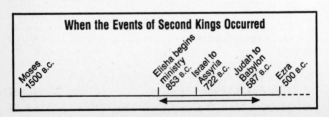

When the Events of Second Kings Occurred

Moses 1500 B.C. — Elisha begins ministry 853 B.C. — Israel to Assyria 722 B.C. — Judah to Babylon 587 B.C. — Ezra 500 B.C.

---◆---

KEYS TO SECOND KINGS

Key Word: *Captivities of the Kingdom*

Second Kings records both the destruction and captivity of Israel by the Assyrians (2 Kin. 17), as well as the destruction and captivity of Judah by the Babylonians (2 Kin. 25).

The book was written selectively, not exhaustively, from a prophetic viewpoint to teach that the decline and collapse of the two kingdoms occurred because of failure on the part of the rulers and people to heed the warnings of God's messengers.

Key Verses: *Second Kings 17:22, 23; 23:27*

Key Chapter: *Second Kings 25*

The last chapter of 2 Kings records the utter destruction of the city of Jerusalem and its glorious temple. Hope is still alive, however, with the remnant in the Babylonian captivity as Evil-Merodach frees Jehoiachin from prison and treats him kindly.

---◆---

Survey of Second Kings

Divided Kingdom (chaps. 1—17)

These chapters record the history of Israel's corruption in a relentless succession of bad kings from Ahaziah to Hoshea. The situation in Judah during this time (Jehoram to Ahaz) is somewhat better, but far from ideal. This dark period in the northern kingdom of Israel is interrupted only by the ministries of such godly prophets as Elijah and Elisha.

Elisha instructs one of his prophetic assistants to anoint Jehu king over Israel. Jehu fulfills the prophecies concerning

The Second Book of the Kings

FOCUS	Divided Kingdom			Surviving Kingdom		
REFERENCE	1:1 ——————— 9:1 ——————— 17:1 ——————— 18:1 ——————— 22:1 ——————— 25:1 ——— 25:30					
DIVISION	Ministry of Elisha Under Ahaziah and Jehoram	Reigns of Ten Kings of Israel and Eight Kings of Judah	Fall of Israel	Reigns of Hezekiah and Two Evil Kings	Reigns of Josiah and Four Evil Kings	Fall of Judah
TOPIC	Israel and Judah			Judah		
LOCATION	Ahaziah to Hoshea			Hezekiah to Zedekiah		
	Israel Deported to Assyria			Judah Deported to Babylonia		
TIME	131 Years (853–722 B.C.)			155 Years (715–560 B.C.)		

Ahab's descendants by putting them to death. He kills Ahab's wife Jezebel, his sons, and the priests of Baal, but does not depart from the calf worship set up by Jeroboam. Meanwhile, in Judah, Jezebel's daughter Athaliah kills all the descendants of David, except for Joash, and usurps the throne. However, Jehoiada the priest eventually removes her from the throne and places Joash in power. Joash restores the temple and serves God.

Syria gains virtual control over Israel, but there is no response to God's chastisement: the kings and people refuse to repent. There is a period of restoration under Jeroboam II, but the continuing series of wicked kings in Israel leads to its overthrow by Assyria.

Surviving Kingdom (chaps. 18—25)

Six years before the overthrow of Israel's capital of Samaria, Hezekiah becomes king of Judah. Because of his exemplary faith and reforms, God spares Jerusalem from Assyria and brings a measure of prosperity to Judah. However, Hezekiah's son Manasseh is so idolatrous that his long reign leads to the downfall of Judah. Even Josiah's later reforms cannot stem the tide of evil, and the four kings who succeed him are exceedingly wicked. Judgment comes with three deportations to Babylon and the destruction of Jerusalem. Still, the book ends on a note of hope with God preserving a remnant for Himself.

Outline of Second Kings

The Book of First Chronicles

◆

KEYS TO FIRST CHRONICLES

Key Word: *Priestly View of David's Reign*

Key Verses: *First Chronicles 17:11–14; 29:11*

Key Chapter: *First Chronicles 17*

Pivotal for the Book of First Chronicles as well as for the rest of the Scriptures is the Davidic Covenant recorded in Second Samuel 7 and First Chronicles 17. God promises David that He will "establish him [David's ultimate offspring, Jesus Christ] in My house and in My kingdom forever; and his throne shall be established forever" (1 Chr. 17:14).

◆

Authorship and Date

Ezra the priest and scribe seems the most likely possibility as the author of 1 and 2 Chronicles. The last two verses of 2 Chronicles are repeated in the first three verses of the Book of Ezra (originally written with Nehemiah as one book), probably indicating they went together in the original version. Most scholars agree that these four books were written and compiled by the same person, but not all accept the theory of Ezra's authorship.

Historical Setting

The Books of First and Second Chronicles cover several centuries of the history of God's covenant people—from the founders of the nation until the end of their captivity in Babylon and Persia about 538 B.C. The stage is set for the return of the Jewish people to Jerusalem after the Persians defeat Babylon and become the dominant power of the ancient world.

When the Events of First Chronicles Occurred

Theological Contribution

The Books of First and Second Chronicles should not only be read as histories, but for their insights into how God has kept faith with His covenant people across the centuries. By selecting events that show how God has kept His promises, the author presents a beautiful doctrine of hope that begins with Adam (1 Chr. 1:1) and stretches to the end of the captivity of God's people thousands of years later (2 Chr. 36:22–23). The clear implication for Christians today is that He is still a God of hope whose ultimate purpose will prevail in the world and in the lives of His people.

Survey of First Chronicles

Royal Line of David (1—9)

These nine chapters are the most comprehensive genealogical tables in the Bible. They trace the family tree of David and Israel in a highly selective manner to show God at work in selecting and preserving a people for Himself from the beginning of human history to the period after the Babylonian exile. The genealogies move from the patriarchal period (Adam to Jacob; 1:1—2:2) to the national period (Judah, Levi, and the other tribes of Israel; 2:3—9:44). The priestly perspective of Chronicles is evident in the special attention given to the tribe of Levi.

Reign of David (10—29)

Compared with 2 Samuel, David's life in 1 Chronicles is seen in an entirely different light. Chronicles completely omits David's struggles with Saul, his seven-year reign in Hebron, his various wives, his sin with Bathsheba, and Absalom's rebellion but adds events not found in 2 Samuel, such as David's preparations for the temple and its worship services.

Only one chapter is given to Saul's reign (10), because his heart was not right with God. David's story begins with his coronation over all Israel after he has already reigned for seven years as king over Judah. Chronicles emphasizes his concern for the things of the Lord, including his return of the ark and his desire to build a temple for God. God establishes His crucial covenant with David (17), and the kingdom is strengthened and expanded under his reign (18—20). His sin in numbering the people is recorded to teach the consequences of disobeying God's law. Most of the rest of the book (22—29) is concerned with David's preparations for the building of the temple and the worship associated with it. David is not allowed to build the temple (28:3), but he designs the plans, gathers the materials, prepares the site, and arranges for the

The First Book of the Chronicles

FOCUS	Royal Line of David		Reign of David			
REFERENCE	1:1 —————————— 10:1 —————— 13:1 ———— 18:1 ———— 21:1 ———— 28:1 —— 29:30					
DIVISION	Genealogies of David and Israel	Accession of David as King	Acquisition of the Ark	Victories of David	Preparation for the Temple	Last Days of David
TOPIC	Genealogy		History			
	Ancestry		Activity			
LOCATION	Israel					
TIME	Thousands of Years		c. 33 Years			

Levites, priests, choirs, porters, soldiers, and stewards. The book closes with his beautiful public prayer of praise and the accession of Solomon.

Outline of First Chronicles

The Book Of Second Chronicles

Background and general themes of 2 Chronicles are discussed under 1 Chronicles (pp. 66–67).

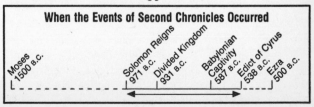

When the Events of Second Chronicles Occurred

Moses 1500 B.C. | Solomon Reigns 971 B.C. | Divided Kingdom 931 B.C. | Babylonian Captivity 587 B.C. | Edict of Cyrus 538 B.C. | Ezra 500 B.C.

◆

KEYS TO SECOND CHRONICLES

Key Word: *Priestly View of Judah*

The Book of Second Chronicles provides topical histories of the end of the united kingdom (Solomon) and the kingdom of Judah. More than historical annals, Chronicles is a *divine editorial* on the spiritual characteristics of the Davidic dynasty.

Key Verses: *Second Chronicles 7:14; 16:9*

Key Chapter: *Second Chronicles 34*

Second Chronicles records the reforms and revivals under such kings as Asa, Jehosphaphat, Joash, Hezekiah, and Josiah.

◆

Survey of Second Chronicles

Solomon's Reign (1—9)

The reign of Solomon brings in Israel's golden age of peace, prosperity, and temple worship. The kingdom is united and its boundaries extend to their greatest point. Solomon's wealth, wisdom, palace, and temple become legendary. His mighty spiritual, political, and architectural feats raise Israel to her zenith. However, it is in keeping with the purpose of Chronicles that six of these nine chapters concern the construction and dedication of the temple.

The Reign of Judah's Kings (10—36)

Unfortunately, Israel's glory is short-lived. Soon after Solomon's death the nation is divided, and both kingdoms begin a downward spiral that can only be delayed by the religious reforms. The nation generally forsakes the temple

The Second Book of the Chronicles

FOCUS	Reign of Solomon		Reigns of the Kings of Judah		
REFERENCE	1:1 ——— 2:1 ———	8:1 ———	10:1 ———	14:1 ———	36:1 – 36:23
DIVISION	Inauguration of Solomon	Completion of the Temple	The Glory of Solomon's Reign	The Division of the Kingdom	The Reforms Under Asa, Jehoshaphat, Joash, Hezekiah, and Josiah	The Fall of Judah
TOPIC	The Temple Is Constructed			The Temple Is Destroyed		
	Splendor			Disaster		
LOCATION	Judah					
TIME	c. 40 Years			c. 393 Years		

and the worship of God, and is soon torn by warfare and unrest. The reformation efforts on the part of some of Judah's kings are valiant, but never last beyond one generation. When the king does serves the Lord, Judah is blessed with political and economic prosperity.

Outline of Second Chronicles

The Book of Ezra

Authorship and Date

In the Hebrew Old Testament, Ezra and Nehemiah appeared as one unbroken book, closely connected in theme and style to the books of First and Second Chronicles. The last two verses of 2 Chronicles are repeated in the first three verses of the Book of Ezra, probably indicating that they belonged together. For this reason, many scholars believe Ezra served as writer and editor-compiler of all four of these books sometime late in the fifth century B.C.

Historical Setting

The Book of Ezra belongs to the postexilic period. These were the years just after a remnant of the nation returned to Jerusalem following their exile of about 50 years in Babylon. The return came about after the defeat of Babylon by the

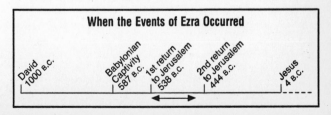

When the Events of Ezra Occurred

David 1000 B.C. | Babylonian Captivity 587 B.C. | 1st return to Jerusalem 538 B.C. | 2nd return to Jerusalem 444 B.C. | Jesus 4 B.C.

◆

KEYS TO EZRA

Key Word: *Temple*

The basic theme of Ezra is the restoration of the Temple and the spiritual, moral, and social restoration of the returned remnant in Jerusalem under the leadership of Zerubbabel and Ezra.

Key Verses: *Ezra 1:3; 7:10*

Key Chapter: *Ezra 6*

Ezra 6 records the completion and dedication of the Temple which stimulates the obedience of the remnant to keep the Passover and separate themselves.

◆

Persian Empire. Unlike the Babylonians, the Persians allowed their subject nations to live in their own native regions under the authority of a ruling governor and practiced religious tolerance.

Theological Contribution

The theme of the Book of Ezra is the restoration of the remnant of God's covenant people in Jerusalem in obedience to His Law. In His providence, God used even the unrighteous Persian kings to work His ultimate will and return His people to their homeland.

Special Consideration

Ezra's treatment of the pagan women whom the Jewish men had married poses a problem to some readers (10:10–19). How could he be so cruel as to insist that these wives be "put away" (divorced) with no means of support? His actions must be understood in light of the drastic situation that faced the Jewish community in Jerusalem following the exile. Only a small remnant of the covenant people had returned, and it was important for them to keep themselves from pagan idolatry and foreign cultural influences at all costs. Ezra must have realized, too, that this was one of the problems which had led to their downfall and captivity as a people in the first place.

Survey of Ezra

The Restoration of the Temple (chaps. 1—6)

Cyrus, king of Persia, issues a proclamation allowing the Jewish people to return to Jerusalem to rebuild their Temple and resettle their native land. About 50,000 of the people return under the leadership of Zerubbabel, a "prince" of Judah (a direct descendant of King David), appointed by Cyrus as governor of Jerusalem (2:64-65). Those who return are from the tribes of Judah, Benjamin, and Levi; but it is evident that representatives from the other ten tribes eventually return as well.

Zerubbabel first restores the altar and the religious feasts before beginning work on the temple itself. The foundation of the temple is laid, but opposition arises and the work ceases. The prophets Haggai and Zechariah exhort the people to get back to building the temple (5:1, 2), and the work begins again under Zerubbabel and Joshua the high priest. Tattenai, a Persian governor, protests to King Darius I about the temple building and challenges their authority to continue. King Darius finds the decree of Cyrus and confirms it, even forcing Tattenai to provide whatever is needed to complete the work.

The Reformation of the People (chaps. 7—10)

A smaller return under Ezra takes place in eighty-one years after the first return under Zerubbabel by the authority of King Artaxerxes I. Less than two thousand men return but

The Book of Ezra

FOCUS	Restoration of the Temple		Reformation of the People	
REFERENCE	1:1 ——————— 3:1 ———————		7:1 ——————— 9:1 ——————— 10:44	
DIVISION	First Return to Jerusalem	Construction of the Temple	Second Return to Jerusalem	Restoration of the People
TOPIC	Zerubbabel		Ezra	
	First Return of 49,897		Second Return of 1,754	
LOCATION	Persia to Jerusalem		Persia to Jerusalem	
TIME	22 Years (538–516 B.C.)		1 Year (458–457 B.C.)	

God uses Ezra to rebuild the people spiritually and morally. When Ezra discovers that the people and the priests have intermarried with foreign women, he identifies with the sin of his people and offers a great intercessory prayer on their behalf. During the gap of fifty-eight years between Ezra 6 and 7, the people fall into a confused spiritual state and Ezra is alarmed. They quickly respond to Ezra's confession and weeping by making a covenant to put away their foreign wives and to live in accordance with God's law. This confession and response to the Word of God brings about a great revival.

Outline of Ezra

The Book of Nehemiah

◆

KEYS TO NEHEMIAH

Key Word: *Walls*

While Ezra deals with the religious restoration of Judah, Nehemiah is primarily concerned with Judah's political and geographical restoration. The first seven chapters are devoted to the rebuilding of Jerusalem's walls, because Jerusalem was the spiritual and political center of Judah. Without walls, Jerusalem could hardly be considered a city at all.

Key Verses: *Nehemiah 6:15, 16; 8:8*

Key Chapter: *Nehemiah 9*

The key to the Old Testament is the covenant, which is its theme and unifying factor. Israel's history can be divided according to the nation's obedience or disobedience to God's conditional covenant: blessings from obedience and destruction from disobedience. Nehemiah 9 records that upon completion of the Jerusalem wall the nation reaffirmed its loyalty to the covenant.

◆

Authorship and Date

As written originally in the Hebrew language, Nehemiah, 1 and 2 Chronicles, and Ezra formed one unbroken book, written probably by the priest Ezra. Most conservative scholars, however, believe Nehemiah contributed some of the material that appears in the book which bears his name (chaps. 1—7, 11—13).

Historical Setting

The Book of Nehemiah is set in that crucial time in Jewish history known as the postexilic period. These were the years after the return of the covenant people to their homeland about 530 B.C. following 70 years of captivity in Babylon and Persia.

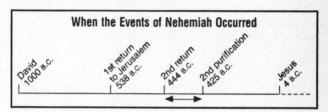

When the Events of Nehemiah Occurred

David 1000 B.C. | 1st return to Jerusalem 538 B.C. | 2nd return 444 B.C. | 2nd purification 425 B.C. | Jesus 4 B.C.

Theological Contribution

Nehemiah is an excellent case study in courageous, resourceful leadership and the power of prayer. Against overwhelming odds, he encouraged the people to "rise up and build" (2:18). Their rapid completion of the wall has been an inspiration to countless Christians across the centuries who have faced the challenge of completing some major task to the glory of God.

Survey of Nehemiah

The Reconstruction of the Wall (chaps. 1—7)

When Nehemiah hears of the second destruction of the Jerusalem walls, his great concern for his people and the welfare of Jerusalem leads him to take bold action. He prays on behalf of his people and then secures Artaxerxes' permission, provision, and protection for the massive project of rebuilding the walls.

The return under Nehemiah in 444 B.C. takes place thir-

The Book of Nehemiah

FOCUS	Reconstruction of the Wall		Restoration of the People	
REFERENCE	1:1 ——————— 3:1 ———————		8:1 ——————— 11:1 ——————— 13:31	
DIVISION	Preparation to Reconstruct the Wall	Reconstruction of the Wall	Renewal of the Covenant	Obedience to the Covenant
TOPIC	Political		Spiritual	
	Construction		Instruction	
LOCATION	Jerusalem			
TIME	19 Years (444–425 B.C.)			

teen years after the return led by Ezra, and ninety-four years after the return led by Zerubbabel. Nehemiah inspects the walls and work begins immediately, but opposition also arises in the form of mockery and conspiracy. Nehemiah sets half of the people on military watch and half on construction. He also deals with internal problems with prayer and action by example.

The Restoration of the People (chaps. 8—13)

The construction of the walls is followed by consecration and consolidation of the people. Ezra the priest is the leader of the spiritual revival (chaps. 8—10), reminiscent of the reforms he led thirteen years earlier (Ezra 9 and 10). Ezra gives the people a marathon reading of the law and the covenant is then renewed with God as the people commit themselves to separate from the Gentiles in marriage and to obey God's commandments.

Lots are drawn to determine who will remain in Jerusalem and who will return to the cities of their inheritance. One-tenth are required to stay in Jerusalem, and the rest of the land is resettled by the people and priests. The walls of Jerusalem are dedicated to the Lord in a joyful ceremony accompanied by music.

Unfortunately, Ezra's revival is short-lived; and Nehemiah, who returned to Persia in 432 B.C. (13:6), makes a second trip to Jerusalem about 425 B.C. to reform the people. He cleanses the Temple, enforces the Sabbath, and requires the people to put away all foreign wives.

Outline of Nehemiah

The Book of Esther

Authorship and Date

For centuries scholars have debated the question of who wrote the Book of Esther. Until new evidence emerges, the author must remain unknown. Esther must have been written some time shortly after 465 B.C. near the end of the reign of the Persian king Xerxes.

Historical Setting

The Book of Esther is valuable historically because it gives us a view of the Jewish people who were scattered throughout the ancient world after the Babylonian exile. When the Persians overthrew the Babylonians, they allowed the Jewish exiles to return to their native land; but thousands of Jewish

◆

KEYS TO ESTHER

Key Word: *Providence*

The Book of Esther was written to show how the Jewish people were protected and preserved by the gracious hand of God from the threat of annihilation. Although God disciplines His covenant people, He never abandons them.

Key Verses: *Esther 4:14; 8:17*

Key Chapter: *Esther 8*

According to the Book of Esther, the salvation of the Jews is accomplished through the second decree of King Ahasuerus, allowing the Jews to defend themselves against their enemies. Chapter 8 records this pivotal event with the accompanying result that "many of the people of the land became Jews" (8:17).

◆

citizens chose to remain in Persia. This is the setting of Esther.

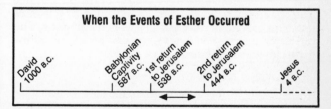

When the Events of Esther Occurred

David 1000 B.C. — Babylonian Captivity 587 B.C. — 1st return to Jerusalem 538 B.C. — 2nd return to Jerusalem 444 B.C. — Jesus 4 B.C.

Theological Contribution

Beginning with Genesis, God had made it clear that He would bless His covenant people and bring a curse upon those who tried to do them harm (Gen. 12:1, 3). Esther shows once again that we can trust God to work out His ultimate purpose of redemption in our lives.

Special Consideration

One unusual fact about this book is that it never mentions the name of God, but a careful reading will reveal that the book does have a spiritual base. Although the enemies of the covenant people may triumph for a season, God holds the key to ultimate victory.

Survey of Esther

The Threat to the Jews (chaps. 1—4)

Ahasuerus (King Xerxes of Persia) provides a lavish banquet and display of royal glory for the people of Susa, and proudly seeks to make Queen Vashti's beauty a part of the program. When she refuses to appear, the king seeks another queen, and Esther wins the royal "beauty pageant." At her cousin Mordecai's instruction, she does not reveal that she is Jewish. With her help, Mordecai is able to warn the king of an assassination plot, and his deed is recorded in the palace records.

Meanwhile, Haman becomes captain of the princes, but Mordecai refuses to bow to him. In retaliation he convinces Ahasuerus to issue an edict that all Jews in the empire will be slain eleven months hence in a single day. Mordecai asks Esther to appeal to the king to spare the Jews.

The Triumph of the Jews (chaps. 5—10)

After fasting, Esther appears before the king to invite him to a banquet along with Haman. At the banquet she requests that they attend a second banquet, as she seeks the right moment to divulge her request. Haman is flattered but later enraged when he sees Mordecai. He takes his wife's suggestion to build a large gallows for his enemy. That night a sleepless

The Book of Esther

FOCUS	Threat to the Jews		Triumph of the Jews	
REFERENCE	1:1 —————— 2:21 ——————	5:1 ——————	8:4 ——————	10:3
DIVISION	Selection of Esther as Queen	Formulation of the Plot by Haman	Triumph of Mordecai over Haman	Triumph of Israel over Her Enemies
TOPIC	Feasts of Ahasuerus		Feasts of Esther and Purim	
	Grave Danger		Great Deliverance	
LOCATION	Persia			
TIME	10 Years (483–473 B.C.)			

Ahasuerus discovers the oversight in rewarding Mordecai and asks Haman's counsel. Haman, mistakenly thinking the king wants to honor him, tells the king how the honor should be bestowed, only to find out that the reward is for Mordecai. At the second banquet Esther makes her plea for her people and accuses Haman of his treachery. The infuriated king has Haman hanged on the gallows intended for Mordecai.

Persian law sealed with the king's ring (3:12) cannot be revoked, but at Esther's request the king issues a new decree to all the provinces that the Jews may assemble and defend themselves on the day when they are attacked by their enemies. The Jews defeat their enemies in their cities throughout the Persian provinces, and Mordecai advances to a position second only to the king.

Outline of Esther

THREE

BOOKS OF POETRY
AND WISDOM

◆

APPROXIMATELY one-third of the Old Testament is written in poetry. This includes entire books (except for short prose sections), such as Job, Psalms, Proverbs, the Song of Solomon, and Lamentations. Many scholars consider the Book of Job to be not only the greatest poem in the Old Testament but also one of the greatest poems in all literature.

The wisdom literature of the Old Testament consists of the Books of Job, Proverbs, and Ecclesiastes, and certain of the Psalms. *Practical wisdom* (for example, Proverbs) consists mainly of wise sayings that offer guidelines for a successful and happy life. *Speculative wisdom* (for example, Job) reflects upon the deeper issues of the meaning of life, the worth and value of life, and the existence of evil in the world.

BOOKS OF POETRY AND WISDOM	
BOOK	**SUMMARY**
Job	An examination of the problems of evil and human suffering
Psalms	The song book or hymnal of ancient Israel
Proverbs	Wise sayings and observations designed to develop proper attitudes and behavior

Ecclesiastes	A philosophical description of the emptiness of life without God
Song of Solomon	A love song portraying the beauty of a human love relationship as a symbol of divine love

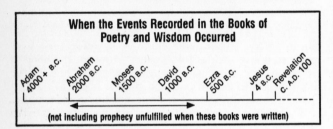

When the Events Recorded in the Books of Poetry and Wisdom Occurred

Adam 4000 + B.C. — Abraham 2000 B.C. — Moses 1500 B.C. — David 1000 B.C. — Ezra 500 B.C. — Jesus 4 B.C. — Revelation C. A.D. 100

(not including prophecy unfulfilled when these books were written)

The Book of Job

Authorship and Date

The author of Job is unknown, and there are no textual hints as to his identity. The non-Hebraic cultural background of this book may point to gentile authorship.

The date of the book's writing is still something of a mystery. Some place it as late as the second century B.C., but many conservative scholars and historical evidence favor about 950 B.C., the golden age of biblical Wisdom literature.

Historical Setting

Job probably lived during the time of the patriarch Abraham, about 2000 to 1800 B.C. Like Abraham, Job's wealth was measured in flocks and herds.

◆

KEYS TO JOB

Key Word: *Sovereignty*

The basic question of the book is, "Why do the righteous suffer if God is loving and all-powerful?" Suffering itself is not the central theme; rather, the focus is on what Job *learns* from his suffering—the sovereignty of God over all creation.

Key Verses: *Job 13:15; 37:23, 24*

Key Chapter: *Job 42*

Upon Job's full recognition of the utter majesty and sovereignty of the Lord, he repents and no longer demands an answer as to the "why" of his plight.

◆

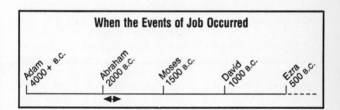

When the Events of Job Occurred

Adam 4000 + B.C.　　Abraham 2000 B.C.　　Moses 1500 B.C.　　David 1000 B.C.　　Ezra 500 B.C.

Theological Contribution

Job teaches us that sometimes the righteous must suffer without knowing the reason why; that is why it is important to trust God in everything. When we see how great He is, like Job, we bow down in humble submission.

Survey of Job

The Dilemma of Job (chaps. 1—2)

Written in the form of a dramatic poem, Job begins with two introductory chapters, in the form of a narrative or prologue, that set the stage for the rest of the book.

Job is considered a wealthy man in the tribal culture of the ancient world. But Satan insists that the integrity of this upright man has never been tested. He accuses Job of serving God only because God has protected him and made him wealthy. God grants permission for the testing to begin.

In rapid fashion, Job's sons and daughters are killed and all his flocks are driven away by his enemies. Finally, Job himself is stricken with a terrible skin disease. In his sorrow he sits mourning on an ash heap, scraping his sores with a piece of pottery while he laments his misfortune.

The Debates of Job (chaps. 3—37)

Job's three friends—Eliphaz, Bildad, and Zophar—arrive to mourn with him and to offer their comfort. But instead of comforting Job, these friends launch into long lectures and philosophical debates to show Job the reasons for his suffering. Job's responses to their simplistic assumptions increase the emotional fervor of the debate cycles. He makes three basic complaints: (1) God does not hear me (13:3, 24; 19:7; 23:3–5; 30:20); (2) God is punishing me (6:4; 7:20; 9:17); and (3) God allows the wicked to prosper (21:7). After Job's closing monologue (chaps. 27—31), Elihu freshens the air with a more perceptive and accurate view than those offered by Eliphaz, Bildad, or Zophar (chaps. 32—37).

The Deliverance of Job (chaps. 38—42)

After Elihu's preparatory discourse, God Himself ends the debate by speaking to Job from the whirlwind. In His first speech God reveals His power and wisdom as Creator and Preserver of the physical and animal world. Job responds by

The Book of Job

FOCUS	Dilemma of Job	Debates of Job				Deliverance of Job
REFERENCE	1:1 ———— 3:1	First Cycle of Debate ———— 15:1	Second Cycle of Debate ———— 22:1	Third Cycle of Debate ———— 27:1	Final Defense of Job ———— 32:1	Solution of Elihu ———— 38:1	Controversy of God with Job ———— 42:17
DIVISION	Controversy of God and Satan		Debate				Controversy of God with Job
TOPIC	Conflict		Debate				Repentance
	Prose		Poetry				Prose
LOCATION	Land of Uz (North Arabia)						
TIME	Patriarchal Period (c. 2000 B.C.)						

acknowledging his own ignorance and insignificance; he can offer no rebuttal (40:3–5). In His second speech God reveals His sovereign authority and challenges Job with two illustrations of His power to control the uncontrollable. This time Job responds by acknowledging his error with a repentant heart (42:1–6). When he acknowledges God's sovereignty over his life, his worldly goods are restored twofold. Job prays for his three friends who have cut him so deeply, but Elihu's speech is never rebuked.

Outline of Job

The Book of Psalms

Authorship, Date and Historical Setting

Most people automatically think of David when they consider the question of who wrote the Book of Psalms. A shepherd boy who rose to become the most famous king of Judah, he was also known as "the sweet psalmist of Israel"

KEYS TO PSALMS

Key Word: *Worship*

The central theme of the Book of Psalms is worship—God is worthy of all praise because of who He is, what He has done, and what He will do. His goodness extends through all time and eternity.

Key Verses: *Psalm 19:14; 145:21*

Key Chapter: *Psalm 100*

So many of the favorite chapters of the Bible are contained in the Book of Psalms that it is difficult to select the key chapter among such psalms as Psalms 1; 22; 23; 24; 37; 72; 100; 101; 119; 121; and 150. The two central themes of worship and praise are beautifully wed in Psalm 100.

(2 Sam 23:1). While it is clear that David wrote many of the individual psalms, he is definitely not the author of the entire collection. Two of the psalms (72 and 127) are attributed to Solomon, David's son and successor. Psalm 90 is a prayer assigned to Moses. Another group of 12 psalms (50 and 73—83) is ascribed to the family of Asaph. The sons of Korah wrote 11 psalms (42, 44—49, 84—85, 87—88). Psalm 88 is attributed to Heman, while Psalm 89 is assigned to Ethan the Ezrahite. With the exception of Solomon and Moses, all these additional authors were priests or Levites who were responsible for providing music for sanctuary worship during David's reign. Fifty of the psalms designate no specific person as author. They were probably written by many different people.

A careful examination of the authorship question, as well as the subject matter covered by the psalms themselves, reveals they span a period of many centuries. The oldest psalm in the collection is probably the prayer of Moses (90), a reflection on the frailty of man as compared to the eternity of God. The latest psalm is probably 137, a song of lament clearly written during the days when the Hebrews were being held captive by the Babylonians, from about 586 to 538 B.C.

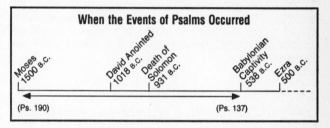

Theological Contribution

We may think of the psalms as a description of our human response to God. At times God is presented in all His majesty and glory, and our response is wonder, awe, and fear. Other psalms portray God as a loving Lord who is involved in our lives, and our response is to draw close to His comfort and security.

The psalms also have a great deal to say about the person and work of Christ: He would be crucified (Ps. 22); He would be a priest like Melchizedek (Ps. 110:4; Heb. 5:6); He would pray for His enemies (Ps. 109:4; Luke 23:34); and His throne would be established forever (Ps. 45:6; Heb. 1:8).

Special Consideration

Psalms provides the best examples in the Bible of the nature of Hebrew poetry. The principle upon which this poetry is based is not rhythm or rhyme but parallelism. In parallelism, one phrase is followed by another that says essentially the same thing but in a more creative, expressive way. Here is a good example of this poetic technique:

The Lord of hosts is with us;
The God of Jacob is our refuge (46:11).

This example is known as *synonymous parallelism* because the second phrase expresses the same thought as the first. But sometimes the succeeding line introduces a thought that is directly opposite to the first idea. This is known as *antithetic parallelism*. Here is a familiar couplet that demonstrates this form:

For the Lord knows the way of the righteous,
But the way of the ungodly shall perish (1:6).

A third kind of parallelism in Hebrew poetry may be called *progressive*, or climbing—in which part of the first line is repeated in the second, but also something more is added. For example:

The floods have lifted up, O Lord,
The floods have lifted up their voice (93:3).

Another literary device which the Hebrew writers used to give their psalms a peculiar style and rhythm was the *alphabetical acrostic*. The best example of this technique is Psalm 119—the longest in the collection—which contains 22 different sections of eight verses each. Each major section is headed by a different letter of the Hebrew alphabet. In the original language, each verse in these major divisions of the psalm begins with the Hebrew letter which appears as the heading for that section. Many modern translations of the Bible include these Hebrew letters as a part of the structure of this psalm. Writing this poem with such a structure required a high degree of literary skill.

Survey of Psalms

In the original Hebrew manuscripts, this long collection of 150 psalms was divided into five sections:

> Book 1 (1–41);
> Book 2 (42–72);
> Book 3 (73–89);
> Book 4 (90–106);
> and Book 5 (107–150).

Each of these major sections closes with a brief prayer of praise, or doxology. Many modern translations of the Bible, including the NKJV, retain this fivefold division.

The following classification divides the psalms into ten types:

(1) *Individual Lament Psalms:* Directly addressed to God, these psalms petition Him to rescue and defend an individual. They have these elements: (a) an introduction (usually a cry to God), (b) the lament, (c) a confession of trust in God, (d) the petition, (e) a declaration or vow of praise. Most psalms are of this type (e.g., 3–7; 12; 13; 22; 25–28; 35; 38–40; 42; 43; 51; 54–57; 59; 61; 63; 64; 69–71; 86; 88; 102; 109; 120; 130; 140–143).

(2) *Communal Lament Psalms:* The only difference is that the nation rather than an individual makes the lament (e.g., 44; 60; 74; 79; 80; 83; 85; 90; and 123).

(3) *Individual Thanksgiving Psalms:* The psalmist publicly acknowledges God's activity on his behalf. These psalms thank God for something He has already done or express confidence in what He will yet do. They have these elements: (a) a proclamation to praise God, (b) a summary statement, (c) a report of deliverance, and (d) a renewed vow of praise (e.g., 18; 30; 32; 34; 40; 41; 66; 106; 116; and 138).

(4) *Communal Thanksgiving Psalms:* In these psalms the acknowledgment is made by the nation rather than by an individual (see 124 and 129).

The Book of Psalms

BOOK	Book I (1–41)	Book II (42–72)	Book III (73–89)	Book IV (90–106)	Book V (107–150)
CHIEF AUTHOR	David	David and Korah	Asaph	Anonymous	David and Anonymous
NUMBER OF PSALMS	41	31	17	17	44
BASIC CONTENT	Songs of Worship	Hymns of National Interest		Anthems of Praise	
TOPICAL LIKENESS TO PENTATEUCH	Genesis: Humanity and Creation	Exodus: Deliverance and Redemption	Leviticus: Worship and Sanctuary	Numbers: Wilderness and Wandering	Deuteronomy: Scripture and Praise
CLOSING DOXOLOGY	41:13	72:18, 19	89:52	106:48	150:1-6
POSSIBLE COMPILER	David	Hezekiah or Josiah		Ezra or Nehemiah	
POSSIBLE DATES OF COMPILATION	c. 1020–970 B.C.	c. 970–610 B.C.		Until c. 430 B.C.	

(5) *General Praise Psalms:* These psalms are more general than the thanksgiving psalms. The psalmist attempts to magnify the name of God and boast about His greatness (see 8; 19; 29; 103; 104; 139; 148; 150). The joyous exclamation "hallelujah" ("praise the LORD!") is found in several of these psalms.

(6) *Descriptive Praise Psalms:* These psalms praise God for His attributes and acts (e.g., 33; 36; 105; 111; 113; 117; 135; 136; 146; 147).

(7) *Enthronement Psalms:* These psalms describe Yahweh's sovereign reign over all (see 47; 93; 96–99). Some anticipate the kingdom rule of Christ.

(8) *Pilgrimage Songs:* Also known as Songs of Zion, these psalms were sung by pilgrims traveling up to Jerusalem for the three annual religious feasts of Passover, Pentecost, and Tabernacles (see 43; 46; 48; 76; 84; 87; 120–134).

(9) *Royal Psalms:* The reigns of the earthly King and the heavenly King are portrayed in most of these psalms (e.g., 2; 18; 20; 21; 45; 72; 89; 101; 110; 132; and 144).

(10) *Wisdom and Didactic Psalms:* The reader is exhorted and instructed in the way of righteousness (see 1; 37; 119).

Other Special Terms

A number of special musical terms (some obscure) are used in the superscriptions of the psalms. "To the Chief Musician" appears in fifty-five psalms indicating that there is a collection of psalms used by the conductor of music in the temple, perhaps for special occasions. "Selah" is used seventy-one times in the psalms and three times in Habakkuk 3. This word may mark a pause, a musical interlude, or a crescendo.

The Book of Proverbs

◆

KEYS TO PROVERBS

Key Word: *Wisdom*

Proverbs is one of the few biblical books that clearly spells out its purpose. The words "wisdom and instruction" in 1:2 complement each other because *wisdom (hokhmah)* means "skill" and *instruction (musar)* means "discipline." No skill is perfected without discipline, and when a person has skill he has freedom to create something beautiful. Proverbs deals with the most fundamental skill of all: practical righteousness before God in every area of life.

Key Verses: *Proverbs 1:5–7 and 3:5, 6*

Key Chapter: *Proverbs 31*

The last chapter of Proverbs is unique in ancient literature, as it reveals a very high and noble view of women.

◆

Authorship and Date

The name of Solomon as author is associated with the Book of Proverbs from the very beginning. Additional evidence of his authorship is found within the book itself, where Solomon is identified as author of the section from 10:1 to 22:16 as well as writer of chapters 25—29.

But what about those portions of Proverbs that clearly are attributed to other writers, such as "the wise" (22:17), Agur (30:1), and King Lemuel (31:1)? Many scholars believe Solomon wrote the basic core of Proverbs but added some writings from other sources, giving proper credit to their writers. Additionally, a second collection of proverbs attributed to Solomon (chaps. 25—29) was not added to the book until more than 200 years after his death.

In its original version the book must have been written and compiled by Solomon some time during his reign from 970 B.C. to 931 B.C. Then, about 720 B.C. the material now contained in chapters 25—29 was added to the book.

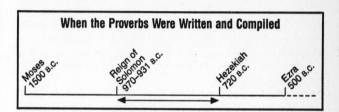

When the Proverbs Were Written and Compiled

Moses 1500 B.C. — Reign of Solomon 970-931 B.C. — Hezekiah 720 B.C. — Ezra 500 B.C.

Theological Contribution

Israel's distinctive contribution to the thinking of the wise men of all nations and times is that true wisdom is centered in respect and reverence for God. This is the great underlying theme of the Book of Proverbs.

Special Consideration

In reading the Book of Proverbs, we need to make sure we do not turn these wise sayings into literal promises. Proverbs are statements of the way things generally turn out in God's world. For example, it is generally true that those who keep God's commandments will enjoy "length of days and long life" (3:2). But this should not be interpreted as an ironclad guarantee. It is important to keep God's laws, no matter how long or short our earthly life may be.

Survey of Proverbs

The Purpose of Proverbs (1:1-7)

The brief prologue states the author, theme, and purpose of the book.

The Proverbs to the Youth (1:8—9:18)

Following the introduction, there is a series of ten exhortations, each beginning with "My son" (1:8—9:18). These messages introduce the concept of wisdom in the format of a father's efforts to persuade his son to pursue the path of wisdom in order to achieve godly success in life. Wisdom rejects the invitation of crime and foolishness, rewards seekers of wisdom on every level, and wisdom's discipline provides freedom and safety (1—4).

Wisdom protects one from illicit sensuality and its consequences, from foolish practices and laziness, and from adultery and the lure of the harlot (5—7).

Wisdom is to be preferred to folly because of its divine origin and rich benefits (8 and 9). There are four kinds of fools, ranging from those who are naive and uncommitted to scoffers who arrogantly despise the way of God. The fool is not mentally deficient; he is self-sufficient, ordering his life as if there were no God.

The Proverbs of Solomon (10:1—24:34)

There is a minimal amount of topical arrangement in these chapters. There are some thematic clusters (e.g., 26:1-12, 13-16, 20-22), but the usual units are one-verse maxims. It is helpful to assemble and organize these proverbs according to such specific themes as money and speech. This Solomonic collection consists of 375 proverbs of Solomon.

Chapters 10—15 contrast right and wrong in practice, and all but nineteen proverbs use antithetic parallelism, that is, parallels of paired opposite principles.

Chapters 16:1—22:16 offers a series of self-evident moral

The Book of Proverbs

FOCUS	Purpose of Proverbs	Proverbs to Youth	Proverbs of Solomon	Proverbs of Solomon (Hezekiah)	Words of Agur	Words of Lemuel
REFERENCE	1:1 ——————	1:8 ——————	10:1 ——————	25:1 ——————	30:1 ——————	31:1 ———— 31:31
DIVISION	Purpose and Theme	Father's Exhortations	First Collection of Solomon	Second Collection of Solomon	Numerical Proverbs	Virtuous Wife
TOPIC	Prologue	Principles of Wisdom			Epilogue	
TOPIC	Commendation of Wisdom		Counsel of Wisdom		Comparisons of Wisdom	
LOCATION	Judah					
TIME	c. 970–720 B.C.					

truths and all but eighteen proverbs use synonymous parallelism, that is, parallels of paired identical or similar principles.

The words of wise men (22:17—24:34) are given in two groups. The first group includes thirty distinct sayings (22:17—24:22), and six more are found in the second group (24:23—34).

The Proverbs Copied by Hezekiah's Men (25:1—29:27)

This second Solomonic collection was copied and arranged by "the men of Hezekiah" (25:1). These proverbs in chapters 25—29 further develop the themes in the first Solomonic collection.

The Words of Agur (30:1-33)

The last two chapters of Proverbs form an appendix of sayings by two otherwise unknown sages, Agur and Lemuel. Most of Agur's material is given in clusters of numerical proverbs.

The Words of King Lemuel (31:1-31)

The last chapter includes an acrostic of twenty-two verses (the first letter of each verse consecutively follows the complete Hebrew alphabet) portraying a virtuous wife (31:10-31).

Outline of Proverbs

The Book of Ecclesiastes

Authorship and Date

King Solomon of Israel, a ruler noted for his great wisdom and vast riches, has traditionally been accepted as the author of Ecclesiastes, though some scholars note that it uses words and phrases that belong to a much later time in Israel's history. The book was probably written some time during 970 to 931 B.C.

◆

KEYS TO ECCLESIASTES

Key Word: *Vanity*

The word *vanity* appears thirty-seven times to express the many things that cannot be understood about life. All earthly goals and ambitions lead to dissatisfaction and frustration when pursued as ends in themselves apart from God.

Key Verses: *Ecclesiastes 2:24 and 12:13, 14*

Key Chapter: *Ecclesiastes 12*

Only when the Preacher views his life from God's perspective "above the sun" does it take on meaning as a precious gift "from the hand of God" (2:24). Chapter 12 resolves the book's extensive inquiry into the meaning of life with the single conclusion, "Fear God and keep His commandments, for this is the whole duty of man" (12:13).

◆

Theological Contribution

The Book of Ecclesiastes has a powerful message for our selfish, materialistic age. It teaches that great accomplishments and earthly possessions alone do not bring lasting happiness. True satisfaction comes from serving God and following His will for our lives.

But another important truth from Ecclesiastes, which we often overlook, is that life is to be enjoyed. "Every man should eat and drink and enjoy the good of all his labor—it is the gift of God" (3:13).

Special Consideration

One of the most moving passages in the Bible is the poem from Ecclesiastes on the proper time for all events: "A time to be born, and a time to die" (3:2). This text, if taken seriously, can restore balance to our living.

Survey of Ecclesiastes

The Thesis That "All Is Vanity" (1:1–11)

After a one-verse introduction, the Preacher states his theme: "Vanity of vanities, all *is* vanity" (1:2). Life under the sun appears to be futile and perplexing. Verses 3–11 illustrate this theme in the endless and apparently meaningless cycles found in nature and history.

The Proof That "All Is Vanity" (1:12—6:12)

The Preacher describes his multiple quest for meaning and satisfaction as he explores his vast personal resources. He begins with wisdom (1:12–18) and moves on to laughter, hedonism, and wine (2:1–3) and then turns to works, women, and wealth (2:4–11); but all lead to emptiness. He realizes that wisdom is far greater than foolishness, but both seem to lead to futility in view of the brevity of life and universality of death (2:12–17). He concludes by acknowledging that contentment and joy are found only in God.

When the Preacher considers the unchanging order of events and the fixed laws of God, Time is short, and there is no eternity on earth (3:1–15). The futility of death seems to cancel the difference between righteousness and wickedness (3:16–22). Chapters 4 and 5 explore the futility in social relationships (oppression, rivalry, covetousness, power) and in religious relationships (formalism, empty prayer, vows). Ultimate meaning can be found only in God.

The Counsel for Living with Vanity (7:1—12:14)

A series of lessons on practical wisdom is given in 7:1—9:12. Levity and pleasure-seeking are seen as superficial and foolish; it is better to have sober depth of thought. Wisdom and self-control provide perspective and strength in coping

The Book of Ecclesiastes

FOCUS	Thesis: "All Is Vanity"		Proof: "Life Is Vain"		Counsel: "Fear God"		
REFERENCE	1:1 ——— 1:4	———	1:12 ——— 3:1	———	7:1 ——— 10:1	——— 12:9	——— 12:14
DIVISION	Introduction of Vanity	Illustrations of Vanity	Proof from Scripture	Proof from Observations	Coping in a Wicked World	Counsel for Uncertainty	Conclusion: Fear and Obey God
TOPIC	Declaration of Vanity		Demonstration of Vanity		Decision from Vanity		
	Subject		Sermons		Summary		
LOCATION	Universe: "Under the Sun"						
TIME	c. 935 B.C.						

with life. One should enjoy prosperity and consider in adversity that God made both. Submission to authority helps one avoid unnecessary hardship, but real justice is often lacking on earth.

Observations on wisdom and folly are found in 9:13—11:6. In view of the unpredictability of circumstances, wisdom is the best course to follow in order to minimize grief and misfortune. Youth is too brief and precious to be squandered in foolishness or evil. A person should live well in the fullness of each day before God and acknowledge Him early in life (11:7—12:7). This section closes with an exquisite allegory of old age (12:1-7).

The Preacher concludes that the "good life" is only attained by revering God. Life will not wait upon the solution of all its problems; nevertheless, real meaning can be found by looking not "under the sun" but beyond the sun to the "one Shepherd" (12:11).

Outline of Ecclesiastes

The Book of Song of Solomon

Authorship and Date

Traditionally, authorship of the Song of Solomon has been assigned to Solomon, since the book itself makes this claim (1:1). But some scholars insist it was a later collection of songs attributed to Solomon because of his reputation as a writer of psalms and proverbs (1 Kin. 4:32). Strong internal evidence clearly supports the traditional view that Solomon himself wrote this song that bears his name. It must have been written early in his reign, probably about 965 B.C.

◆

KEYS TO SONG OF SOLOMON

Key Word: *Love in Marriage*

The purpose of this book depends on the viewpoint taken as to its primary thrust:

Fictional: To portray Solomon's attraction and marriage to a poor but beautiful girl from the country.

Allegorical: To present God's love for His bride Israel or Christ's love for His Church.

Historical: To record Solomon's actual romance with a Shulamite woman. The various scenes in the book exalt the joys of love in courtship and marriage and offers a proper perspective of human love.

Key Verses: *Song of Solomon 7:10 and 8:7*

◆

Historical Setting

With his large harem, how could King Solomon write such a beautiful love song to one specific wife? Perhaps his union with the Shulamite woman was the only authentic marriage

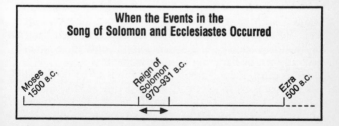

**When the Events in the
Song of Solomon and Ecclesiastes Occurred**

Moses
1500 B.C.

Reign of
Solomon
970–931 B.C.

Ezra
500 B.C.

relationship which Solomon ever knew. Most of his marriages were political arrangements with other nations. In contrast, the Shulamite woman was not a cultured princess but a lowly vineyard keeper whose skin had been darkened by her long exposure to the sun (1:6).

Theological Contribution

The great message of the Song of Solomon is the beauty of love between a man and a woman as experienced in the relationship of marriage. In its frank but beautiful language, the song praises the sexual and physical side of marriage as a natural and proper part of God's plan, reflecting His purpose and desire for the human race (Gen. 2:24). Like Genesis, the Song of Solomon says a bold *Yes!* to the beauty and sanctity of married love.

But this book also points beyond human love to the great Author of love. Authentic love is possible in the world because God brought love into being and planted that emotion in the hearts of His people. Even husbands and wives should remember that the love which they share for one another is not a product of their human goodness but the love of God working in our lives.

Special Consideration

The symbols and images that the groom uses to describe the beauty of his Shulamite bride may seem strange to modern readers. He portrays her hair as "a flock of goats, going down from Mount Gilead" (4:1). Her neck, he says, is like "the tower of David, built for an armory, on which hang a thousand bucklers" (4:4). Such compliments today would certainly not be flattering to most women!

In his use of these symbols, the groom is reflecting the cultural patterns of the ancient world. To those who lived in Solomon's time, the rippling effect of a flock of goats moving down a hillside was, indeed, a thing of beauty. And a stately tower atop a city wall reflected an aura of stability and nobility. The Shulamite woman would have been very pleased at such creative compliments from her poetic groom.

Survey of Song of Solomon

The Beginning of Love (1:1—5:1)

King Solomon has a vineyard in the country of the Shulamite (6:13; 8:11). The Shulamite must work in the vineyard with her brothers (1:6; 8:11, 12); and when Solomon visits the area, he wins her heart and eventually takes her to the palace in Jerusalem as his bride. She is tanned from hours of work outside in the vineyard, but she is "fairest among women" (1:6, 8).

Chapters 1—3 gives a series of recollections of the courtship:

- the bride's longing for affection (1:2—8)
- expressions of mutual love (1:9—2:7)
- a springtime visit to the bride's home (2:8—17)
- the Shulamite's dream of separation (3:1—5)
- the ornate wedding procession (3:6—11).

In 4:1—5:1, Solomon praises his bride from head to foot with a superb chain of similes and metaphors. Her virginity is compared to "a garden enclosed" (4:12), and the garden is entered when the marriage is consummated (4:16—5:1). The union is commended, possibly by God, in 5:1.

The Broadening of Love (5:2—8:14)

Some time after the wedding, the Shulamite has a troubled dream (5:2) in the palace while Solomon is away. In her dream Solomon comes to her door, but she answers too late—he is gone. She panics and searches for him late at night in Jerusalem.

Upon his return, Solomon assures her of his love and

The Song of Solomon

FOCUS	Beginning of Love		Broadening of Love	
REFERENCE 1:1 —————— 3:6 —————— 5:2 —————— 7:11 —————— 8:14				
DIVISION	Falling in Love	United in Love	Struggling in Love	Growing in Love
TOPIC	Courtship	Wedding	Problem	Progress
	Fostering of Love	Fulfillment of Love	Frustration of Love	Faithfulness of Love
LOCATION	Israel			
TIME	c. 1 Year			

praises her beauty (6:4—7:10). The Shulamite begins to think of her country home and tries to persuade her beloved to return there with her (7:11—8:4).

The journey takes place in 8:5–7 and their relationship continues to deepen. Their love will not be overthrown by jealousy or circumstances. At her homecoming (8:8–14) the Shulamite reflects on her brothers' care for her when she was young (8:8, 9). She remains virtuous ("I *am* a wall," 8:10) and is now in a position to look out for her brothers' welfare (8:11, 12). The song concludes with a dual invitation of lover and beloved (8:13, 14).

Outline of Song of Solomon

FOUR

BOOKS OF THE MAJOR PROPHETS

◆

THE last seventeen books of the Old Testament are books of prophecy. As a unit, these books make up about one-fourth of the total Bible, and were written across a period of about 450 years.

The prophets of Old Testament times were divinely chosen spokesmen who received and related God's messages, whether in oral, visual, or written form. The terms *major prophets* and *minor prophets* may suggest that some of these spokesmen for God are more important than others, but this is clearly not the case. As the Bible was compiled across the centuries, the longest prophetic books—Isaiah, Jeremiah, Lamentations, Ezekiel, and Daniel—were placed at the beginning of the prophetic section and are referred to as the major prophets.

BOOKS OF THE MAJOR PROPHETS

BOOK	SUMMARY
Isaiah	The outstanding prophet of condemnation and messianic consolation
Jeremiah	A message of judgment against Judah's moral and spiritual decay
Lamentations	Jeremiah's five poems of lament over fallen Jerusalem

Ezekiel	A prophecy of judgment during the Babylonian Captivity
Daniel	A book of prophecy about the end time

The timeline below shows the period during which the historical events of these books occurred. It does not indicate the generally accepted opinions regarding the time for fulfillment of the predictive prophecy included in these books.

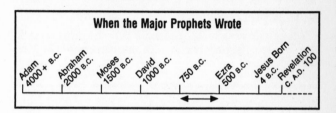

When the Major Prophets Wrote

Adam 4000 + B.C. — Abraham 2000 B.C. — Moses 1500 B.C. — David 1000 B.C. — 750 B.C. — Ezra 500 B.C. — Jesus Born 4 B.C. — Revelation c. A.D. 100

The Book of Isaiah

Authorship, Date, and Historical Setting

Isaiah gives us few facts about himself, but we do know he was "the son of Amoz" (1:1). The quality of his writing indicates he was well educated and that he probably came from an upper-class family. Married, he had two children to whom he gave symbolic names to show that God was about to bring judgment against the nation of Judah.

He was called to his prophetic ministry "in the year that King Uzziah [Azariah] died" (6:1)—about 740 B.C.—through a stirring vision of God as he worshiped in the Temple. He prophesied for more than 40 years to the nation of Judah during a time of great moral and political upheaval.

◆

KEYS TO ISAIAH

Key Word: *Salvation Is of the Lord*

The basic theme of this book, sometimes called "the fifth gospel," is found in Isaiah's name: "Salvation Is of the Lord." Humanity has great need for salvation, and only God's great provision will suffice.

Key Verses: *Isaiah 9:6, 7 and 53:6*

Key Chapter: *Isaiah 53*

Along with Psalm 22, Isaiah 53 lists the most remarkable and specific prophecies of the atonement of the Messiah.

◆

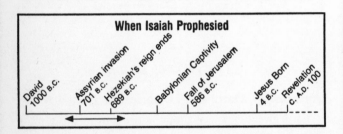

Theological Contribution

The Book of Isaiah presents more insights into the nature of God than any other book of the Old Testament. God's holiness is the first thing that impresses the prophet when he sees Him in all His glory in the Temple (6:1–8).

God is interested in the salvation of His people. He is the sovereign ruler of history and the only one who has the power to save.

God's ultimate purpose of salvation will be realized through the *coming Messiah*, our Lord and Savior Jesus Christ. When Jesus begins His public ministry in His hometown of Nazareth, He quotes from Isaiah (61:1–2; Luke 4:18–19) to show that this prophecy is being fulfilled in His life and ministry.

Survey of Isaiah

Prophecies of Condemnation (chaps. 1—35)

Isaiah's first message of condemnation is aimed at his own countrymen in Judah (chaps. 1—12). Judah is riddled with moral and spiritual disease; the people are neglecting God as they bow to ritualism and selfishness. But God graciously invites them to repent and return to Him because this is their only hope of avoiding judgment. Isaiah's call to proclaim God's message is found in chapter 6, and this is followed by the book of Immanuel (chaps. 7—12). These chapters repeatedly refer to the Messiah and anticipate the blessing of His future reign.

The prophet moves from local to regional judgment as he proclaims a series of oracles against the surrounding nations (chaps. 13—23). Isaiah's little apocalypse (chaps. 24—27) depicts universal tribulation followed by the blessings of the kingdom. Chapters 28—33 pronounce six woes on Israel and Judah for specific sins. Isaiah's prophetic condemnation closes with a general picture of international devastation that will precede universal blessing (chaps. 34 and 35).

Historical Parenthesis (chaps. 36—39)

This historical parenthesis looks back to the Assyrian invasion of Judah in 701 B.C. and anticipates the coming Babylonian invasion of Judah. Judah escapes captivity by Assyria (36 and 37; 2 Kin. 18 and 19), but they will not escape from the hands of Babylon (38 and 39; 2 Kin. 20). God answers King Hezekiah's prayers and delivers Judah from Assyrian de-

The Book of Isaiah

FOCUS	Prophecies of Condemnation				Historical Parenthesis	Prophecies of Comfort		
REFERENCE	1:1 ——— 13:1	13:1 ——— 24:1	24:1 ——— 28:1	28:1 ——— 36:1	36:1 ——— 40:1	40:1 ——— 49:1	49:1 ——— 58:1	58:1 ——— 66:24
DIVISION	Prophecies Against — Judah	Prophecies Against — The Nations	Prophecies of — Day of Lord	Prophecies of — Judgment & Blessing	Hezekiah's Salvation, Sickness, and Sin	Israel's Deliverance	Israel's Deliverer	Israel's Glorious Future
TOPIC	Prophetic				Historic	Messianic		
TOPIC	Judgment				Transition	Hope		
LOCATION	Israel and Judah							
TIME	c. 740–680 B.C.							

struction by Sennacherib. Hezekiah also turns to the Lord in his illness and is granted a fifteen-year extension of his life. But he foolishly shows all his treasures to the Babylonian messengers, and Isaiah tells him that the Babylonians will one day carry his treasure and descendants to their land.

Prophecies of Comfort (chaps. 40—66)

Having pronounced Judah's divine condemnation, Isaiah comforts them with God's promises of hope and restoration. The basis for this hope is the sovereignty and majesty of God (chaps. 40—48). Babylon will indeed carry them off; but Babylon will finally be judged and destroyed, and God's people will be released from captivity.

Chapters 49—57 concentrate on the coming Messiah who will be their Savior and suffering Servant. The heart of this stunning prophecy occurs in chapter 53, as Isaiah develops the description of God's servant to its highest point. The servant's suffering and death and the redemptive nature of His mission are clearly foretold. Although humankind deserved God's judgment because "we have turned, every one, to his own way" (53:6), God sent His servant to take away our sins. According to Isaiah, it is through His suffering that we are made right with God, since "the Lord has laid on Him the iniquity of us all" (53:6). All who acknowledge their sins and trust in Him will be delivered (chaps. 58—66). In that day Jerusalem will be rebuilt, Israel's borders will be enlarged, and the Messiah will reign in Zion. God's people will confess their sins and His enemies will be judged. Peace, prosperity, and justice will prevail, and God will make all things new.

Outline of Isaiah

The Book of Jeremiah

Authorship and Date

Most conservative scholars agree that the author of the Book of Jeremiah was the famous prophet of that name. After prophesying against Judah for about 20 years, the

◆

KEYS TO JEREMIAH

Key Word: *Judah's Last Hour*

In Jeremiah, God is seen as patient and holy: He delays judgment and appeals to His people to repent before it is too late. Judah's time for repentance will soon pass.

Key Verses: *Jeremiah 7:23, 24 and 8:11, 12*

Key Chapter: *Jeremiah 31*

Amid all the judgment and condemnation by Jeremiah are the wonderful promises of Jeremiah 31. Even though Judah has broken the covenants of her great King, God will make a new covenant and write it on their hearts.

◆

prophet Jeremiah was commanded by God to put his messages in written form. He dictated these to his scribe or secretary, Baruch, who wrote them on a scroll (36:1–4). Because Jeremiah had been banned from entering the royal court, he sent Baruch to read the messages to King Jehoiakim. To show his contempt for Jeremiah and his message, the king cut the scroll apart and threw it in the fire (36:22–23). Jeremiah promptly dictated his book to Baruch again, adding "many similar words" (36:32) that had not been included in the first scroll.

This clear description of how a second version of Jeremiah came to be written shows the book was composed in several different stages during the prophet's ministry. Baruch must have put the book in final form shortly after Jeremiah's death, not long after 585 B.C.

Historical Setting

The Book of Jeremiah belongs to a chaotic time in the history of God's covenant people. Jeremiah's native land, the

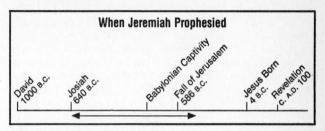

southern kingdom of Judah, was caught in a power squeeze between three great powers of the ancient world: Egypt, Assyria, and Babylon.

When Jeremiah Prophesied

David 1000 B.C.   Josiah 640 B.C.   Babylonian Captivity   Fall of Jerusalem 586 B.C.   Jesus Born 4 B.C.   Revelation c. A.D. 100

Theological Contribution

Jeremiah's greatest theological contribution was his concept of the new covenant (31:31–34). A new covenant between God and His people was necessary because the old covenant had failed so miserably.

Special Consideration

Jeremiah was a master at using figures of speech, metaphors, and symbolic behavior to drive home his messages. He carried a yoke around his neck to show the citizens of Judah they should submit to the inevitable rule of the pagan Babylonians (27:1–12). He described a potter who marred a piece of clay, then reshaped it into a perfect vessel to teach submission; he purchased a plot of land in his hometown to symbolize his hope for the future.

Survey of Jeremiah

The Call of Jeremiah (chap. 1)

Jeremiah is called and sanctified before birth to be God's prophet. This introductory chapter surveys the identification, inauguration, and instructions of the prophet.

The Prophecies to Judah (chaps. 2—45)

Jeremiah's message is communicated through a variety of parables, sermons, and object lessons. In a series of twelve graphic messages, Jeremiah lists the causes of Judah's coming judgment. God has bound Judah to Himself; but like a rotten waistband, they have become corrupt and useless. Jeremiah offers a confession for the people, but their sin is too great; the prophet can only lament for them. As a sign of imminent judgment Jeremiah is forbidden to marry and participate in the feasts. Because the nation does not trust God or keep the Sabbath, the land will receive a sabbath rest when they are in captivity. Jerusalem will be invaded and the rulers and people will be deported to Babylon. Restoration will only come under the new Shepherd, the Messiah, the nation's future King. Jeremiah announces the duration of the captivity as seventy years, in contrast to the messages of the false prophets who insist it will not happen.

Because of his message (2:25), Jeremiah suffers misery and opposition (chaps. 26—45). He is rejected by the prophets and priests who call for his death, but he is spared by the elders and officials. In his sign of the yoke he proclaims the unpopular message that Judah must submit to divine discipline. But he assures the nation of restoration and hope under a new covenant (chaps. 30—33). A remnant will be delivered and there will be a coming time of blessing.

Jeremiah's personal experiences and sufferings are the focal point of chapters 34—45 as opposition against the prophet mounts. He is imprisoned, and after the destruction of the city, Jeremiah is taken to Egypt by fleeing Jews. There he prophesies that Nebuchadnezzar will invade Egypt as well.

The Prophecies to the Gentiles (chaps. 46—51)

These chapters are a series of prophetic oracles against nine nations: Egypt, Philistia, Moab, Ammon, Edom, Damascus (Syria), Arabia, Elam, and Babylon. Only Egypt, Moab, Ammon, and Elam are given a promise of restoration.

The Book of Jeremiah

FOCUS	Call of Jeremiah	Prophecies to Judah					Prophecies to the Gentiles	Fall of Jerusalem
REFERENCE	1:1 ————	2:1 ————	26:1 ————	30:1 ————	34:1 ————		46:1 ————	52:1 ———— 52:34
DIVISION	Prophetic Commission	Condemnation of Judah	Conflicts of Jeremiah	Future Restoration of Jerusalem	Present Fall of Jerusalem		Condemnation of Nine Nations	Historic Conclusion
TOPIC	Call	Before the Fall		Ministry	The Fall		After the Fall	Retrospect
LOCATION		Judah					Surrounding Nations	Babylon
TIME				c. 640–580 B.C.				

The Fall of Jerusalem (chap. 52)

Jeremiah's forty-year declaration of doom was finally vindicated in an event so significant that it is recorded in detail four times in the Scriptures (2 Kin. 25; 2 Chr. 36; Jer. 39; 52). In this historical supplement, Jerusalem is captured, destroyed, and plundered, and the captives taken to Babylon.

Outline of Jeremiah

The Book of Lamentations

◆

KEYS TO LAMENTATIONS

Key Word: *Lamentations*

Three themes run through the five laments of Jeremiah. The most prominent is the theme of mourning but with confession of sin and an acknowledgment of God's righteous judgment comes a note of hope in God's future restoration of His people.

Key Verses: *Lamentations 2:5, 6 and 3:22, 23*

Key Chapter: *Lamentations 3*

Lamentations 3:22–25 expresses a magnificent faith in the mercy of God—especially when placed against the dark backdrop of chapters 1, 2, 4, and 5.

◆

Authorship, Date, and Historical Setting

Lamentations itself gives no clue concerning its author, but many conservative Bible scholars agree on the prophet Jeremiah, who prophesied in Jerusalem during this period of his nation's history. The book is realistic in its portrayal of

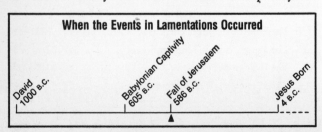

When the Events in Lamentations Occurred

David 1000 B.C. — Babylonian Captivity 605 B.C. — Fall of Jerusalem 586 B.C. — Jesus Born 4 B.C.

conditions in Jerusalem just before its fall to Babylonian forces under Nebuchadnezzar, suggesting an author who was an eyewitness of these events. This supports Jeremiah's authorship. The date of the writing was probably some time shortly after the fall of the city in 587 or 586 B.C.

Theological Contribution

Jerusalem was the site of the Temple of God, the place where God's presence dwelt and where sacrifice could be made to Him. In later years Jerusalem became the focal point of God's final work of salvation in the person of Jesus Christ. The Book of Lamentations reminds us of the central role which this city has always played in God's work of redemption in the world.

Special Consideration

Lamentations has many strange expressions such as *daughter of Zion* (2:1), *daughter of Judah* (2:5), and *daughter of Jerusalem* (2:15). These do not refer to daughters of these cities but to the cities themselves as daughters of the Lord. As such they remind us of the profound sorrow associated with God's judgment of His sinful people; yet, since they remain daughters, these cities speak of great hope during desperate times.

Survey of Lamentations

The Destruction of Jerusalem (chap. 1)

This poem consists of a lamentation by Jeremiah (1:1–11) and a lamentation by the personified Jerusalem (1:12–22). The city has been left desolate because of its grievous sins, and her enemies "mocked at her downfall" (1:7).

The Anger of God (chap. 2)

Through the Babylonians, God has terminated all religious observances, removed the priests, prophets, and kings, and razed the temple and palaces. Jeremiah grieves over the suffer-

The Book of Lamentations

FOCUS	Destruction of Jerusalem	Anger of Jehovah	Prayer for Mercy	Siege of Jerusalem	Prayer for Restoration
REFERENCE	1:1 ———————	2:1 ———————	3:1 ———————	4:1 ———————	5:1 ——————— 5:22
DIVISION	Mourning City	Broken People	Suffering Prophet	Ruined Kingdom	Penitent Nation
TOPIC	Grief	Cause	Hope	Repentance	Prayer
LOCATION	Jerusalem				
TIME	c. 586 B.C.				

ing the people brought on themselves through rebellion against God.

The Prayer for Mercy (chap. 3)

In the first eighteen verses, Jeremiah enters into the miseries and despair of his people and makes them his own. However, there is an abrupt turn in verses 19–39 as the prophet reflects on the faithfulness and loyal love of the compassionate God of Israel. These truths enable him to find comfort and hope in spite of his dismal circumstances, and he petitions God for deliverance.

The Siege of Jerusalem (chap. 4)

The prophet rehearses the siege of Jerusalem and remembers the suffering and starvation of rich and poor. He also reviews the causes of the siege, especially the sins of the prophets and priests and their foolish trust in human aid. This poem closes with a warning to Edom of future punishment and a glimmer of hope for Jerusalem.

The Prayer for Restoration (chap. 5)

Jeremiah's last elegy is a melancholy description of his people's lamentable state. Their punishment is complete.

Outline of Lamentations

The Book of Ezekiel

Authorship, Date, and Historical Setting

The author of this book was clearly the prophet Ezekiel, a spokesman for the Lord who lived among the Jewish captives in Babylon, though some scholars have questioned Ezekiel's authorship. Ezekiel begins his prophetic ministry "in the fifth year of King Jehoiachin's captivity" (1:2), about 597 B.C. Ezekiel must have prophesied for at least 20 years among the captives, until 573 B.C. The Babylonians took captives from Jerusalem in 605 B.C., 597 B.C., and 587—586 B.C., when Nebuchadnezzar destroyed the city.

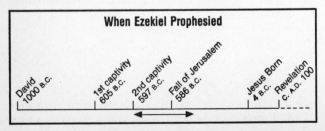

When Ezekiel Prophesied

David 1000 B.C. — 1st captivity 605 B.C. — 2nd captivity 597 B.C. — Fall of Jerusalem 586 B.C. — Jesus Born 4 B.C. — Revelation C. A.D. 100

◆

KEYS TO EZEKIEL

Key Word: *The Future Restoration of Israel*

The broad purpose of Ezekiel is to remind the generation born during the Babylonian exile of the cause of Israel's current destruction, of the coming judgment on the Gentile nations, and of the coming national restoration of Israel.

Key Verses: *Ezekiel 36:24–26 and 36:33–35*

Key Chapter: *Ezekiel 37*

Central to the hope of the restoration of Israel is the vision of the valley of the dry bones. Ezekiel 37 outlines with clear steps Israel's future.

◆

Theological Contribution

One of the greatest insights of the Book of Ezekiel is its teaching of individual responsibility. The Jewish people had such a strong sense of group identity as God's covenant people that they tended to gloss over their need as individuals to follow God and His will. He also makes a clear reference to the Messiah, a prophecy fulfilled when Jesus was born in Bethlehem more than 500 years later.

Special Consideration

In his use of parables, symbolic behavior, and object lessons to drive home his messages, the prophet Ezekiel reminds us of the great prophet Jeremiah. Ezekiel portrayed God's covenant people as a helpless newborn child (16:12), as a lioness who cared carefully for her cubs (19:1–9), as a sturdy cedar (17:1–10), and as a doomed and useless vine (chap. 15). He also carried his belongings about to show that

God would allow His people to be carried into exile by the Babylonians (12:1–16).

Survey of Ezekiel

The Commission of Ezekiel (chaps. 1—3)

God gives Ezekiel an overwhelming vision of His divine glory and commissions him to be His prophet.

The Judgment on Judah (chaps. 4—24)

Ezekiel directs his prophecies against the nation God chose for Himself. The prophet's signs and sermons (chaps. 4—7) point to the certainty of Judah's judgment. In chapters 8—11, Judah's past sins and coming doom are seen in a series of visions of the abominations in the temple, the slaying of the wicked, and the departing glory of God. The priests and princes are condemned as the glory leaves the temple, moves to the Mount of Olives, and disappears in the east.

Chapters 12—24 speak of the causes and extent of Judah's coming judgment. Judah's prophets are counterfeits and her elders are idolators. They have become a fruitless vine and an adulterous wife. Babylon will swoop down like an eagle and pluck them up, and they will not be aided by Egypt. The people are responsible for their own sins, and they are not being unjustly judged for the sins of their ancestors. Judah has been unfaithful, but God promises that her judgment ultimately will be followed by restoration.

The Judgment on the Gentiles (chaps. 25—32)

Judah's nearest neighbors may gloat over her destruction, but they too will suffer the fate of siege and destruction by Babylon. Ezekiel shows the full circle of judgment on the nations that surround Judah by following them in a clockwise circuit: Ammon, Moab, Edom, Philistia, Tyre, and Sidon (25—28). Many scholars believe that the "king of Tyre"

The Book of Ezekiel

FOCUS	Commission of Ezekiel		Judgment on Judah	Judgment on Gentiles	Restoration of Israel	
REFERENCE	1:1 ——————— 2:1 ————		4:1 ———————	25:1 ———————	33:1 ——————— 40:1 ——————— 48:35	
DIVISION	Ezekiel Sees the Glory	Ezekiel Is Commissioned to the Work	Signs, Messages, Visions, and Parables of Judgment	Judgment on Surrounding Nations	Return of Israel to the Lord	Restoration of Israel in the Kingdom
TOPIC	Before the Siege (c. 592–587 B.C.)			During the Siege (c. 586 B.C.)	After the Siege (c. 585–570 B.C.)	
	Judah's Fall			Judah's Foes	Judah's Future	
LOCATION	Babylon					
TIME	c. 597–573 B.C.					

in 28:11–19 may be Satan, the real power behind the nation.

Chapters 29—32 contain a series of oracles against Egypt. Unlike the nations in chapters 25—28 destroyed by Nebuchadnezzar, Egypt will continue to exist, but as "the lowliest of kingdoms" (29:15).

The Restoration of Israel (chaps. 33—48)

After the overthrow of Jerusalem, Ezekiel's message no longer centers on coming judgment but on comfort and consolation. God's people will be regathered and restored. The vision of the valley of dry bones pictures the reanimation of the nation by the Spirit of God. Israel and Judah will be purified and reunited. There will be an invasion by the northern armies of Gog, but Israel will be saved.

In 572 B.C., fourteen years after the destruction of Jerusalem, Ezekiel returns in a vision to the fallen city and is given detailed specifications for the reconstruction of the Temple, the city, and the land (40—48). After an intricate description of the new outer court, inner court, and temple (40—42), Ezekiel views the return of the glory of the Lord to the Temple from the east. Regulations concerning worship in the coming Temple (43—46) are followed by revelations concerning the new land and city (47 and 48).

Outline of Ezekiel

The Book of Daniel

Authorship and Date

Most conservative scholars believe the Book of Daniel was written by the prophet and statesman of that name who lived as a captive of Babylon and Persia for more than 50 years after he was taken into captivity in 605 B.C. But this theory is rejected by some scholars, who object to the specific details of the prophetic visions that Daniel records.

Daniel's prophecies, according to these critics, are not "prophecies" at all, but were written after these events and were attributed to Daniel to show that these great events of world history would eventually happen. According to evi-

---

KEYS TO DANIEL

Key Word: *God's Program for Israel*

Daniel was written to encourage the exiled Jews by revealing God's sovereign program for Israel during and after the period of gentile domination. The "Times of the Gentiles" began with the Babylonian captivity, and Israel would suffer under gentile powers for many years. But this period is not permanent, and a time will come when God will establish the messianic kingdom which will last forever.

Key Verses: *Daniel 2:20–22 and Daniel 2:44*

Key Chapter: *Daniel 9*

Daniel's prophecy of the seventy weeks (9:24–27) provides the chronological frame for messianic prediction from the time of Daniel to the establishment of the kingdom on earth.

---

dence in the book itself, Daniel's captivity lasted from the time of Nebuchadnezzar's reign in Babylon (1:1–6) into the reign of Cyrus of Persia (10:1), about 536 B.C. He must have written his book some time during this period or shortly thereafter.

Historical Setting

The Book of Daniel clearly spans that period among God's covenant people known as the Babylonian captivity. Nebuchadnezzar took captives from Judah on three separate occasions, beginning in 605 B.C. Among this first group taken were Daniel and his companions. Daniel's prayer to God toward the end of the book (chap. 9) is dated at 538 B.C., the very year that Cyrus of Persia issued his decree making it possible for some of the captives to return to Jerusalem to restore their land and rebuild the Temple (Ezra 1:1–4).

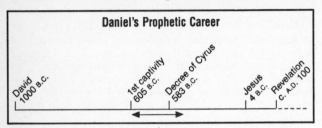

Daniel's Prophetic Career

David 1000 B.C.

1st captivity 605 B.C.

Decree of Cyrus 583 B.C.

Jesus 4 B.C.

Revelation c. A.D. 100

Theological Contribution

The major contribution of the Book of Daniel arises from its nature as apocalyptic prophecy. Highly symbolic in language, the prophecy was related to the events of Daniel's near future, but even today it contains a message for the future.

Special Consideration

Chapter 9 of Daniel is a fascinating passage; it combines the best of biblical piety and biblical prophecy. Daniel's study of the prophecy of the 70 years of captivity from the prophet Jeremiah (Jer. 25) led him to pray for God's intervention on behalf of His people (9:1–19). The Lord's answer came through the angel Gabriel, who gave Daniel the prophecy of the seventy weeks, or 70 sevens (9:20–27). The 70 sevens as envisioned by the prophet are usually interpreted as years. Thus, the prophecy deals with the next 490 years in the future of God's covenant people.

Perhaps the round numbers in this prophecy should be our clue that it is dangerous to try to pin its fulfillment to a specific day or year. But we can say for sure that the end of the 483 years spoken of by Daniel would bring us to the general period of the ministry of the Lord Jesus Christ. The final week in the prophecy is symbolic of the age between the ascension of Jesus and His second coming.

Survey of Daniel

The Personal History of Daniel (chap. 1)

The first chapter sets the stage for the rest of the book by introducing Daniel and his three friends, Hananiah, Mishael, and Azariah. These four young Hebrew men are taken captive in one of the Babylonian raids against Judah in 605 B.C. Intelligent and promising, they are placed in special training as servants in the court of King Nebuchadnezzar; then their names and diets are changed to reflect Babylonian culture in an attempt to take away their Jewish identity. But Daniel and his friends rise to the challenge, proving their Jewish food superior to the diet of the Babylonians. The young men increase in wisdom and knowledge, gaining favor in the king's court.

The Prophetic Plan for the Gentiles (2—7)

In the second major section of the book (chaps. 2—7), Daniel and his friends meet several additional tests to prove that although they are being held captive by a pagan people, the God whom they worshiped is still in control.

Only Daniel can relate and interpret Nebuchadnezzar's disturbing dream of the great statue (chap. 2). God empowers Daniel to foretell the way in which He will sovereignly raise and depose four gentile empires. The Messiah's kingdom will end the times of the Gentiles. Because of his position revealed in the dream, Nebuchadnezzar erects a golden image and demands that all bow to it (chap. 3). The persecution and preservation of Daniel's friends in the fiery furnace again illustrate the power of God.

After Nebuchadnezzar refuses to respond to the warning

The Book of Daniel

FOCUS	History of Daniel	Prophetic Plan for the Gentiles				Prophetic Plan of Israel		
REFERENCE	1:1 ———	2:1 ———	5:1 ———	6:1 ———	7:1 ———	8:1 ———	9:1 ———	10:1 ——— 12:13
DIVISION	Personal Life of Daniel	Visions of Nebuchadnezzar	Vision of Belshazzar	Decree of Darius	Four Beasts	Vision of Ram and Male-Goat	Vision of Seventy Weeks	Vision of Israel's Future
TOPIC	Daniel's Background	Daniel Interprets Others' Dreams				Angel Interprets Daniel's Dreams		
	Hebrew	Aramaic				Hebrew		
LOCATION	Babylon or Persia							
TIME	c. 605–536 B.C.							

of his vision of the tree (chap. 4), he is humbled until he acknowledges the supremacy of God and the foolishness of his pride. The feast of Belshazzar marks the end of the Babylonian kingdom (chap. 5). Belshazzar is judged because of his arrogant defiance of God.

In the reign of Darius, a plot against Daniel backfires when he is divinely delivered in the den of lions (chap. 6). Daniel's courageous faith is rewarded, and Darius learns a lesson about the might of the God of Israel.

The vision of the four beasts (chap. 7) supplements the four-part statue vision of chapter 2 in its portrayal of the Babylonian, Persian, Greek, and Roman empires.

The Prophetic Plan for Israel (chaps. 8–12)

The focus in chapter 8 narrows to a vision of the ram and goat that shows Israel under the Medo-Persian and Grecian empires. Alexander the Great is the large horn of 8:21 and Antiochus Epiphanes is the little horn of 8:9. After Daniel's prayer of confession for his people, he is privileged to receive the revelation of the seventy weeks, including the Messiah's atoning death (9). This gives the chronology of God's perfect plan for the redemption and deliverance of His people. Following is a great vision that gives amazing details of Israel's future history (chaps. 10 and 11). Chapter 11 chronicles the coming kings of Persia and Greece, the wars between the Ptolemies of Egypt and the Seleucids of Syria, and the persecution led by Antiochus. God's people will be saved out of tribulation and resurrected (chap. 12).

Outline of Daniel

FIVE

BOOKS OF THE MINOR PROPHETS

♦

THE last twelve books of the Old Testament became known as the books of the minor prophets because they are generally shorter and they were placed after the five major prophets. They were written across a period of about 400 years in the history of the nations of Judah and Israel, spanning the Assyrian, Babylonian, and Persian Empires. Two were prophets to the northern kingdom (Amos, Hosea); six were prophets to the southern kingdom (Obadiah, Joel, Micah, Nahum, Zephaniah, Habakkuk); one delivered God's message to a pagan nation (Jonah); and three were postexilic prophets (Haggai, Zechariah, Malachi).

BOOKS OF THE MINOR PROPHETS

BOOK	SUMMARY
Hosea	A message of Israel's condemnation followed by God's forgiveness
Joel	A prediction of foreign invasion as a form of judgment by God
Amos	A prophecy of eight pronouncements of judgment against Israel
Obadiah	A prophesy of the destruction of Edom

Jonah	A reluctant prophet who led Nineveh to repentance
Micah	A prediction of judgment and a promise of messianic restoration
Nahum	A prophecy of the destruction of Nineveh
Habakkuk	A prophet who questioned God and praised His approaching judgment against Judah
Zephaniah	A prediction of destructive judgment followed by tremendous blessing
Haggai	A call to rebuild the Temple
Zechariah	A messianic prophecy calling for the completion of the Temple
Malachi	A prophecy of destruction followed by messianic blessing

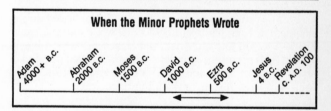

When the Minor Prophets Wrote

Adam 4000 + B.C. | Abraham 2000 B.C. | Moses 1500 B.C. | David 1000 B.C. | Ezra 500 B.C. | Jesus 4 B.C. | Revelation C. A.D. 100

The Book of Hosea

Authorship and Date

The undisputed author of this book is the prophet Hosea, who identifies himself in the book as "the son of Beeri"

◆

KEYS TO HOSEA

Key Word: *The Loyal Love of God for Israel*

The themes of chapters 1—3 echo throughout the rest of the book. The adultery of Gomer (chap. 1) illustrates the sin of Israel (chaps. 4—7); the degradation of Gomer (chap. 2) represents the judgment of Israel (chaps. 8—10); and Hosea's redemption of Gomer (chap. 3) pictures the restoration of Israel (chaps. 11—14). More than any other Old Testament prophet, Hosea's personal experiences illustrate his prophetic message.

Key Verses: *Hosea 4:1; 11:7-9*

Key Chapter: *Hosea 4*

The nation of Israel has left the knowledge of the truth and followed the idolatrous ways of their pagan neighbors. Central to the book is Hosea 4:6.

◆

(1:1). The prophet says that he lived and prophesied during the reign of King Jeroboam II of Israel while four successive kings—Uzziah, Jotham, Ahaz, and Hezekiah—were ruling in Judah. This means his prophetic ministry covered a period of about 40 years, from about 755 B.C. to about 715 B.C. His book was written sometime during these years.

Historical Setting

Hosea prophesied during the twilight years of the northern kingdom of Israel, a time of rapid moral decline. Worship of false gods was mixed with worship of the one true God. Weakened by internal strife, Israel collapsed in 722 B.C. when the nation of Assyria destroyed Samaria, Israel's capital city.

The Book of Joel

◆

KEYS TO JOEL

Key Word: *The Great and Terrible Day of the Lord*

The key theme of Joel is the day of the Lord in retrospect and prospect. Joel uses the terrible locust plague that has recently occurred in Judah to illustrate the coming day of judgment.

Key Verses: *Joel 2:11, 28, 29*

Key Chapter: *Joel 2*

The prophet calls for Judah's repentance and promises God's repentance (2:13, 14) from His planned judgment upon Judah if they do indeed turn to Him.

◆

Authorship and Date

The author of this book was the prophet Joel, who identifies himself in the introduction as "the son of Pethuel" (1:1). His many references to agriculture (1:7, 10–12) may indicate he was a farmer or a herdsman.

Unlike most of the other Old Testament prophets, Joel mentions no kings of Judah or Israel and no historical events that might give us some indication about when he wrote his prophecy. The similarity of Joel's concept of the day of the Lord to the language of the prophet Zephaniah (Joel 2:2; Zeph. 1:14–16) may indicate they were contemporaries. Zephaniah prophesied shortly before the fall of Jerusalem and the nation of Judah in 587 B.C.

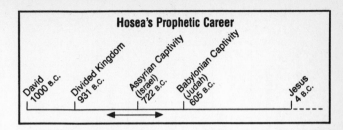

Theological Contribution

Many people believe the Old Testament portrays God's wrath, while the New Testament pictures His love. But the Book of Hosea includes tender expressions of steadfast love among this prophet's descriptions of judgment. Hosea ranks with Deuteronomy and the Gospel of John as major biblical treatises on the love of God.

Special Consideration

Few events in the Bible have been debated as strongly as Hosea's marriage. The command for a man of God to marry a harlot is so startling that interpreters have offered many different explanations, but the plain meaning of the text is that Hosea married a prostitute at God's direct command. In this way, through his own tormented life Hosea could present a striking picture of the pain in God's heart because of the harlotries of His covenant people.

Survey of Hosea

The Adulterous Wife and Faithful Husband (chaps. 1—3)

Hosea marries a woman named Gomer who bears him three children appropriately named by God as signs to Israel. Jezreel, Lo-Ruhamah, and Lo-Ammi mean "God Scatters,"

The Book of Hosea

FOCUS	Adulterous Wife and Faithful Husband			Adulterous Israel and Faithful Lord			
REFERENCE	1:1 —— 2:2	—— 3:1	—— 4:1	—— 6:4	—— 9:1	—— 11:1	—— 14:9
DIVISION	Prophetic Marriage	Application of Gomer to Israel	Restoration of Gomer	Spiritual Adultery of Israel	Refusal of Israel to Repent	Judgment of Israel by God	Restoration of Israel to God
TOPIC	Marriage of Hosea — Personal			Message of Hosea — National			
LOCATION	Northern Kingdom of Israel						
TIME	c. 755–715 B.C.						

"Not Pitied," and "Not My People." Similarly, God will judge and scatter Israel because of her sin.

Gomer seeks other lovers and deserts Hosea. In spite of the depth to which her sin carries her, Hosea redeems her from the slave market and restores her.

The Adulterous Israel and Faithful Lord (chaps. 4—14)

Because of his own painful experience, Hosea can feel some of the sorrow of God over the sinfulness of His people. His loyal love for Gomer is a reflection of God's concern for Israel. Israel has fallen into the dregs of sin and is hardened against God's gracious last appeal to return. Even now God wants to heal and redeem them (7:1, 13), but in their arrogance and idolatry they rebel.

Chapters 9 and 10 give the verdict: Israel's disobedience will lead to her dispersion. God is holy (chaps. 4—7) and just (chaps. 8—10), but He is also loving and gracious (chaps. 11—14). God must discipline, but because of His endless love, He will ultimately save and restore His wayward people.

Outline of Hosea

Historical Setting

If Joel did write his book about 600 B.C., he would have lived in the frantic final years of the nation of Judah. After the Babylonian army destroyed Jerusalem in 587/586 B.C. the leading citizens of Judah were carried into captivity in Babylon.

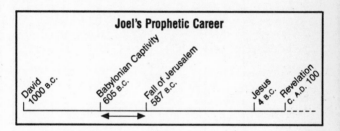

Joel's Prophetic Career

David 1000 B.C. · Babylonian Captivity 605 B.C. · Fall of Jerusalem 587 B.C. · Jesus 4 B.C. · Revelation C. A.D. 100

Theological Contribution

The Book of Joel is remarkable because it shows that a message from God can often come packaged in the form of a natural disaster. This prophet teaches us that the Lord may use a natural disaster to stir in His people a renewed awareness of His will.

Special Consideration

Readers of Joel are always impressed with the prediction of the future outpouring of the Holy Spirit (2:28–32). The apostle Peter used this passage to explain the exciting events of Pentecost to his hearers (Acts 2:16–21). Just as Joel predicted, the Holy Spirit was poured out on all these early followers of Jesus who were gathered in Jerusalem seeking God's will and praying for His divine guidance.

The Book of Joel

FOCUS	Day of the Lord in Retrospect		Day of the Lord in Prospect	
REFERENCE	1:1 ——————— 1:13 ———————	2:1 ———————	2:28 ———————	3:21
DIVISION	Past Day of the Locust	Past Day of the Drought	Imminent Day of the Lord	Ultimate Day of the Lord
	Historical Invasion		Prophetic Invasion	
TOPIC	Past Judgment on Judah		Future Judgment and Restoration of Judah	
LOCATION	Southern Kingdom of Judah			
TIME	c. 600 B.C.			

Survey of Joel

The Day of the Lord in Retrospect (1:1–20)

Joel begins with an account of a recent locust plague that
has devastated the land. The black cloud of insects has
stripped the grapevines and fruit trees and ruined the grain
harvest. The economy has been brought to a further stand-
still by a drought and the people are in a desperate situation.

The Day of the Lord in Prospect (2:1–3:21)

Compared to the terrible day of the Lord, the destruction
by the locusts will seem insignificant. The land will be invaded by a swarming army, and the desolation caused by this
army will be dreadful (2:11).

Even so, it is not too late for the people to avert disaster.
The prophetic warning is designed to bring them to the point
of repentance (2:12–17). God's gracious offer falls on deaf
ears. Ultimately, the swarming, creeping, stripping, and
gnawing locusts (1:4; 2:25) will come again in a fiercer form.
But God promises that judgment will be followed by great
blessing in a material (2:18–27) and spiritual (2:28–32) sense.

These rich promises are followed by a solemn description
of the judgment of all nations in the valley of decision (3:14)
in the end times. The nations will give an account of themselves to the God of Israel who will judge those who have
rebelled against Him. God alone controls the course of history (3:17). Joel ends with the kingdom blessings upon the
remnant of faithful Judah (3:20).

Outline of Joel

The Book of Amos

❖

KEYS TO AMOS

Key Word: *The Judgment of Israel*

The basic theme of Amos is the coming judgment of Israel because of the holiness of God and the sinfulness of His covenant people.

Key Verses: *Amos 3:1, 2; 8:11, 12*

Key Chapter: *Amos 9*

Set in the midst of the harsh judgments of Amos are some of the greatest prophecies of restoration of Israel anywhere in Scripture. Within the scope of just five verses the future of Israel becomes clear, as the Abrahamic, Davidic, and Palestinian covenants are focused on their climactic fulfillment in the return of the Messiah.

❖

Authorship, Date, and Historical Setting

The author of this book is clearly Amos, humble herdsman, or shepherd, of Tekoa (1:1), a village near Jerusalem in the southern kingdom of Judah. God calls him to deliver His message of judgment to the people who live in Israel, Judah's sister nation to the north. Amos indicated in his book that he prophesied during the reigns of King Uzziah (Azariah) in Judah and King Jeroboam II in Israel (1:1). This places his prophecy at about 760 B.C. He must have written the book some time after this date, perhaps after returning to his home in Tekoa.

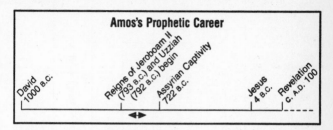

Amos's Prophetic Career

David 1000 B.C. — Reigns of Jeroboam II (793 B.C.) and Uzziah (792 B.C.) begin — Assyrian Captivity 722 B.C. — Jesus 4 B.C. — Revelation c. A.D. 100

Theological Contribution

Amos is known as the great "prophet of righteousness" of the Old Testament. His book underlines the principle that religion demands righteous behavior. True religion is not a matter of observing feast days and offering burnt offerings but seeking God's will, treating others with justice, and following God's commands.

Special Consideration

The Book of Amos is one of the most eloquent cries for justice and righteousness to be found in the Bible. Amos was an humble shepherd who dared to deliver God's message to the wealthy and influential people of his day. His message is just as timely for our world.

Survey of Amos

The Eight Prophecies (1:1—2:16)

Amos begins with the nations that surround Israel as his catalog of catastrophes gradually spirals in on Israel herself. Seven times God declares, "I will send a fire," a symbol of judgment.

The Book of Amos

FOCUS	Eight Prophecies	Three Sermons	Five Visions	Five Promises
REFERENCE	1:1 ———————	3:1 ———————	7:1 ———————	9:1 ——————— 9:15
DIVISION	Judgment of Israel and Surrounding Nations	Sin of Israel: Present, Past, and Future	Pictures of the Judgment of Israel	Restoration of Israel
	Pronouncements of Judgment	Provocations for Judgment	Future of Judgment	Promises After Judgment
TOPIC		Judgment		Hope
LOCATION	Surrounding Nations	Northern Kingdom of Israel		
TIME	c. 760–753 B.C.			

The Three Sermons (3:1—6:14)

Next Amos delivers three sermons. The first (chap. 3) is a general pronouncement of judgment because of Israel's iniquities. The second sermon (chap. 4) exposes the crimes of the people and describes the ways God has chastened them in order to draw them back to Himself. The third (chaps. 5—6) lists the sins of the house of Israel and calls the people to repent. But their refusal to turn to God will lead to their exile.

The Five Visions (7:1—9:10)

Amos's three sermons are followed by five visions of coming judgment upon the northern kingdom. The first two judgments of locusts and fire do not come to pass because of Amos' intercession. The third vision of the plumb line is followed by the only narrative section in the book (7:10–17). The fourth vision pictures Israel as a basket of rotten fruit, overripe for judgment. The fifth vision is a relentless portrayal of Israel's unavoidable judgment.

The Five Promises (9:11—15)

Amos has hammered upon the theme of divine retribution with oracles, sermons, and visions. Nevertheless, he ends his book on a note of consolation. God promises to reinstate the Davidic line, to renew the land, and to restore the people after their season of judgment had come to an end.

Outline of Amos

The Book of Obadiah

Authorship and Date

The author clearly identifies himself as the prophet Obadiah, but this is all we know about him. Most scholars believe the great humiliation of Israel which the prophet mentions was the siege of Jerusalem by the Babylonians, beginning in 605 B.C. and ending with its final destruction in 587 B.C. Thus, the book must have been written shortly after the fall of the city.

Historical Setting

Centuries earlier, twin brothers, Jacob and Esau, went their separate ways (Gen. 27; 36), but the Bible reports many clashes between these two nations, the Edomites and Israel.

One notable example was the refusal of the Edomites to let the Israelites cross their land as they traveled toward the land

◆

KEYS TO OBADIAH

Key Word: *The Judgment of Edom*

The major theme of Obadiah is a declaration of Edom's coming doom because of its arrogance and cruelty to Judah.

Key Verses: *Obadiah 10 and 21*

◆

of Canaan (Num. 20:14–21). But the final insult to Israel must have been Edom's participation in the looting of Jerusalem after the city fell to the Babylonians.

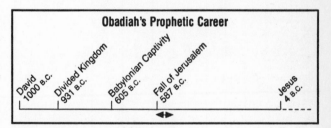

Obadiah's Prophetic Career

David 1000 B.C. | Divided Kingdom 931 B.C. | Babylonian Captivity 605 B.C. | Fall of Jerusalem 587 B.C. | Jesus 4 B.C.

Theological Contribution

God declared in the Book of Genesis that He would bless the rest of the world through Abraham and his descendants. He also promised to protect His special people against any who would try to do them harm (Gen. 12:1–3). This promise is affirmed in the Book of Obadiah, as God keeps faith with His people, in spite of their unworthiness and disobedience.

The Book of Obadiah

FOCUS	Judgment of Edom			Restoration of Israel
REFERENCE	1:1 ———————— 10	15	19	21
DIVISION	Predictions of Judgment	Reasons for Judgment	Results of Judgment	Possession of Edom by Israel
TOPIC	Prediction of Judgment			Victory of Israel
	Defeat of Israel			Prediction of Possession
LOCATION	Edom and Israel			
TIME	c. 586–539 B.C.			

Survey of Obadiah

The Judgment of Edom (vv. 1–18)

The first section of Obadiah makes it clear that the coming overthrow of Edom is a certainty, not a condition. Edom is arrogant (v. 3) because of its secure position in Mount Seir, a mountainous region south of the Dead Sea. But when God destroys Edom it will be totally ransacked. Nothing will avert God's complete judgment. Verses 10–14 describe Edom's major crime of gloating over the invasion of Jerusalem. Edom rejoiced when foreigners plundered Jerusalem, and became as one of them.

The Restoration of Israel (v. 19–21)

The closing verses give hope to God's people that they will possess not only their own land, but also that of Edom and Philistia.

Outline of Obadiah

The Book of Jonah

Authorship and Date

The traditional view is that the prophet Jonah wrote this book. This would place its writing at about 760 B.C., since this prophet—"the son of Amittai" (1:1)—is the same Jonah who prophesied during the reign of Jeroboam II of Israel,

◆

KEYS TO JONAH

Key Word: *The Revival in Nineveh*

God's loving concern for the Gentiles is not a truth disclosed only in the New Testament. More than seven centuries before Christ, God commissioned the Hebrew prophet Jonah to proclaim a message of repentance to the Assyrians.

Key Verses: *Jonah 2:8, 9; 4:2*

Key Chapter: *Jonah 3*

The third chapter of Jonah records perhaps the greatest revival of all time as the entire city of Nineveh "[believes] God, and [proclaims] a fast," and cries out to God.

◆

from 793 to 753 B.C. (2 Kin. 14:25). The only other thing we know about Jonah is that he was a native of the village of Gath Hepher in Israel.

Historical Setting

The prophet Jonah visited Nineveh during the glorious days of the Assyrian empire. From about 885 to 625 B.C., the Assyrians dominated the ancient world. Numerous passages

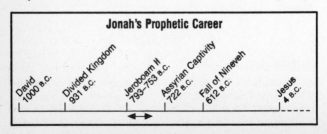

Jonah's Prophetic Career

David 1000 B.C. — Divided Kingdom 931 B.C. — Jeroboam II 793-753 B.C. — Assyrian Captivity 722 B.C. — Fall of Nineveh 612 B.C. — Jesus 4 B.C.

in the Old Testament report advances of Assyrian military forces against the neighboring kingdoms of Judah and Israel during these years. Israel finally fell to Assyrian forces about 722 B.C.

Theological Contribution

One of the great truths emphasized by this book is that God can use people who do not want to be used by Him. Jonah was practically driven to Nineveh against his will, but his grudging message still struck a responsive chord in the Assyrians. However, the greatest insight of the book is that God desires to show mercy and grace to all the peoples of the world. No one nation or group can claim exclusive rights to His love.

Special Consideration

Too much attention has been focused on the "great fish" (1:17) that swallowed Jonah and then spat him out on the shore. We solve nothing by debating whether a fish could swallow a man or whether a person could remain alive for three days in the stomach of such a creature. The point of this part of the story is that God worked a miracle to preserve the life of His prophet so he could get to Nineveh to carry out God's orders.

Survey of Jonah

The First Commission of Jonah (chaps. 1—2)

This chapter records the commission of Jonah (1:1, 2), the disobedience of Jonah (1:3), and the judgment on Jonah (1:4–17). Jonah does not want to see God spare the notoriously cruel Assyrians. Instead of going five hundred miles northeast to Nineveh, Jonah attempts to go two thousand miles west to Tarshish (Spain).

God prepares a "great fish" to accomplish His desired result. The fish and its divinely appointed rendezvous with

The Book of Jonah

FOCUS	First Commission of Jonah				Second Commission of Jonah			
REFERENCE	1:1 ——— 1:4	——— 2:1	——— 2:10	3:1 ———	3:5 ———	4:1 ———	4:4 — 4:11
DIVISION	Disobedience to the First Call	Judgment on Jonah Exacted	Prayer of Jonah in the Fish	Deliverance of Jonah from the Fish	Obedience to the Second Call	Judgment on Nineveh Averted	Prayer of Jonah	Rebuke of Jonah
TOPIC	God's Mercy upon Jonah				God's Mercy upon Nineveh			
	"I Won't Go."		"I Will Go."		"I'm Here."		"I Shouldn't Have Come."	
LOCATION	The Great Sea				The Great City			
TIME	c. 760 B.C.							

the sinking prophet became a powerful reminder to Jonah of the sovereignty of God in every circumstance. While inside the fish (2), Jonah utters a declarative praise psalm which alludes to several psalms that were racing through his mind (Ps. 3:8; 31:22; 42:7; 69:1).

In his unique "prayer closet," Jonah offers thanksgiving for his deliverance from drowning. When he acknowledges that "salvation *is* of the LORD" (2:9), he is finally willing to obey and be used by God. After he is cast up on the shore, Jonah has a long time to reflect on his experiences during his eastward trek of five hundred miles to Nineveh.

The Second Commission of Jonah (chaps. 3—4)

Jonah obeys his second commission to go to Nineveh (3:1–4) where he becomes "a sign to the Ninevites" (Luke 11:30). The prophet is a walking object lesson from God, his skin no doubt bleached from his stay in the fish. Jonah's words of coming judgment are followed by a proclamation by the king of the city to fast and repent. Because of His great mercy, God "relented from the disaster that He had said He would bring upon them" (3:10).

In the final chapter, God's love and grace are contrasted with Jonah's anger and lack of compassion. He is unhappy with the good results of his message because he knows God will now spare Nineveh. God uses a plant, a worm, and a wind to teach Jonah a lesson in compassion. He is forced to see his lack of a divine perspective makes his repentance a greater problem than the repentance of Nineveh.

Outline of Jonah

The Book of Micah

◆

KEYS TO MICAH

Key Word: *The Judgment and Restoration of Judah*

Micah exposes the injustice of Judah and the righteousness and justice of God. About one-third of the book indicts Israel and Judah for specific sins. Another third of Micah predicts the judgment that will come as a result of those sins. The remaining third of the book is a message of hope and consolation. God's justice will triumph and the divine Deliverer will come.

Key Verses: *Micah 6:8; 7:18*

Key Chapters: *Micah 6; 7*

The closing section of Micah describes a courtroom scene. God has a controversy against His people, and He calls the mountains and hills together to form the jury as He sets forth His case. There can only be one verdict: guilty.

Nevertheless, the book closes on a note of hope. The same God who executes judgment also delights to extend mercy (7:18, 7).

◆

Authorship and Date

This book was written by the prophet Micah, a native of the village of Moresheth (1:1) in southern Judah near the Philistine city of Gath. Since Micah championed the rights of the poor, he was probably a humble farmer or herdsman himself, although he shows a remarkable knowledge of Jerusalem and Samaria, the capital cities of the nations of Judah and Israel. Micah also tells us that he prophesied "in the days of Jotham, Ahaz, and Hezekiah, kings of Judah" (1:1). The reigns of these three kings stretched from about 750 B.C. to 687 B.C.; so his book was probably written some time during this period.

Historical Setting

The Book of Micah belongs to that turbulent period during which the Assyrians launched their drive for supremacy throughout the ancient world. Micah probably saw his prophecy of judgment against Israel fulfilled, since the Assyrians defeated this nation in 722 B.C.

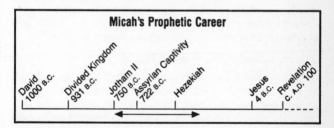

Micah's Prophetic Career

David 1000 B.C. — Divided Kingdom 931 B.C. — Jotham II 750 B.C. — Assyrian Captivity 722 B.C. — Hezekiah — Jesus 4 B.C. — Revelation c. A.D. 100

Theological Contribution

The mixture of judgment and promise in the Book of Micah is a striking characteristic of the Old Testament prophets. These contrasting passages give real insight into the character of God. In His wrath He remembers mercy; He cannot maintain His anger forever. God was determined to maintain His holiness, and so He acted in judgment on those who had broken His covenant. But He was just as determined to fulfill the promises He had made to Abraham centuries earlier.

Perhaps the greatest contribution of the Book of Micah is its clear prediction of the ultimate fulfillment of the covenant: a coming Savior.

Survey of Micah

The Prediction of Judgment (chaps. 1—3)

Micah begins by launching into a general declaration of the condemnation of Israel (Samaria) and Judah (Jerusalem). Both kingdoms will be overthrown because of their rampant treachery. Micah uses a series of wordplays on the names of several cities of Judah in his lamentation over Judah's coming destruction (1:10–16). This is followed by some of the specific causes for judgment: premeditated schemes, covetousness, and cruelty. Nevertheless, God will regather a remnant of His people (2:12, 13). The prophet then systematically condemns the princes (3:1–4) and the prophets (3:5–8) and concludes with a warning of coming judgment (3:9–12).

The Prediction of Restoration (chaps. 4—5)

Micah then moves into a two-chapter message of hope, which describes the reinstitution of the kingdom (4:1–5) and the intervening captivity of the kingdom (4:6–5:1), concluding with the prophecy of the birth of the Messiah (5:2). This messianic verse is stunning in its accuracy because it names the specific town where the Messiah was born—the village of Bethlehem in the territory of the tribe of Judah.

The Plea for Repentance (chaps. 6 and 7)

In His two controversies with His people, God calls them into court and presents an unanswerable case against them.

The Book of Micah

FOCUS	Prediction of Judgment		Prediction of Restoration			Plea for Repentance		
REFERENCE	1:1 ———	3:1 ———	4:1 ———	4:6 ———	5:2 ———	6:1 ———	6:10 ———	7:7 ———7:20
DIVISION	Judgment of People	Judgment of Leadership	Promise of Coming Kingdom	Promise of Coming Captivities	Promise of Coming King	First Plea of God	Second Plea of God	Promise of Final Salvation
TOPIC	Punishment		Promise			Pardon		
	Retribution		Restoration			Repentance		
LOCATION	Judah—Israel							
TIME	c. 735–710 B.C.							

Authentic worship consists of following God's will and dealing justly with other people, not empty rituals. Micah concludes with a sublime series of promises that the Lord will pardon their iniquity and renew their nation in accordance with His covenant.

Outline of Micah

The Book of Nahum

Authorship and Date

This book was written by a prophet known as "Nahum the Elkoshite" (1:1). This brief identification tells us all we know about this spokesman for the Lord. Even the location of his home, Elkosh, is uncertain. The book was probably written about 612 B.C. shortly before Nineveh fell.

Historical Setting

For more than 100 years before Nahum's day, Assyria had been one of the dominant powers of the ancient world. The

◆

KEYS TO NAHUM

Key Word: *The Judgment of Nineveh*

If ever a city deserved the title "Here to Stay," Nineveh was that city. But Nahum declares that Nineveh will fall.

Key Verses: *Nahum 1:7, 8; 3:5–7*

Key Chapter: *Nahum 1*

Nahum 1:2–8 portrays the patience, power, holiness, and justice of the living God. He is slow to wrath, but God settles His accounts in full. This book concerns the downfall of Assyria, but it is written for the benefit of the surviving kingdom of Judah.

◆

northern kingdom of Israel fell to Assyrian forces in 722 B.C. Some prophets taught that this pagan nation was used as an instrument of God's judgment against His wayward people. But now it was Assyria's turn to feel the force of God's wrath. The armies of Nabopolassar of Babylon stormed Nineveh in 612 B.C. The entire Assyrian Empire crumbled three years later under the relentless assault of this aggressive Babylonian ruler.

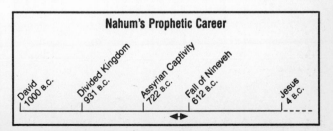

Nahum's Prophetic Career

David 1000 B.C. — Divided Kingdom 931 B.C. — Assyrian Captivity 722 B.C. — Fall of Nineveh 612 B.C. — Jesus 4 B.C.

The Book of Nahum

FOCUS	Destruction of Nineveh Decreed		Destruction of Nineveh Described		Destruction of Nineveh Deserved	
REFERENCE	1:1	1:9	2:1	2:3	3:1	3:12 ———— 3:19
DIVISION	General Principles of Divine Judgment	Destruction of Nineveh and Deliverance of Judah	The Call to Battle	Description of the Destruction of Nineveh	Reasons for the Destruction of Nineveh	Inevitable Destruction of Nineveh
TOPIC	Verdict of Vengeance		Vision of Vengeance		Vindication of Vengeance	
	What God Will Do		How God Will Do It		Why God Will Do It	
LOCATION	In Judah Against Nineveh, Capital of Assyria					
TIME	c. 612 B.C.					

Theological Contribution

This book teaches the sure judgment of God against those who oppose His will and abuse His people. Although God sometimes uses a pagan nation as an instrument of His judgment, He will also judge that nation by His standards of righteousness and holiness.

Survey of Nahum

The Destruction of Nineveh Is Decreed (chap. 1)

Nahum begins with a very clear description of the character of God. Because of His righteousness, He is a God of vengeance (1:2). God is also characterized by patience (1:3) and power (1:3–6). He is gracious to all who respond to Him, but those who rebel against Him will be overthrown (1:7, 8). God is holy, and Nineveh stands condemned because of her sins (1:9–14). Nothing can stand in the way of judgment, and this is a message of comfort to the people of Judah (1:15).

The Destruction of Nineveh Is Described (chap. 2)

Assyria will be conquered, but Judah will be restored (2:1, 2). Nahum's description of the siege of Nineveh (2:3–7) and the sack of Nineveh (2:8–13) is one of the most vivid portraits of battle in Scripture.

The Destruction of Nineveh Is Deserved (chap. 3)

Nahum closes his brief book of judgment with God's reason for Nineveh's coming overthrow. The city is characterized by cruelty and corruption (3:1–7). Just as Assyria crushed the Egyptian capital city of Thebes (No Amon), Assyria's capital city will also be destroyed (3:8–10). Nineveh is fortified so well that defeat seems impossible, but God proclaims that its destruction is inevitable (3:11–19).

Outline of Nahum

The Book of Habakkuk

Authorship and Date

Nothing is known about the prophet Habakkuk except his name. Since the book speaks of the coming destruction of Judah, it had to be written some time before Jerusalem was destroyed by the Babylonians in 587 B.C. The most likely time for its composition is probably about 600 B.C.

Historical Setting

The Book of Habakkuk belongs to that turbulent era in ancient history when the balance of power was shifting from

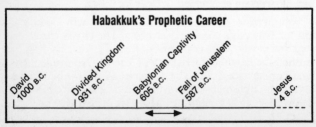

Habakkuk's Prophetic Career

David 1000 B.C.   Divided Kingdom 931 B.C.   Babylonian Captivity 605 B.C.   Fall of Jerusalem 587 B.C.   Jesus 4 B.C.

◆

KEYS TO HABAKKUK

Key Word: *"The Just Shall Live by His Faith"*

Habakkuk struggles in his faith when he sees men flagrantly violate God's law and distort justice on every level, without fear of divine intervention. He wants to know why God allows this growing iniquity to go unpunished. God's answer satisfies Habakkuk that he can trust Him even in the worst of circumstances because of His matchless wisdom, goodness, and power.

Key Verses: *Habakkuk 2:4; 3:17–19*

Key Chapter: *Habakkuk 3*

The Book of Habakkuk builds to a triumphant climax reached in the last three verses (3:17–19). The beginning of the book and the ending stand in stark contrast: mystery to certainty, questioning to affirming, and complaint to confidence.

◆

the Assyrians to the Babylonians. Assyria's domination came to an end with the destruction of its capital city, Nineveh, by the invading Babylonians in 612 B.C. Less than 20 years after Habakkuk wrote his book, the Babylonians also destroyed Jerusalem and carried the leading citizens of Judah into captivity.

Theological Contribution

The question-and-answer technique of the prophet Habakkuk teaches a valuable lesson about the nature of God. That God allows Himself to be questioned by one of His followers is an indication of His longsuffering mercy and grace.

The theme of God's judgment against unrighteousness also is woven throughout the book. God soon will punish His wayward people for their transgression, but He also will punish the pagan Babylonians because of their great sin. God's acts of judgment are in accord with His holiness, righteousness, and mercy.

Special Consideration

Paul's famous declaration, "The just shall live by faith" (Rom. 1:17), is a direct quotation from Habakkuk 2:4. In this brief prophetic book, we find the seeds of the glorious gospel of our Lord and Savior Jesus Christ.

Survey of Habakkuk

The Problems of Habakkuk (chaps. 1—2)

Habakkuk's first dialogue with God takes place in 1:1–11. In 1:1–4, the prophet asks God how long He will allow the wickedness of Judah to go unpunished. The people of Judah sin with impunity, and justice is perverted. God's startling answer is given in 1:5–11. He is raising up the fierce Babylonians as His rod of judgment upon sinful Judah. The Chaldeans will come against Judah swiftly, violently, and completely. The coming storm from the east will be God's answer to Judah's crimes.

This answer leads to Habakkuk's second dialogue with God (1:12—2:20). The prophet is more perplexed than ever and asks how the righteous God can punish Judah with a nation that is even more wicked (1:12—2:1). Habakkuk stands upon a watchtower to wait for God's reply, and the Lord answers with a series of five woes (2:5–20).

The Babylonians will not escape His terrible judgment, but Judah is guilty of the same offenses and stands under the same condemnation.

The Book of Habakkuk

FOCUS	Problems of Habakkuk			Praise of Habakkuk
REFERENCE	1:1 —— 1:5 ——	1:12 ——	2:2 ——	3:1 —— 3:19
DIVISION	First Problem of Habakkuk	First Reply of God	Second Problem of Habakkuk	Second Reply of God	Prayer of Praise of Habakkuk
TOPIC	Faith Troubled				Faith Triumphant
	What God Is Doing				Who God Is
LOCATION	The Nation of Judah				
TIME	c. 607 B.C.				

The Praise of Habakkuk (chap. 3)

Habakkuk begins by questioning God, but he concludes his book with a psalm of praise for the person (3:1–3), power (3:4–12), and plan (3:13–19) of God. He now acknowledges God's wisdom in the coming invasion of Judah, and although it terrifies him, he will trust the Lord.

Outline of Habakkuk

The Book of Zephaniah

Authorship and Date

Scholars are in general agreement that Zephaniah the prophet wrote this book that bears his name. In his introduction (1:1), the author traces his ancestry back four generations to Hezekiah, a former king of Judah noted for his faithfulness to God. The book also tells how Zephaniah the prophet ministered during the days of Josiah, a godly king who reigned over the nation of Judah from about 641 to about 609 B.C. Most scholars place the writing of the book at about 627 B.C.

◆

KEYS TO ZEPHANIAH

Key Word: *The Day of the Lord*

God is holy and must vindicate His righteousness by calling all the nations of the world into account before Him. The sovereign God will judge not only His own people but also the whole world. Wrath and mercy, severity and kindness, cannot be separated in the character of God.

Key Verses: *Zephaniah 1:14, 15; 2:3*

Key Chapter: *Zephaniah 3*

The last chapter of Zephaniah records the two distinct parts of the day of the Lord: judgment and restoration. Following the conversion of the nation, Israel finally is fully restored. Under the righteous rule of God, Israel fully inherits the blessings contained in the biblical covenants.

◆

Historical Setting

This book belongs to a dark period in Judah's history. About 100 years before Zephaniah's time, Judah's sister nation, the northern kingdom of Israel, had fallen to a foreign power because of its sin and idolatry. Zephaniah sensed that the same thing was about to happen to the southern kingdom of Judah—and for precisely the same reason.

Under the leadership of two successive evil kings, Manasseh and Amon, the people of Judah had fallen into worship of false gods. Not even a brief religious renewal under the good king Josiah was enough to turn the tide of paganism and false worship that carried Judah toward certain destruction. Judgment came to the nation in 587 B.C., when the invading Babylonians destroyed the city of Jerusalem and carried its leading citizens into captivity in Babylon.

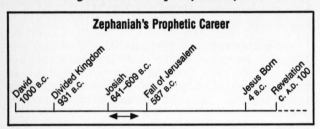

Zephaniah's Prophetic Career

David 1000 B.C. | Divided Kingdom 931 B.C. | Josiah 641–609 B.C. | Fall of Jerusalem 587 B.C. | Jesus Born 4 B.C. | Revelation C. A.D. 100

Theological Contribution

The judgment of the Lord portrayed by the prophet Zephaniah springs from His nature as a God of holiness. Because God demands holiness and righteousness in His people, He will judge those who continue to sin and rebel (1:17). But the Lord also is merciful and faithful to His promise.

Survey of Zephaniah

The Judgment in the Day of the Lord (1:1—3:8)

The prophetic oracle begins with an awesome statement of God's coming judgment upon the entire earth because of the sins of men (1:2, 3). Zephaniah then concentrates on the judgment of Judah (1:4–18), listing some of the offenses that will cause it to come. Judah is polluted with idolatrous priests who promote the worship of Baal and nature, and her officials and princes are completely corrupt. Therefore, the day of the Lord is imminent; and it will be characterized by terror, desolation, and distress. However, by His grace, God appeals to His people to repent and humble themselves to avert the coming disaster before it is too late (2:1–3).

Zephaniah pronounces God's coming judgment upon the

The Book of Zephaniah

FOCUS	Judgment in the Day of the Lord				Salvation in the Day of the Lord	
REFERENCE	1:1 ——— 1:4 ———	2:4 ———	3:1 ———	3:8 ———	3:9 ——— 3:14 ——— 3:20	
DIVISION	Judgment on the Whole Earth	Judgment on the Nation of Judah	Judgment on the Nations Surrounding Judah	Judgment on the City of Jerusalem	Judgment on the Whole Earth	Promise of Conversion	Promise of Restoration
TOPIC	Day of Wrath				Day of Joy	
LOCATION	Judgment on Judah				Restoration for Judah	
	Judah and the Nations					
TIME	c. 630 B.C.					

nations that surround Judah: Philistia (west), Moab and Ammon (east), Ethiopia (south), and Assyria (north) (2:4–15). Then he focuses on Jerusalem, the center of God's dealings but a city characterized by spiritual rebellion and moral treachery (3:1–7).

The Salvation in the Day of the Lord (3:9–20)

After a broad statement of the judgment of all nations (3:8), Zephaniah changes the tone of the remainder of his book to blessing; for this, too, is an aspect of the day of the Lord. The nation will be cleansed and will call on the name of the Lord (3:9, 10). The remnant of Israel will be regathered, redeemed, and restored (3:11–20). They will rejoice in their Redeemer, and He will be in their midst.

Outline of Zephaniah

The Book of Haggai

Authorship and Date

This book was written by the prophet Haggai, whose name means "festive." Like those whom he encouraged, he

◆

KEYS TO HAGGAI

Key Word: *The Reconstruction of the Temple*

Haggai's basic theme is clear: the remnant must reorder its priorities and complete the temple before it can expect the blessing of God upon its efforts.

Key Verses: *Haggai 1:7, 8; 2:7–9*

Key Chapter: *Haggai 2*

Verses 6–9 record some of the most startling prophecies in Scripture: "I will shake heaven and earth, the sea and dry land" (the Tribulation) and "they shall come to the Desire of All Nations" and "in this place I will give peace" (the second coming of the Messiah).

◆

probably spent many years in captivity in Babylon before returning to his native land. He delivered these messages of encouragement "in the second year of King Darius" (1:1), a Persian ruler. This dates his book precisely in 520 B.C.

Historical Setting

Haggai takes us back to one of the most turbulent periods in Judah's history. For more than 50 years they were held

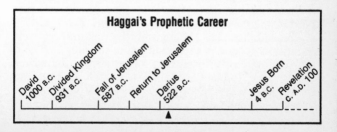

Haggai's Prophetic Career

David 1000 B.C. — Divided Kingdom 931 B.C. — Fall of Jerusalem 587 B.C. — Return to Jerusalem — Darius 522 B.C. — Jesus Born 4 B.C. — Revelation C. A.D. 100

captive by the Babylonians. But they were allowed to return to their native land, beginning about 530 B.C., after Babylon fell to the conquering Persians.

Theological Contribution

Haggai urged the people to put rebuilding the Temple at the top of their list of priorities. The rebuilt Temple in Jerusalem was important as a place of worship and sacrifice. Centuries later, at the death of Jesus "the veil of the Temple was torn in two" (Luke 23:45), demonstrating that He had given Himself as the eternal sacrifice on our behalf.

Special Consideration

The Book of Haggai ends with a beautiful promise of the coming of the Messiah. Meanwhile, God's special servant, Zerubbabel, was to serve as a "signet ring" (2:23), a sign or promise of hope for the full restoration of God's covenant people in their native land.

Survey of Haggai

The Completion of the Latter Temple (1:1–15)

When the remnant returns from Babylon under Zerubbabel, they begin to rebuild the Temple of the Lord. However, the work soon stops and the people find excuses to ignore it as the years pass. They have no problem in building rich dwellings for themselves (1:4), while they claim that the time for building the temple has not yet come (1:2).

God withdraws His blessing and they sink into economic depression because of their indifference to God. God communicates directly through His prophet Haggai, Zerubbabel the governor, Joshua the high priest, and all the people respond; and twenty-three days later they again begin to work on the Temple.

The Book of Haggai

FOCUS	Completion of the Latter Temple	Glory of the Latter Temple	Present Blessings of Obedience	Future Blessings Through Promise
REFERENCE	1:1 ———————	2:1 ———————	2:10 ———————	2:20 ——————— 2:23
DIVISION	"Consider Your Ways . . . My House That Is in Ruins."	"The Glory of This Latter Temple Shall Be Greater."	"From This Day I Will Bless You."	"I Will Shake Heaven and Earth."
TOPIC	The Temple of God		The Blessings of God	
	First Rebuke (Present)	First Encouragement (Future)	Second Rebuke (Present)	Second Encouragement (Future)
LOCATION	Jerusalem			
TIME	September 1 520 B.C.	October 21 520 B.C.	December 24 520 B.C.	December 24 520 B.C.

The Glory of the Latter Temple (2:1–9)

In a few short weeks, the enthusiasm of the people sours into discouragement; the elders remember the glory of Solomon's Temple and bemoan the puniness of the present Temple (see Ezra 3:8–13). Haggai's prophetic word of encouragement reminds the people of God's covenant promises in the past (2:4, 5), and of His confident plans for the future (2:6–9).

The Present Blessings of Obedience (2:10–19)

Haggai's message to the priests illustrates the concept of contamination (2:11–13) and applies it to the nation (2:14–19). The Lord requires holiness and obedience, and the contamination of sin blocks the blessing of God.

The Future Blessings of Promise (2:20–23)

On the same day that Haggai addresses the priests, he gives a second message to Zerubbabel. God will move in judgment, and in His power He will overthrow the nations of the earth (2:21, 22). At that time, Zerubbabel, a symbol of the Messiah to come, will be honored.

Outline of Haggai

The Book of Zechariah

◆

KEYS TO ZECHARIAH

Key Word: *Prepare for the Messiah*

The first eight chapters frequently allude to the Temple and encourage the people to complete their great work on the new sanctuary. As they build the Temple, they are building their future, because that very structure will be used by the Messiah when He comes to bring salvation.

Key Verses: *Zechariah 8:3; 9:9*

Key Chapter: *Zechariah 14*

Zechariah builds to a tremendous climax in the fourteenth chapter, where he discloses the last siege of Jerusalem and the ultimate holiness of Jerusalem and her people.

◆

Authorship, Date, and Historical Setting

Most conservative scholars agree that the entire book of Zechariah was written by the prophet of that name, who identifies himself in the book's introduction as "the son of Berechiah" (1:1), although some scholars insist the second major section of the book, chapters 9—14, was added by an unknown author 30 or 40 years later. Most likely, these prophecies were delivered and then reduced to writing over a period of about 45 years—from 520 to 475 B.C.

Zechariah probably was a priest as well as a prophet—an unusual circumstance because most of the prophets of Israel spoke out against the priestly class. He was probably born in

Babylon while the Jewish people were in captivity and returned with his family with the first wave of captives who reached Jerusalem under Zerubbabel about 530 B.C.

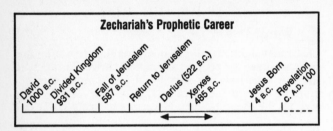

Theological Contribution

One of the greatest contributions of the Book of Zechariah is the merger of the priestly and prophetic elements in Israel's history, a preparation for the understanding of Christ as both priest and prophet. Zechariah is also noted for his development of an apocalyptic-prophetic style—highly symbolized and visionary language concerning the events of the endtime. In this, his writing stands apart with the Books of Daniel and Revelation.

Special Considerations

Zechariah 12:10 is a remarkable verse that speaks of the response of the nation of Israel to Jesus Christ as Savior and Lord. It describes a day in the future when the Jewish people (the house of David and the inhabitants of Jerusalem) will recognize the significance of the death of Jesus, be saved. But the most startling thing about Zechariah 12:10 is the phrase "Then they will look on Me whom they have pierced." In speaking through the prophet Zechariah, the Lord identifies Himself as the one who will be pierced.

Survey of Zechariah

The Eight Visions (chaps. 1—6)

The book opens with an introductory appeal to the people to repent and return to God, unlike their fathers who rejected the warnings of the prophets (1:1–6). A few months later, Zechariah has a series of eight night visions, evidently in one troubled night (February 15, 519 B.C.; 1:7). The first five are visions of comfort, and the last three are visions of judgment:

(1) The horseman among the myrtle trees—God will rebuild Zion and His people (1:7–17).
(2) The four horns and craftsmen—Israel's oppressors will be judged (1:18–21).
(3) The man with a measuring line—God will protect and glorify Jerusalem (2:1–13).
(4) The cleansing of Joshua the high priest—Israel will be cleansed and restored by the coming Branch (3:1–10).
(5) The golden lampstand—God's Spirit is empowering Zerubbabel and Joshua (4:1–14).
(6) The flying scroll—individual sin will be judged (5:1–4).
(7) The woman in the basket—national sin will be removed (5:5–11).
(8) The four chariots—God's judgment will descend on the nations (6:1–8). The crowning of Joshua (6:9–15) anticipates the coming of the Branch who will be King and Priest (the composite crown).

The Four Messages (chaps. 7—8)

In response to a question about the continuation of the fasts (7:1–3), God gives Zechariah a series of four messages:

• a rebuke of empty ritualism (7:4–7);
• a reminder of past disobedience (7:8–14);
• the restoration and consolation of Israel (8:1–17);
• and the recovery of joy in the kingdom (8:18–23).

The Book of Zechariah

FOCUS	Eight Visions			Four Messages	Two Burdens	
REFERENCE	1:1	1:7	6:9	7:1	9:1	12:1 — 14:21
DIVISION	Call to Repentance	Eight Visions	Crowning of Joshua	Question of Fasting	First Burden: Rejection of the Messiah	Second Burden: Reign of the Messiah
TOPIC	Pictures			Problem	Prediction	
	Israel's Fortune			Israel's Fastings	Israel's Future	
LOCATION	Jerusalem					
TIME	While Building the Temple (520–518 B.C.)				After Building the Temple (c. 480–470 B.C.)	

The Two Burdens (chaps. 9—14)

The first burden (9—11) concerns the first advent and rejection of Israel's coming King. Alexander the Great will conquer Israel's neighbors, but will spare Jerusalem (9:1—8) which will be preserved for her King (the Messiah; 9:9, 10). Israel will succeed against Greece (the Maccabean revolt; 9:11—17), and although they will later be scattered, the Messiah will bless them and bring them back (10:1—11:3). Israel will reject her Shepherd-King and be led astray by false shepherds (11:4—17).

The second burden (12—14) concerns the second advent of Christ and the acceptance of Israel's King. The nations will attack Jerusalem, but the Messiah will come and deliver His people (12). They will be cleansed of impurity and falsehood (13), and the Messiah will come in power to judge the nations and reign in Jerusalem over the whole earth (14).

Outline of Zechariah

The Book of Malachi

◆

KEYS TO MALACHI

Key Word: *An Appeal to Backsliders*

The divine dialogue in Malachi's prophecy is designed as an appeal to break through the barrier of Israel's disbelief, disappointment, and discouragement. God reveals His continuing love in spite of Israel's lethargy. His appeal in this oracle is for the people and priests to stop and realize that their lack of blessing is not caused by God's lack of concern, but by their disobedience of the covenant law.

Key Verses: *Malachi 2:17–3:1; 4:5, 6*

Key Chapter: *Malachi 3*

The last book of the Old Testament concludes with a dramatic prophecy of the coming of the Messiah and John the Baptist: "I send My messenger, and he will prepare the way before Me" (3:1).

◆

Authorship and Date

Although nothing is known about this person, the weight of tradition has assumed the book was written by a prophet

named Malachi, about 1,000 years after the time of Moses,
the first prophet and Bible writer. The prophecy can be specifically dated at about 450 B.C.

Historical Setting

Malachi was addressed to the nation of Israel about 100
years after its return from captivity in Babylon. At first the
people had been enthusiastic about rebuilding Jerusalem and
the Temple and restoring their system of worship, but their
zeal soon began to wane. They began to question God's
providence as their faith degenerated into cynicism.

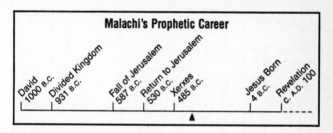

Malachi's Prophetic Career

David 1000 B.C. · Divided Kingdom 931 B.C. · Fall of Jerusalem 587 B.C. · Return to Jerusalem 530 B.C. · Xerxes 485 B.C. · Jesus Born 4 B.C. · Revelation c. A.D. 100

Theological Contribution

The prophecy of Malachi is noted for its vivid portrayal of
the love of God as well as His might and power. Israel needed
to be reminded of these truths at a time when widespread
doubt had dashed expectations of the Messiah.

Special Consideration

Malachi leaves us with the feeling that the story is not yet
finished, that God still has promises to fulfill on behalf of His
people. After Malachi came 400 long years of silence. But
when the time was right, heaven would burst forth in song at
the arrival of the Messiah.

The Book of Malachi

FOCUS	Privilege of the Nation	Pollution of the Nation		Promise to the Nation		
REFERENCE	1:1 ———	1:6 ———	2:10 ———	3:16 ———	4:1 ———	4:4 ——— 4:6
DIVISION	Love of God for the Nation	Sin of the Priests	Sin of the People	Book of Remembrance	Coming of Christ	Coming of Elijah
TOPIC	Past	Present		Future		
	Care of God	Complaint of God		Coming of God		
LOCATION	Jerusalem					
TIME	c. 450 B.C.					

Survey of Malachi

The Privilege of the Nation (1:1–5)

The Israelites blind themselves to God's love for them. Wallowing in the problems of the present, they are forgetful of God's works for them in the past. God gives them a reminder of His special love by contrasting the fates of Esau (Edom) and Jacob (Israel).

The Pollution of the Nation (1:6—3:15)

The priests have lost all respect for God's name and in their greed offer only diseased and imperfect animals on the altar. The people are indicted for their treachery in divorcing the wives of their youth in order to marry foreign women (2:10–16). In response to their questioning the justice of God, they receive a promise of the Messiah's coming but also a warning of the judgment that He will bring (2:17—3:6).

The people have robbed God of the tithes and offerings due Him, but God is ready to bless them with abundance if they will put Him first (3:7–12). The final problem is the arrogant challenge to the character of God (3:13–15).

The Promise to the Nation (3:16—4:6)

The Lord assures His people that a time is coming when the wicked will be judged and those who fear Him will be blessed, but the prophecy ends on the bitter word *curse*. Although the people are finally cured of idolatry, there is little spiritual progress in Israel's history. Sin abounds, and the need for the coming Messiah is greater than ever.

Outline of Malachi

PART TWO

♦

THE NEW TESTAMENT

WRITTEN about 400 years after the close of the Old Testament, the New Testament completes the cosmic story of God's plan to bring salvation upon the earth. The word *testament* is best translated as "covenant." The New Testament embodies the new covenant of which Jesus was mediator (Jer. 31:31–34; Heb. 9:15). This new covenant was sealed with the atoning death of Jesus Christ.

The New Testament opens with five narrative books—the four Gospels and the Acts of the Apostles. The Gospels deal with the ministry, death, and resurrection of Jesus. The Book of Acts continues the story of the development of the early church across the next thirty years.

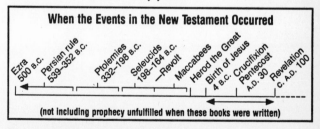

When the Events in the New Testament Occurred

Ezra 500 B.C.
Persian rule 539–352 B.C.
Ptolemies 332–198 B.C.
Seleucids 198–164 B.C. —Revolt
Maccabees
Herod the Great
Birth of Jesus 4 B.C.
Crucifixion Pentecost A.D. 30
Revelation C. A.D. 100

(not including prophecy unfulfilled when these books were written)

Twenty-one letters, or epistles, follow the historical narratives. The last book in the New Testament, the Revelation of John, portrays through visions and symbolic language the accomplishment of God's purpose in the world and the ultimate triumph of Christ.

The twenty-seven books of the New Testament were written over a period of about 50 years in Greek, the international language of the people.

SIX

THE GOSPELS

◆

THE early church placed the Gospels of Matthew, Mark, Luke, and John at the beginning of the New Testament as the theological backdrop for the rest of the New Testament. These four accounts provide a composite picture of the person and work of the Savior, working together to give depth and clarity to our understanding of the most unique figure in human history. In them He is seen as divine and human, the sovereign servant, the God-man.

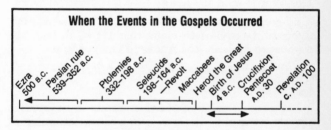

When the Events in the Gospels Occurred

THE GOSPELS

BOOK	SUMMARY
Matthew	Christ presented as the teacher who is greater than Moses
Mark	Probably the earliest of the Gospels, focusing on Jesus as Suffering Servant

Luke	Fullest biography of Christ, focusing on Jesus as the keystone in the history of salvation
John	The most symbolic Gospel, which presents Christ as the divine Son of God who came to earth in human form

The Book of Matthew

◆

KEYS TO MATTHEW

Key Word: *Jesus the King*

By quoting repeatedly from the Old Testament, Matthew validates Christ's claim that He is, in fact, the prophesied Messiah (the Anointed One) of Israel.

Key Verses: *Matthew 16:16–19 and 28:18–20*

Key Chapter: *Matthew 12*

The turning point of Matthew comes in the twelfth chapter when the Pharisees, acting as the leadership of the nation of Israel, formally reject Jesus Christ as the Messiah. Christ's ministry changes immediately with His new teaching of parables, increased attention given to His disciples, and His repeated statement that His death is now near.

◆

Authorship and Date

Matthew is an anonymous gospel, but the actual author probably was a Palestinian Jew who used the Gospel of Mark, plus a Greek translation of Matthew's Aramaic "oracles," and composed the gospel in Greek. The name of the gospel, therefore, stems from the apostle Matthew on whom the author draws, in part, to compose his work.

Theological Contribution

Matthew's main subject is the "kingdom of heaven" or "kingdom of God." This kingdom is mentioned 51 times in the Gospel of Matthew, twice as often as in any other gospel. The kingdom is already here in Jesus (12:28), but it is not yet fulfilled (13:43; 25:34). The kingdom cannot be earned (19:23); it can be received only by those who recognize that they do not deserve it (5:3; 21:31). The kingdom extends like a fishing net, gathering people from every part of society (13:47), offering new life in the life-changing presence of God (8:11). The kingdom is more valuable than a precious gem (13:45–46), and it excludes any and all competitors for its allegiance (6:33).

The kingdom of God means the rule or reign of God—in the entire universe, in the world, and in our hearts. The primary indication of the presence of the kingdom in the world is the transformation of life, both individually and socially.

Special Considerations

The Gospel of Matthew has at least five special considerations that will be mentioned briefly here:

- Matthew sought to prove to the Jews that Jesus was the Christ, the fulfillment of Old Testament prophecy. A recurring statement that occurs in this gospel is, "All this was done that it might be fulfilled which was spoken by the Lord through the prophet" (1:22; also 2:15, 17, 23).
- Matthew has a special interest in the church, which by the time this gospel was written had become the dominant factor in the lives of Christians. Indeed, Matthew is the only gospel to mention the word *church* (16:18; 18:17).

- Matthew has a strong interest in eschatology (the doctrine of last things)—that is, in the second coming of Jesus, the end of the age, and the final judgment (chap. 25).
- Matthew has a great interest in the teachings of Jesus, especially concerning the kingdom of God (chaps. 5—7; 10; 13; 18; 24—25).
- Matthew writes to show that Jesus is the King to whom God has given power and authority to redeem and to judge humankind (1:1–17; 2:2; 21:1–11; 27:11, 37; 28:18).

Survey of Matthew

The Presentation of the King (1:1—4:11)

The promise to Abraham was that "in you all the families of the earth shall be blessed" (Gen. 12:3). Jesus Christ, the Savior of the world, is "the Son of Abraham" (1:1). However, He is also "the Son of David"; and as David's direct descendant, He is qualified to be Israel's King.

The magi know that the "King of the Jews" (2:2) has been born and come to worship Him. John the Baptist, the messianic forerunner who breaks the four hundred years of prophetic silence, also bears witness of Him (cf. Mal. 3:1). The sinlessness of the King is proved when He overcomes the satanic temptations to disobey the will of the Father.

The Proclamation of the King (4:12—7:29)

In this section, Matthew uses a topical rather than a chronological arrangement of his material in order to develop a crucial pattern in Christ's ministry. The words of the Lord found in the Sermon on the Mount presents new laws and standards for God's people (chaps. 5—7).

The Power of the King (8:1—11:1)

The works of the Lord are presented in a series of ten miracles (chaps. 8—9) that reveal His authority over every realm (disease, demons, death, and nature). Thus, the words of the Lord are supported by His works; His claims are verified by His credentials.

The Progressive Rejection of the King (11:2—16:12)

Here we note a series of reactions to Christ's words and works. Because of increasing opposition, Jesus begins to spend proportionately more time with His disciples as He prepares them for His coming death and departure.

The Preparation of the King's Disciples (16:13—20:28)

In a series of discourses, Jesus communicates the significance of accepting or rejecting His offer of righteousness. His teaching in 16:13—21:11 is primarily directed to those who accept Him.

The Presentation and Rejection of the King (20:29—27:66)

The majority of Christ's words in this section are aimed at those who reject their King. The Lord predicts the terrible judgment that will fall on Jerusalem, resulting in the dispersion of the Jewish people. Looking beyond these events (fulfilled in A.D. 70), He also describes His second coming as the Judge and Lord of the earth.

The Proof of the King (28)

Authenticating His words and works are the empty tomb, resurrection, and appearances, all proving that Jesus Christ is indeed the prophesied Messiah, the very Son of God.

Christ's final ministry in Judea (beginning in 19:1) reaches a climax at the cross as the King willingly gives up His life to redeem sinful persons. Jesus endures awesome human hatred in this great demonstration of divine love (cf. Rom. 5:7, 8). His perfect sacrifice is acceptable, and this gospel concludes with His glorious resurrection.

The Gospel According to Matthew

FOCUS	Offer of the King			Rejection of the King			
REFERENCE	1:1 ———	4:12 ———	8:1 ———	11:2 ———	16:13 ———	20:29 ———	28:1 — 28:20
DIVISION	Presentation of the King	Proclamation of the King	Power of the King	Progressive Rejection of the King	Preparation of the King's Disciples	Presentation and Rejection of the King	Proof of the King
TOPIC	Teaching the Throngs				Teaching the Twelve		
	Chronological	Thematic			Chronological		
LOCATION	Bethlehem and Nazareth	Galilee			Judea		
TIME	c. 4 B.C.—A.D. 30 or 33						

Outline of Matthew

The Gospel of Mark

◆

KEYS TO MARK

Key Word: *Jesus the Servant*

Mark's theme is captured well in 10:45 because Jesus is portrayed in this book as a Servant and as the Redeemer of men (cf. Phil. 2:5–11). Mark shows his gentile readers how the Son of God—rejected by His own people—achieved ultimate victory through apparent defeat.

Key Verses: *Mark 10:43–45 and 8:34–37*

Key Chapter: *Mark 8*

Mark 8 is a pivotal chapter showing the change of emphasis in Jesus' ministry after Peter's confession, "You are the Christ." After this point Jesus begins to fortify His men for His forthcoming suffering and death.

◆

Authorship and Date

The Gospel of Mark nowhere mentions the name of its author. Tradition unanimously ascribes this gospel to John Mark, a native of Jerusalem (Acts 12:12), and later an associate of both Peter (1 Pet. 5:13) and Paul (2 Tim. 4:11). If Mark composed his gospel while in the services of Peter, and Peter died in Rome between A.D. 64 and A.D. 68, then the gospel would have been written in Italy in the late 60's.

Theological Contribution

One of Mark's key objectives is to portray Jesus as God's Son. At decisive points in his story, he reveals the mystery of Jesus' person. At the baptism (1:11) and Transfiguration (9:7) the Father in heaven calls Jesus "My beloved Son," thus indicating that Jesus shares a unique relationship with the Father. Demons recognize Jesus as God's Son, too (1:24; 3:11; 5:7), testifying that Jesus is equipped with God's authority and power.

However, Jesus is powerful according to the model of the Suffering Servant of Isaiah. He must be obedient to the will of the Father, even to death on a cross. He is human, for He appears sorrowful (14:34), disappointed (8:12), displeased (10:14), angry (11:15–17), amazed (6:6), and fatigued (4:38).

For Mark, faith and discipleship have no meaning apart from following the *suffering* Son of God. Faith is not a magic that works independently of the believer's participation (6:1–6); rather, it draws the believer into intimate union with Jesus as Lord (9:14–29). As the Son of Man serves in self-abasement, so too must His disciples serve (10:42–45). Discipleship with Christ leads to self-denial and suffering. This, however, is not a matter of religious desire to suffer; rather, when one loses his life, he finds it in Christ (8:35).

Special Consideration

The ending of the Gospel of Mark poses a problem. The two oldest and most important manuscripts of the Greek New Testament (Sinaiticus and Vaticanus) end with the words, "For they were afraid" (16:8). Other manuscripts add, in whole or in part, the material making up verses 9–20. This longer ending, however, is unlike Mark 1:1—16:8 in style and content; it contains material presented exactly as it is in Matthew and Luke. It has long been debated whether Mark intended to end his gospel at 16:8, or whether the original ending was lost and a secondary ending (vv. 9–20) was later added.

It seems unlikely that, having begun the gospel with a bold introduction (1:10), Mark would end it on a note of fear (16:8). It also would seem logical that one who drafted a gospel along the lines of the early Christian preaching would not have omitted a central feature like the resurrection (1 Cor. 15:3–26). These reasons suggest that the shorter ending of Mark (at 16:8) is not the original (or intended) ending—for whatever reason—and that verses 9–20 are a later addition supplied to compensate for the omission.

Survey of Mark

To Serve (chaps. 1—10)

Mark passes over the birth and early years of Jesus' life and begins with the events that immediately precede the inauguration of His public ministry—His baptism by John and His temptation by Satan (1:1–13). The first four chapters emphasize the words of the Servant while chapters 5—7 accent His works. However, in both sections there is a frequent alternation between Christ's messages and miracles in order to reveal His person and power. Though He has come to serve others, Jesus' authority prevails over many realms.

Although Jesus has already been teaching and testing His disciples (see chap. 4), His ministry with them becomes more

The Gospel According to Mark

FOCUS	To Serve		To Sacrifice	
REFERENCE 1:1 ———— 2:13 ————		8:27 ———— 11:1 ————	16:1 ———— 16:20	
DIVISION	Presentation of the Servant	Opposition to the Servant	Instruction by the Servant	Rejection of the Servant	Resurrection of the Servant
TOPIC	Sayings and Signs		Sufferings	
	c. 3 Years	c. 6 Months	8 Days	
LOCATION	Galilee and Perea		Judea and Jerusalem	
TIME	c. A.D. 29–30 or 33			

intense from this point on as He begins to prepare them for His departure. The religious leaders are growing more antagonistic, and Christ's "hour" is only about six months away. Mark 8:31 is the pivotal point in the gospel as the son of Man speaks clearly to His disciples about His coming death and resurrection.

To Sacrifice (chaps. 11—16)

Mark allots a disproportionate space to the last weeks of the Servant's redemptive ministry. During the last seven days in Jerusalem, hostility from the chief priests, scribes, elders, Pharisees, Herodians, and Sadducees reaches crisis proportions as Jesus publicly refutes their arguments in the temple. After His last supper with the disciples, Jesus offers no resistance to His arrest, abuse, and agonizing crucifixion. His willingness to bear countless human sins in atonement is the epitome of servanthood.

Outline of Mark

The Gospel of Luke

Authorship and Date

The author does not identify himself by name, but he does tell us a good deal about himself. An educated man with the best command of Greek of any New Testament writer, he counts among his acquaintances a person of high social standing, the "most excellent" Theophilus, to whom he addresses both Luke (1:3) and Acts (1:1). As a Gentile, the author is interested in Gentiles; he is equally disinterested in matters purely Jewish. Later tradition identifies the author as Luke, the companion of Paul. The Gospel of Luke probably was written sometime shortly after A.D. 70.

Theological Contribution

Luke, the most universal in outlook of all the gospels, portrays Jesus as a man with compassion for all peoples. Luke is also the most socially-minded of the gospels. Jesus blesses the poor, the hungry, those who weep, and the excluded (6:20–23). In His parables He takes the side of a beggar who sits

◆

KEYS TO LUKE

Key Word: *Jesus the Son of Man*

Luke portrays Christ in His fullest humanity by devoting more of his writing to Christ's feelings and humanity than any other gospel.

Key Verses: *Luke 1:3, 4 and 19:10*

Key Chapter: *Luke 15*

Captured in the three parables of the Lost Sheep, Lost Coin, and Lost Son is the crux of this gospel: that God through Christ has come to seek and to save that which was lost.

◆

outside the gate of a rich man (16:19–31) and celebrates a tax collector who shies away from the Temple because of his sinfulness (18:9–14). Jesus reaches out to a widowed mother who had lost her only son (7:11–17) and to a sinful woman (7:36–50). In another parable the hero of mercy is a despised Samaritan (10:25–37); and after a healing, a Samaritan is praised for his gratitude (17:11–19). The open arms of the Father, as in the parable of the Prodigal Son (15:11–32), await all who return to Him.

Special Consideration

For Luke the coming of Christ is good news; and his gospel is one of *joy*. The births of John and Jesus are echoed by songs of praise from Mary (1:46–55), Zacharias (1:67–79), the angels (2:14), and Simeon (2:29–32). Even the unborn leap for joy (1:44). The note of joy that rings from Gabriel at the Annunciation (1:32–33) ultimately is repeated by the apostles at the end of the gospel (24:52–53).

Luke is also a gospel of the *Holy Spirit*. Unlike the other evangelists, Luke emphasizes the activity of the Spirit in the ministry of Jesus. John the Baptist and his parents are filled with the Spirit (1:15, 41, 67), as is Simeon (2:25–35). Jesus begins His ministry "in the power of the Spirit" (4:14; also 4:1, 18; 10:21), and He promises the Spirit to His disciples in their hour of need (12:12).

Finally, Luke is a gospel of *prayer*. The multitude prays as Zacharias serves at the altar (1:10). Mary prays at the news of salvation (1:46–55). Jesus prays at His baptism (3:21), when He chooses His disciples (6:12), at Peter's confession (9:18), and at His transfiguration (9:29). In the solitude of prayer Jesus takes the first steps of ministry (5:16), falls to His knees on the Mount of Olives (22:39–46) and gives His final breath back to God.

Survey of Luke

The Introduction of the Son of Man (1:1–4:13)

Luke places a strong emphasis on the ancestry, birth, and early years of the Perfect Man and of His forerunner John the Baptist. Their infancy stories are intertwined as Luke records their birth announcements, advents, and Temple presentations. Jesus prepares over thirty years (summarized in one verse, 2:52) for a public ministry of only three years. The ancestry of the Son of Man is traced back to the first man Adam, and His ministry commences after His baptism and temptation.

The Ministry of the Son of Man (4:14–9:50)

The authority of the Son of Man over every realm is demonstrated in 4:14—6:49. In this section His authority over demons, disease, nature, the effects of sin, tradition, and all people is presented as a prelude to His diverse ministry of preaching, healing, and discipling (7:1–9:50).

The Gospel According to Luke

FOCUS	Introduction of the Son of Man	Ministry of the Son of Man	Rejection of the Son of Man	Crucifixion and Resurrection of the Son of Man
REFERENCE	1:1 ——————	4:14 ——————	9:51 ——————	19:28 —————— 24:53
DIVISION	Advent	Activities	Antagonism and Admonition	Application and Authentication
TOPIC		Seeking the Lost		Saving the Lost
	Miracles Prominent		Teaching Prominent	
LOCATION	Israel	Galilee	Israel	Jerusalem
TIME			c. 4 B.C.—A.D. 30 or 33	

The Rejection of the Son of Man (9:51–19:27)

The dual response of growing belief and growing rejection has already been introduced in the gospel (cf. 4:14 and 6:11), but from this time forward the intensity of opposition to the ministry of the Son of Man increases. When the religious leaders accuse Him of being demonized, Jesus pronounces a series of divine woes upon them (11).

Knowing that He is on His last journey to Jerusalem, Jesus instructs His disciples on a number of practical matters including prayer, covetousness, faithfulness, repentance, humility, discipleship, evangelism, money, forgiveness, service, thankfulness, the Second Advent, and salvation (12:1–19:27).

The Crucifixion and Resurrection of the Son of Man (19:28–24:53)

After His triumphal entry into Jerusalem, Jesus encounters the opposition of the priests, Sadducees, and scribes and predicts the overthrow of Jerusalem (19:28–21:38). The Son of Man instructs His disciples for the last time before His betrayal in Gethsemane. The three religious and three civil trials culminate in His crucifixion.

The glory and foundation of the Christian message is the historical resurrection of Jesus Christ. The Lord conquers the grave as He has promised, and appears on a number of occasions to His disciples before His ascension to the Father.

Outline of Luke

Part One: Introduction of the Son of Man (1:1–4:13)

Part Three: The Rejection of the
Son of Man (9:51–19:27)

The Gospel of John

Authorship and Date

Like the other gospels, John comes to us as an anonymous book. Tradition agrees that the author was John the Apostle, who was exiled to the island of Patmos in the Aegean Sea and who later died in Ephesus sometime after Trajan became emperor of Rome in A.D. 98. That places the date sometime around the close of the first century.

◆

KEYS TO JOHN

Key Word: *Believe*

The fourth gospel has the clearest statement of purpose in the Bible: "But these are written that you may believe that Jesus is the Christ, the Son of God, and that believing you may have life in His name" (20:31). John selected the signs he used for the specific purpose of creating intellectual ("that you may believe") and spiritual ("that believing you may have life") conviction about the Son of God.

Key Verses: *John 1:11–13 and John 20:30, 31*

Key Chapter: *John 3*

John 3:16 is without doubt the most quoted and preached verse in all of Scripture. Captured in it is the gospel in its clearest and simplest form: that salvation is a gift of God and is obtainable only through belief.

◆

Theological Contribution

John writes with a modest vocabulary, but his words are charged with symbolism. Terms like *believe, love, truth, world, light* and *darkness, above* and *below, name, witness, sin, judgment, (eternal) life, glory, bread, water,* and *hour* are the key words of this gospel. In John 3:16–21, a passage of less than 150 words in Greek, seven of these terms occur.

The world is where God reveals truth (8:32), light (8:12), and life (14:6) in His Son Jesus Christ. The world is also where persons must decide for or against the witness of Christ, and the decision is judgment (3:18). Sin is to misjudge Jesus—to fail to receive Him as the bread of life (6:35), or not to walk in Him as the light of the world (8:12). The Son has come from above to glorify the Father (17:1), and He does so in His "hour" (12:23; 13:1)—through His suffering on the cross.

In the synoptic gospels—Matthew, Mark, and Luke—Jesus utters short sayings. Longer discourses, such as the Sermon on the Mount (Matthew 5—7), are either collections of sayings on various themes, or, like Matthew 13, mostly parables.

John, on the other hand, records no parables and few of the brief sayings so common to the synoptics. Rather, he expands upon an incident, for example, Nicodemus (chap. 3); or he takes up an image, for example, light (chap. 8).These discourses are blended so completely with John's own style that frequently the reader cannot tell whether it is John or Jesus speaking (3:16).

The Gospel of John expresses the uniqueness of the Son's relationship with the Father. John begins with the preexistence of Jesus: "In the beginning was the Word" (1:1). Jesus is divine ("the Word was God," 1:1), but He is also human ("the Word became flesh," 1:14).

He also introduces Jesus by seven key titles: Word, Lamb of God, Rabbi, Messiah, King of Israel, Son of God, and Son of Man. Only in John do we find the "I am" sayings: "I am the bread of life" (6:35), "I am the light of the world" (8:12), "before Abraham was, I AM" (8:58), "I am the door of the sheep" (10:7), "I am the good shepherd" (10:11), "I and My Father are one" (10:30), "I am the way, the truth, and the life" (14:6), and "I am the vine" (15:5). In each of these sayings the "I" identifies Jesus with the name of God, "I AM" (Ex. 3:14).

Special Consideration

Our present Gospel of John contains a story that probably was not written by the original author. The account of the woman caught in adultery (7:53—8:11) differs markedly in style from the rest of John. It is not found in the earlier and better manuscripts of the book, although there is no reason to doubt that it portrays an actual event in Jesus' ministry.

Survey of John

The Incarnation of the Son of God (1:1-18)

This prologue dates the nature of Jesus, introduces His forerunner, clarifies His mission, and notes the rejection and acceptance He will find during His ministry.

The Presentation of the Son of God (1:19—4:54)

In this section Christ is under careful consideration and scrutiny by Israel. He is introduced by John the Baptist who directs his own disciples to Christ. John carefully selects seven miracles out of the many that Christ accomplished (cf. 21:25) in order to build a concise case for His deity, for they symbolize the life-changing results of belief in Jesus.

The Opposition to the Son of God (5:1—12:50)

John's unusual pattern in these chapters is to record the reactions of belief and disbelief after the performance of one miracle before moving to the next. In a series of growing confrontations, John portrays the intense opposition that will culminate in the Lord's final rejection on the cross. Even though many people received Him, the inevitable crucifixion is foreshadowed in several places (2:4, 21, 22; 7:6, 39; 11:51, 52; 12:16).

The Preparation of the Disciples by the Son of God (13:1—17:26)

John surveys the incarnation and public ministry of Jesus in twelve chapters, but radically changes the pace in the next five chapters to give a detailed account of a few crucial hours. In this clear and vivid recollection of Jesus' last discourse to His intimate disciples, John captures the Lord's words of

The Gospel According to John

FOCUS	Incarnation of the Son of God	Presentation of the Son of God	Opposition to the Son of God	Preparation of the Disciples	Crucifixion and Resurrection of the Son of God
REFERENCE	1:1 ———	1:19 ———	5:1 ———	13:1 ———	18:1 ——— 21:25
DIVISION	Introduction to Christ	Revelation of Christ	Rejection of Christ	Revelation of Christ	Rejection of Christ
				Upper Room Discourse	Supreme Miracle
TOPIC		Seven Miracles			
		That You Might Believe		That You Might Have Life	
LOCATION			Israel		
TIME		A Few Years		A Few Hours	A Few Weeks

comfort and assurance to a group of fearful and confused followers.

Jesus knows that in less than twenty-four hours He will be on the cross. Therefore, His last words speak of all the resources that will be at the disciples' disposal after His departure. They will be indwelled and empowered by the Triune Godhead. The Upper Room Discourse contains the message of the epistles in capsule form as it reveals God's pattern for Christian living.

The Crucifixion and Resurrection of the Son of God (18:1–21:25)

After recording Christ's high priestly prayer on behalf of His disciples and all who believe in Him, John immediately launches into a dramatic description of Christ's arrest and trials before Annas, Caiaphas, and Pilate.

In His crucifixion, Jesus willingly fulfills John the Baptist's prophetic words: "Behold! The Lamb of God who takes away the sin of the world!" (1:29). John closes his gospel with a particularly detailed account of the post-resurrection appearances of the Lord. The Resurrection is the ultimate sign that points to Jesus as the Son of God.

Outline of John ·

Part One: The Incarnation of the
Son of God (1:1–18)

Part Two: The Presentation of the
Son of God (1:19—4:54)

Part Three: The Opposition to the
Son of God (5:1–12:50)

SEVEN

ACTS: A HISTORY OF THE EARLY CHURCH

♦

The Book of Acts

ACTS is the historical link between the Gospels and the Epistles. It is the only book that carries on the story from the ascension of Jesus to the period of the Epistles. In one generation the church makes the transition from a primarily Jewish to a predominantly Gentile membership.

A HISTORY OF THE EARLY CHURCH

BOOK	SUMMARY
Acts	A history of the expansion of the early church

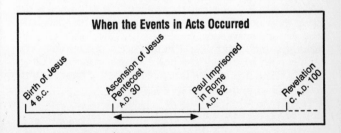

When the Events in Acts Occurred

Birth of Jesus
4 B.C.

Ascension of Jesus
Pentecost
A.D. 30

Paul Imprisoned
in Rome
A.D. 62

Revelation
c. A.D. 100

◆

KEYS TO ACTS

Key Word: _Empowered for Witness_

Because of Luke's strong emphasis on the ministry of the Holy Spirit, this book could be regarded as "The Acts of the Spirit of Christ working in and through the Apostles."

Key Verses: _Acts 1:8 and 2:42–47_

Key Chapter: _Acts 2_

Chapter 2 records the earth-changing events of the Day of Pentecost when the Holy Spirit comes, fulfilling Christ's command to wait until the Holy Spirit arrives to empower and direct the witness. The Spirit transforms a small group of fearful men into a thriving, worldwide church that is ever moving forward and fulfilling the Great Commission.

◆

Authorship and Date

There can be little doubt that the Book of Acts and the Gospel of Luke come from the same author. Addressed to the same individual, Theophilus, the similarities between Luke and Acts in literary style, vocabulary, and theological ideas are unmistakable. If the gospel were written in the early 70's, Acts would have been composed shortly thereafter. Other scholars date Acts as early as A.D. 62 because it ends abruptly with Paul's imprisonment in Rome.

Theological Contribution

The Acts of the Apostles could be justly entitled, "The Acts of the Holy Spirit," for the Spirit is mentioned nearly 60 times in the book. In His parting words, Jesus reminds the disciples of the promise of the Father (1:4–8); ten days later the power of the Spirit descends at Pentecost (2:1–4). It is a reversal of the Tower of Babel, where language became confused and nations were separated by misunderstanding (Gen. 11:1-9).

Special Consideration

Nearly one-fifth of Acts consists of speeches, primarily from Peter, Stephen, and Paul. Common to each of the speeches is the earliest basic framework of gospel proclamation.

1. The promises of God in the Old Testament are now fulfilled.
2. The Messiah has come in Jesus of Nazareth, who did good and mighty works by the power of God, was crucified according to the purpose of God, was raised from the dead, and now reigns by the power of God, and come again to judge and restore all things for the purpose of God.
3. All who hear should repent and be baptized.

Survey of Acts

Witness in Jerusalem (1:1—8:4)

After appearing to His disciples for "forty days" (1:3), the Lord tells them to wait in Jerusalem for the fulfillment of His promise concerning the Holy Spirit. Ten days after His ascension, this promise is significantly fulfilled as the disciples are suddenly empowered and filled with the Holy Spirit. Three thousand persons respond with saving faith to Peter's powerful sermon.

After dramatically healing a man who was lame from birth, Peter delivers a second crucial message to the people of Israel resulting in thousands of additional responses. The apostles are imprisoned and persecuted because of their witness. Ananias and Sapphira receive the ultimate form of discipline because of their treachery; seven men, including Stephen and Philip, are selected to assist the apostles.

Stephen is brought before the Sanhedrin; in his defense, Stephen surveys the Scriptures to prove that the Man they condemned and killed was the Messiah Himself. The members of the Sanhedrin react to Stephen's words by dragging him out of the city and making him the first Christian martyr.

Witness in Judea and Samaria (8:5—12:25)

Philip goes to the province of Samaria and successfully proclaims the new message to a people hated by the Jews. Peter and John confirm his work and exercise their apostolic authority by imparting the Holy Spirit to these new members of the body of Christ. God sovereignly transforms Saul the persecutor into Paul the apostle to the Gentiles, but He uses Peter to introduce the gospel to the Gentiles.

In a special vision Peter realizes that Christ has broken down the barrier between Jew and Gentile. After Cornelius and other Gentiles come to Christ through his preaching, Peter convinces the Jewish believers in Jerusalem that "the Gentiles had also received the word of God" (11:1). Even while experiencing more and more persecution, the church continues to increase, spreading throughout the Roman Empire.

Witness to the End of the Earth (13—28)

Beginning with chapter 13, Luke switches the focus of Acts from Peter to Paul. Antioch in Syria gradually replaces Jerusalem as the headquarters of the church, and all three of Paul's missionary journeys originate from that city. The first journey (A.D. 48–49) concentrates on the Galatian cities of Pisidian Antioch, Iconium, Lystra, and Derbe.

After this journey, a council is held among the apostles and elders of the church in Jerusalem to determine that the gen-

The Acts of the Apostles

FOCUS	Witness in Jerusalem		Witness in Judea and Samaria	Witness to the End of the Earth	
REFERENCE	1:1 ——— 3:1 ———		8:5 ———	13:1 ——— 21:17 —	28:31
DIVISION	Power of the Church	Progress of the Church	Expansion of the Church	Paul's Three Journeys	Paul's Trials
TOPIC	Jews		Samaritans	Gentiles	
	Peter		Philip	Paul	
LOCATION	Jerusalem		Judea and Samaria	Uttermost Part	
TIME	2 or 5 Years (A.D. 30 or 33-35)		13 Years (A.D. 35-48)	14 Years (A.D. 48-62)	

tile converts need not submit to the law of Moses. The second missionary journey (A.D. 50–52) brings Paul once again to the Galatian churches, and then for the first time on to Macedonia and Greece. Paul spends much of his time in the cities of Philippi, Thessalonica, and Corinth, and later returns to Jerusalem and Antioch.

In his third missionary journey (A.D. 53–57), Paul spends almost three years in the Asian city of Ephesus before visiting Macedonia and Greece for the second time. Although he is warned not to go to Jerusalem, Paul cannot be dissuaded.

It is not long before Paul is falsely accused of bringing Gentiles into the Temple. Only the Roman commander's intervention prevents his being killed by the mob. Paul's defense before the people and before the Sanhedrin evokes violent reactions. When the commander learns of a conspiracy to assassinate Paul, he sends his prisoner to Felix, the governor in Caesarea. During his two-year imprisonment there (A.D. 57–59), Paul defends the Christian faith before Felix, Festus, and Agrippa. His appeal to Caesar requires a long voyage to Rome, where he is placed under house arrest until his trial.

Outline of Acts

EIGHT

THE EPISTLES (LETTERS) OF THE APOSTLE PAUL

◆

THE USE OF THE LETTER as a medium of divine revelation was unheard of until the time of Paul and his contemporaries. Through them Paul, under the inspiration of the Holy Spirit, was able to address specific problems and issues of his time with perspectives that are universal and timeless.

EPISTLES (LETTERS) OF THE APOSTLE PAUL

BOOK	SUMMARY
Romans	An explanation of the Christian faith for both Jews and Gentiles, addressed to the church at Rome
1 Corinthians	Instructions to the church at Corinth
2 Corinthians	Paul's defense and explanation of his apostleship
Galatians	An account of the necessity of salvation by divine grace rather than the law, to the churches at Galatia
Ephesians	A letter to the church at Ephesus explaining the believer's position in Christ

Philippians	A joyful letter to the church at Philippi, telling of Paul's conquering faith during imprisonment
Colossians	An account of the supremacy of Christ, written to the church of Colossae
1 and 2 Thessalonians	Instructions to the church at Thessalonica about the coming of the Lord
1 and 2 Timothy	Manuals of leadership for the young pastor at Ephesus
Titus	A manual of Christian conduct for church leaders, written to a young pastor at Crete
Philemon	An appeal for Christian unity and forgiveness for a runaway slave

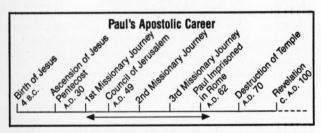

Paul's Apostolic Career

Birth of Jesus 4 B.C. · Ascension of Jesus Pentecost A.D. 30 · 1st Missionary Journey · Council of Jerusalem A.D. 49 · 2nd Missionary Journey · 3rd Missionary Journey · Paul Imprisoned in Rome A.D. 62 · Destruction of Temple A.D. 70 · Revelation C. A.D. 100

The Epistle to the Romans

Authorship and Date

There can be no doubt that Romans is an exposition of the content of the gospel by the strongest thinker in the early church—the apostle Paul. The epistle bears Paul's name as

◆

KEYS TO ROMANS

Key Word: *The Righteousness of God*

The theme of Romans is found in 1:16, 17: God offers the gift of His righteousness to everyone who comes to Christ by faith.

Key Verses: *Romans 1:16, 17 and 3:21–25*

Key Chapters: *Romans 6–8*

Foundational to all teaching on the spiritual life is the central passage of Romans 6–8. The answers to the questions of how to be delivered from sin, how to live a balanced life under grace, and how to live the victorious Christian life through the power of the Holy Spirit are all contained here.

◆

author (1:1). Paul most likely wrote the epistle during his third missionary journey in the spring of A.D. 56 or 57, as he finalized plans to visit Rome (Acts 19:21).

Historical Setting

Romans was written to a church that Paul did not found and had not visited. He wrote the letter to give an account of his gospel in preparation for a personal visit (1:11). Paul wrote most probably from Corinth, where he was completing the collection of money from the Macedonian and Achaian Christians for the "poor saints" in Jerusalem.

Theological Contribution

The great theme of Romans is *God's power to save*. The Romans understood power; when Paul wrote this epistle to the capital of the ancient world, Rome ruled supreme. The gospel, however, is nothing to be ashamed of in comparison; for it, too, is power—indeed the "power of God to salvation for everyone" (1:16).

Survey of Romans

The Revelation of the Righteousness of God (chaps 1—8)

The prologue (1:1–17) consists of a salutation (1:1–7), a statement of Paul's desire to minister in Rome (1:8–15), and the theme of the book: salvation, righteousness, and faith (1:16, 17).

In 1:18—3:20, Paul builds a solid case for the condemnation of all people under the holy God. The Gentiles are without excuse because they have suppressed the knowledge of God they received from nature and their conscience (1:18–32). The Jews are also under the condemnation of God, and Paul overcomes every objection they could raise to this conclusion (2:1—3:8). The divine verdict (3:9–20) is universal: "all have sinned and fall short of the glory of God" (3:23).

The section on justification (3:21—5:21) centers on and develops the theme of God's provision for human need. In Christ, God is both Judge and Savior. Justification is by grace (the source of salvation; 3:21–24), by blood (the basis of salvation; 3:25, 26), and by faith (the conduit of salvation; 3:27–31).

Chapter 4 illustrates the principle of justification by faith apart from works in the life of Abraham. Justification issues in reconciliation between God and humanity (5:1–11). Paul contrasts the two Adams and the opposite results of their two acts. The righteousness of the second Adam is imputed to all who trust in Him, leading to reconciliation (5:12–21).

Chapter 6 describes the believer's relationship to sin: in this position one is dead to the principle of sin (6:1–14) and the practice of sin (6:15–23). The reality of identification with Christ is the basis for the sanctified Christian life. After describing the Christian's emancipation from the Law (7),

Paul's Epistle to the Romans

FOCUS	Revelation of God's Righteousness		Vindication of God's Righteousness			Application of God's Righteousness	
REFERENCE	1:1 ——— 3:21 ———	6:1 ———	9:1 ———	9:30 ———	11:1 ———	12:1 ——— 14:1—16:27	
DIVISION	Need for God's Righteousness	Imputation of God's Righteousness	Demonstration of God's Righteousness	Israel's Past: Election	Israel's Present: Rejection	Israel's Future: Restoration	Christian Duties	Christian Liberties
TOPIC	Sin	Salvation	Sanctification	Sovereignty			Service	
	Doctrinal						Behavioral	
LOCATION	Probably Written in Corinth							
TIME	c. A.D. 56–57							

Paul looks at the work of the Holy Spirit who indwells and empowers every believer (8:1–17). The next major topic after condemnation, justification, and sanctification is glorification (8:18–39). All Christians can anticipate a time when they will be perfectly conformed to Jesus Christ not only in their position (present) but also in their practice (the future resurrection).

The Vindication of the Righteousness of God (chaps. 9—11)

It appears that God has rejected His people, Israel, but it is really Israel who has rejected her Messiah. God's rejection of Israel is only partial (there is a spiritual remnant that has trusted in Christ) and temporary (they will be grafted back; 11:23–27).

The Application of the Righteousness of God (chaps. 12—16)

The salvation described in the first eleven chapters should transform a Christian's life in relation to God (12:1, 2), society (12:3–21), higher powers (13:1–7); and one's neighbors (13:8–14). In chapters 14 and 15 the apostle discusses the whole concept of Christian liberty, noting its principles (14) and its practice (15:1–13). A changed life is not a condition for salvation, but it should be the natural outcome of saving faith. The epistle closes with Paul's statement of his plans (15:14–33), a long series of personal greetings (16:1–16), and an admonition followed by a doxology (16:17–27).

Outline of Romans

Part One: The Revelation of God's Righteousness (1:1–8:39)

The First Epistle to the Corinthians

---◆---

KEYS TO FIRST CORINTHIANS

Key Word: *Correction of Carnal Living*

The cross of Christ is a message that is designed to transform the lives of believers and make them different as people and as a corporate body from the surrounding world. However, the Corinthians are destroying their Christian testimony because of immorality and disunity.

Key Verses: *First Corinthians 6:19, 20 and 10:12, 13*

Key Chapter: *First Corinthians 13*

This chapter has won the hearts of people across the world as the best definition of "love" ever penned.

---◆---

Authorship and Date

First and Second Corinthians bear the unmistakable marks of Pauline authorship (1 Cor. 1:1; 2 Cor. 2:1). This first epistle was written from Ephesus (1 Cor. 16:8) during Paul's third missionary journey, perhaps in A.D. 56. The second letter followed some 12 to 15 months later from Macedonia, where Paul met Titus and received news of the church's repentance (2 Cor. 2:12–17).

Historical Setting

Acts 18:1–8 records the founding of the Corinthian church. During his second missionary journey, Paul went alone from Athens to Corinth in about A.D. 51. There he labored with a Jewish-Christian couple, Aquila and Priscilla, who recently had been expelled from Rome by the emperor Claudius because they were Jews. Silas and Timothy also joined Paul in Corinth. When Paul left Corinth 18 months later, a Christian congregation flourished. The congregation was composed primarily of former pagans (1 Cor. 12:2)

It is reasonably certain that Paul wrote four letters and paid perhaps three visits to the church in Corinth. During his third missionary journey, Paul received word about immorality in the young congregation at Corinth. He wrote a letter (which has since been lost) that apparently failed to achieve its purpose. Some time later Paul learned (1 Cor. 1:11; 16:17) that the sexual problems persisted, along with many others. Paul responded by writing a second letter (1 Corinthians), but this letter also failed to correct the abuses at Corinth.

Paul then apparently made a visit to Corinth, during which he was rebuffed (2 Cor. 2:1). From Ephesus Paul then wrote a third letter in which he spared no punches in his contest with the willful Corinthians. This letter, which he sent by Titus, has also been lost. Many scholars believe it has been attached to 2 Corinthians and preserved as chapters 10—13 of his epistle.

In anxiety over the possible effect of this drastic letter, and impatient over Titus' delay in returning, Paul traveled north from Ephesus to Macedonia. There Titus met him and, to Paul's relief and joy, reported that the Corinthians had punished the ringleader of the opposition and repented (2 Cor. 2:5–11). Paul then wrote a fourth letter (2 Corinthians), recounting his former anxiety and expressing his joy over the reform in Corinth.

Theological Contribution

The problems which Paul faced in the church of Corinth were complex and explosive. The correspondence which resulted is rich and profound in theological insight. Corinth, like its neighboring city of Athens, symbolized Greek culture in its desire for wisdom and power. Paul relied instead on the irony of the cross, "to the Jews a stumbling block and to the Greeks foolishness" (1 Cor. 1:23).

The foolishness of the gospel—indeed, its offensiveness to cultured Greeks—was indication of its power to save.

Special Considerations

First Corinthians contains the earliest record of the Lord's Supper (1 Cor. 11:23–26). The immortal last words of Christ, "This cup is the new covenant in my blood" (11:24–25), recall His past death and anticipate His future return.

Survey of First Corinthians

Answer to the Report of Divisions (chaps. 1—4)

Personality cults centering around Paul, Apollos, and Peter have led to divisions and false pride among the Corinthians (chap. 1). It is not their wisdom or cleverness that has brought them in Christ, because divine wisdom is contrary to human wisdom. The truth of the gospel is spiritually apprehended (chap. 2). Factions that exist among the saints at Corinth are indications of their spiritual immaturity (chap. 3). They should pride themselves in Christ, not in human leaders who are merely His servants (chap. 4).

Answer to Report of Fornication (chaps. 5-6)

The next problem Paul addresses is that of incest between a member of the church and his stepmother (chap. 5). The Corinthians have exercised no church discipline in this matter, and Paul orders them to remove the offender from their fellowship until he repents. Another source of poor testimony is the legal action of believer against believer in civil courts (6:1–8). They must learn to arbitrate their differences within the Christian community. Paul concludes this section with a warning against immorality in general (6:9–20).

Paul's First Epistle to the Corinthians

FOCUS	Answer to Chloe's Report of Divisions		Answer to Report of Fornication			Answer to Letter of Questions				
REFERENCE	1:1 ———	1:18 ———	5:1 ———	6:1 ———	6:12 ———	7:1 ———	8:1 ———	11:2 ———	15:1 ———	16:1 — 16:24
DIVISION	Report of Divisions	Reason for Divisions	Incest	Litigation	Immorality	Marriage	Offerings to Idols	Public Worship	Resurrection	Collection for Jerusalem
TOPIC	Divisions in the Church		Disorder in the Church			Difficulties in the Church				
	Concern		Condemnation			Counsel				
LOCATION	Written in Ephesus									
TIME	c. A.D. 56									

Answer to Letter of Questions (chaps. 7—16)

In these chapters the apostle Paul gives authoritative answers to thorny questions raised by the Corinthians. His first counsel concerns the issues of marriage, celibacy, divorce, and remarriage (chap. 7). The next three chapters are related to the problem of meat offered to idols (8:1—11:1). Paul illustrates from his own life the twin principles of Christian liberty and the law of love, and he concludes that believers must sometimes limit their liberty for the sake of weaker brothers (cf. Rom. 14).

The apostle then turns to matters concerning public worship, including improper observance of the Lord's Supper and the selfish use of spiritual gifts (11:2—14:40). Gifts are to be exercised in love for the edification of the whole body.

The Corinthians also have problems with the Resurrection, which Paul seeks to correct (15). The epistle closes with Paul's instruction for the collection he will make for the saints in Jerusalem (16:1–4), followed by miscellaneous exhortations and greetings (16:5–24).

Outline of First Corinthians

The Second Epistle to the Corinthians

◆

KEYS TO SECOND CORINTHIANS

Key Word: *Paul's Defense of His Ministry*

The major theme of 2 Corinthians is Paul's defense of his apostolic credentials and authority.

Key Verses: *Second Corinthians 4:5, 6 and 5:17–19*

Key Chapters: *Second Corinthians 8 and 9*

These chapters are one unit and comprise the most complete revelation of God's plan for giving found anywhere in the Scriptures.

◆

Background and general themes of 2 Corinthians are discussed under 1 Corinthians (pp. 254–259).

Theological Contribution

Second Corinthians is probably best known for its teaching on Christian ministry. Paul marvels at the treasure of the gospel which God entrusts to human servants. Indeed, the weakness of the servant only highlights the message of salvation (4:1–15).

Survey of Second Corinthians

Paul's Explanation of His Ministry (chaps. 1—7)

After his salutation and thanksgiving for God's comfort in his afflictions and perils (1:1–11), Paul explains why he has delayed his planned visit to Corinth. It is not a matter of vacillation: the apostle wants them to have enough time to repent (1:12—2:4). Paul graciously asks them to restore the repentant offender to fellowship (2:5–13).

Paul's Second Epistle to the Corinthians

FOCUS	Explanation of Paul's Ministry			Collection for the Saints		Vindication of Paul's Apostleship		
REFERENCE	1:1 ——— 2:14	——— 6:11		——— 8:1	——— 8:7	——— 10:1	——— 11:1	——— 12:14 ——— 13:14
DIVISION	His Change of Plans	Philosophy of Ministry	Exhortations to the Corinthians	Example of the Macedonians	Exhortation to the Corinthians	Answers His Accusers	Defends His Apostleship	Announces His Upcoming Visit
TOPIC	Character of Paul			Collection for Saints		Credentials of Paul		
	Ephesus to Macedonia: Change of Itinerary			Macedonia: Preparation for Visit		To Corinth: Imminent Visit		
LOCATION	Written in Macedonia							
TIME	c. A.D. 56							

At this point, Paul embarks on an extended defense of his ministry in terms of his message, circumstances, motives, and conduct (2:14—6:10). He then admonishes the believers to separate themselves from defilement (6:11—7:1), and expresses his comfort at Titus's news of their change of heart (7:2–16).

Paul's Collection for the Saints (chaps. 8—9)

The example of the Macedonians' liberal giving for the needy brethren in Jerusalem (8:1–6) is followed by an appeal to the Corinthians to keep their promise by doing the same (8:7—9:15). In this connection, Paul commends the messengers he has sent to Corinth to make arrangements for the large gift they have promised.

Paul's Vindication of His Apostleship (chaps. 10—13)

Paul concludes with a defense of his apostolic authority and credentials directed to the still rebellious minority in the Corinthian church. His meekness in no way diminishes his authority as an apostle (10). He is forced to boast about his knowledge, integrity, accomplishments, sufferings, visions, and miracles (11:1—12:13). He reveals his plans to visit them for the third time and urges them to repent so that he will not have to use severity when he comes (12:14—13:10). The letter ends with an exhortation, greetings, and a benediction (13:11–14).

Outline of Second Corinthians

The Epistle to the Galatians

◆

KEYS TO GALATIANS

Key Word: *Freedom from the Law*

This epistle shows that the believer is no longer under the law but is saved by faith alone. Galatians is the Christian's Declaration of Independence.

Key Verses: *Galatians 2:20, 21 and 5:1*

Key Chapter: *Galatians 5*

The impact of the truth concerning freedom is staggering: freedom must not be used "as an opportunity for the flesh, but through love serve one another" (5:13). This chapter records the power, "Walk in the Spirit" (5:16), and the results, "the fruit of the Spirit" (5:22), of that freedom.

◆

Authorship and Date

No epistle in the New Testament has better claim to come from Paul than does Galatians. The epistle bears his name (1:1), tells his story (1:11—2:14), and expounds the truth that occupied his life—justification by faith in Jesus Christ (2:16). The date of the epistle is less certain.

Historical Setting

After Paul had evangelized the churches of Galatia, he received disturbing news that they were falling away from the gospel he had taught them (1:6). Certain religious activists had visited Galatia after Paul's departure, persuading the

Christians there that the gospel presented by Paul was insufficient for salvation (1:7).

Theological Contribution

The gospel that Paul had delivered to the Galatians was not his own, nor was he taught it; but it came "through the revelation of Jesus Christ" (1:11–12). Those who presumed to change it were meddling with the very plan of God: that Jews and Gentiles are justified before God by faith alone (1:7–8).

Survey of Galatians

The Gospel of Grace Defended (chaps. 1—2)

Paul affirms his divinely given apostleship and presents the gospel (1:1–5) because it has been distorted by false teachers among the Galatians (1:6–10). Paul launches into his biographical argument for the true gospel of justification by faith in showing that he received his message not from men but directly from God (1:11–24). When he submits his teaching of Christian liberty to the apostles in Jerusalem, they all acknowledge the validity and authority of his message (2:1–10). Paul also must correct Peter on the matter of freedom from the law (2:11–21).

The Gospel of Grace Explained (chaps. 3—4)

In this section Paul uses eight lines of reasoning to develop his theological defense of justification by faith:

(1) The Galatians began by faith (3:1–5).
(2) Abraham was justified by faith (3:6–9).
(3) Christ has redeemed all who trust Him (3:10–14).
(4) Abraham' promise was not nullified by the law (3:15–18).
(5) The law was to drive men to faith (3:19–22).
(6) Believers are no longer bound by the law (3:23–4:7).
(7) The Galatians must regain their freedom in Christ (4:8–20).
(8) Abraham's two sons allegorically reveal the superiority of the Abrahamic promise to the Mosaic Law (4:21–31).

Paul's Epistle to the Galatians

FOCUS	Gospel of Grace Defended		Gospel of Grace Explained		Gospel of Grace Applied	
REFERENCE	1:1 ——————— 2:1	——————— 3:1	——————— 4:1	——————— 5:1	——————— 6:1	——————— 6:18
DIVISION	Paul's Apostleship	Paul's Authority	Bondage of Law	Freedom of Grace	Fruit of the Spirit	Fruits of the Spirit
TOPIC	Biographical Explanation		Doctrinal Exposition		Practical Exhortation	
	Authentication of Liberty	Argumentation for Liberty			Application of Liberty	
LOCATION	South Galatian Theory: Syrian Antioch North Galatian Theory: Ephesus or Macedonia					
TIME	South Galatian Theory: A.D. 48 North Galatian Theory: A.D. 53–56					

The Gospel of Grace Applied (chaps. 5—6)

The Judaizers seek to place the Galatians under bondage to their perverted gospel of justification by law, but Paul warns them that law and grace are two contrary principles (5:1–12). The opposite extreme of legalism is license or antinomianism (5:13–6:10).

The Christian is not only set free from bondage of law, but he is also free of the bondage of sin because of the power of the indwelling Spirit. Liberty is not an excuse to indulge in the deeds of the flesh; rather, it provides the privilege of bearing the fruit of the Spirit by walking in dependence upon Him. This letter closes with a contrast between the Judaizers—who are motivated by pride and a desire to avoid persecution—and Paul, who has suffered for the true gospel, but boasts only in Christ (6:11–18).

Outline of Galatians

The Epistle to the Ephesians

◆

KEYS TO EPHESIANS

Key Word: *Building the Body of Christ*

Ephesians focuses on the believer's responsibility to walk in accordance with his heavenly calling in Christ Jesus and encouraging the body of Christ to maturity in Him.

Key Verses: *Ephesians 2:8–10 and 4:1–3*

Key Chapter: *Ephesians 6*

Even though the Christian is blessed "with every spiritual blessing in the heavenly places in Christ" (1:3), spiritual warfare is still the daily experience of the Christian while in the world.

◆

Authorship and Date

Ephesians bears the name of Paul (1:1; 3:1), and it sets forth many of the great Pauline themes. Ephesians has a number of notable differences from the undisputed letters of Paul; possibly it was intended as a circular or "open letter" to a number of communities surrounding Ephesus. Paul probably wrote Ephesians about the same time as the Epistle to the Colossians, from prison in the late 50's or early 60's.

Theological Contribution

The theme of Ephesians is the relationship between the heavenly Lord Jesus Christ and His earthly body, the church. Christ now reigns "far above all principality and power and might and dominion" (1:21) and has "put all things under His feet" (1:22). Exalted though He is, so fully does He identify with the church that He considers it His body, which He fills with His presence (1:23; 3:19; 4:10). The marriage relationship between husband and wife is a beautiful analogy for expressing Christ's love, sacrifice, and lordship over the church (5:22–32).

Special Consideration

The term *heavenly places* (1:3; 1:20; 2:6; 3:10; 6:12) is not the same as heaven, for in one instance Paul speaks of "spiritual hosts of wickedness in the heavenly places" (6:12). "Heavenly places" implies the unseen, spiritual world beyond our physical sense. It is the region where the most difficult, and yet authentic, Christian discipleship is lived out–the world of decisions, attitudes, temptations, and commitments. It is the battleground of good and evil (6:12).

Survey of Ephesians

The Position of the Christian (1:1–3:21)

After a two-verse prologue, in one long Greek sentence Paul extols the triune God for the riches of redemption (1:3–14). This hymn to God's grace praises the Father for choosing us (1:3–6), the Son for redeeming us (1:7–12), and the Spirit for sealing us (1:13, 14). The saving work of each divine Person is to the praise of the glory of His grace (1:6, 12, 14). Before continuing, Paul offers the first of two very significant prayers (1:15–23; cf. 3:14–21). Here he asks that the readers receive spiritual illumination.

Next, Paul describes the power of God's grace by contrasting their former condition with their present spiritual life in Christ, a salvation attained not by human works but by divine grace (2:1–10). This redemption includes Jews, yet also extends to Gentiles (2:11–22). This is a mystery that has now

Paul's Epistle to the Ephesians

FOCUS	The Position of the Christian			The Practice of the Christian		
REFERENCE	1:1 — 1:15 —	2:1 —	3:14 —	4:1 — 4:17 —	5:22 —	6:10 — 6:24
DIVISION	Praise for Redemption	Prayer for Revelation	Position of the Christian	Prayer for Realization	Unity in the Church	Holiness in Life	Responsibilities at Home and Work	Conduct in the Conflict
TOPIC	Belief			Behavior		
	Privileges of the Christian			Responsibilites of the Christian		
LOCATION	Rome					
TIME	A.D. 60–61					

been revealed (3:1–13). Paul's second prayer (3:14–21) expresses his desire that the readers be strengthened with the power of the Spirit and fully apprehend the love of Christ.

The Practice of the Christian (4:1—6:20)

The pivotal verse of Ephesians is 4:1, because it draws a sharp line between the doctrinal and the practical divisions of this book. There is a cause and effect relationship between chapters 1–3 and 4–6 because the spiritual walk of a Christian must be rooted in spiritual wealth. Paul exhorts the readers to "put off, concerning your former conduct, the old man" (4:22) and "put on the new man" (4:24). They are also to maintain a walk of holiness as children of light (5:1–21). Every relationship (wives, husbands, children, parents, slaves, and masters) must be transformed by their new life in Christ (5:22—6:9). Paul's colorful description of the spiritual warfare and the armor of God (6:10–20) is followed by a word about Tychicus and then a benediction (6:21–24).

Outline of Ephesians

The Epistle to the Philippians

Authorship and Date

There can be little doubt that Philippians comes from Paul. The entire epistle bears the stamp of his language and style; the setting pictures Paul's imprisonments; and the recipients correspond with what we know of the church at Philippi.

During his second missionary journey, in A.D. 49, Paul sensed the Lord called him to visit Macedonia (Acts 16:6–10). At Philippi he founded the first Christian congregation

---

◆

KEYS TO PHILIPPIANS

Key Word: *To Live Is Christ*

Central to Philippians is the concept of "For to me, to live *is* Christ, and to die *is* gain" (1:21).

Key Verses: *Philippians 1:21 and 4:12*

Key Chapter: *Philippians 2*

The grandeur of the truth of the New Testament seldom exceeds the revelation of the humility of Jesus Christ when He left heaven to become a servant of man.

◆

---

on European soil (Acts 16:11–40). A lifelong supportive relationship developed between the Philippians and Paul (Phil. 1:5; 4:15). He visited the church again during his third missionary journey (Acts 20:1, 6).

At the time he wrote Philippians, Paul was in prison awaiting trial, probably A.D. 60 (Phil. 1:7). The Philippian Christians came to Paul's aid by sending a gift, perhaps of money, through Epaphroditus (4:18). During his stay with Paul, Epaphroditus fell desperately ill. But he recovered and Paul sent him back to Philippi. Paul sent this letter with Epaphroditus to relieve the anxiety of the Philippians over their beloved fellow-worker (2:25–30).

Theological Contribution

The focus of Paul's thoughts in this epistle is the Christ-centered life, the hallmark of which is joy. Paul has surrendered everything to Christ and can say, "For to me, to live is Christ" (1:1), "to be a prisoner for Christ" (1:13), "to live and die in Christ" (1:20), "and to give up all to win Christ" (3:7–8). Because Paul's only motive is to "know Him"

(3:10), he shares in the power of Christ and "can do all things through Christ," who is his joy and strength (4:13).

Special Consideration

Nowhere is the mind of Christ presented to the Christian more strongly than in Philippians 2:1–11. Appealing to the Philippians to be of "one mind" (2:2) in pursuing humility, Paul cites the example of the incarnation of God in Jesus Christ. Unlike Adam, who sought to be equal with God (Gen. 3:5), Christ did not try to grasp for equality with God. Instead, being God, he poured Himself out and took upon Himself the form of a slave, to the point of dying the death of a common criminal.

Survey of Philippians

Paul's Account of His Present Circumstances (chap. 1)

Paul's usual salutation (1:1, 2) is followed by his thanksgiving, warm regard, and prayer on behalf of the Philippians (1:3–11). Paul shares the circumstances of his imprisonment and rejoices in the spread of the gospel in spite of and because of his situation (1:12–26). As he considers the outcome of his approaching trial, he expresses his willingness to "depart and be with Christ" (1:23) or to continue in ministry. Paul encourages the Philippians to remain steadfast in the face of opposition and coming persecution (1:27–30).

Paul's Appeal to Have the Mind of Christ (chap. 2)

Paul exhorts the Philippians to have a spirit of unity and mutual concern by embracing the attitude of humility (2:1–4), the greatest example of which is the incarnation and crucifixion of Christ (2:5–11). Paul asks the Philippians to apply this attitude to their lives (2:12–18), and he gives two more examples of sacrifice, the ministries of Timothy and Epaphroditus (2:19–30).

Paul's Epistle to the Philippians

FOCUS	Account of Circumstances	The Mind of Christ	The Knowledge of Christ	The Peace of Christ
REFERENCE 1:1 ———————	2:1 ———————	3:1 ———————	4:1 ——————— 4:23
DIVISION	Partake of Christ	People of Christ	Pursuit of Christ	Power of Christ
TOPIC	Suffering	Submission	Salvation	Sanctification
	Experience	Examples	Exhortation	
LOCATION	Rome			
TIME	c. A.D. 60			

Paul's Appeal to Have the Knowledge of Christ (chap. 3)

It appears that Paul is about to close his letter when he launches into a warning about the continuing problem of legalism (3:1–9) revealing autobiographical details about his previous attainments in Judaism. Compared to the goal of knowing Christ, those pursuits are as nothing.

Paul's Appeal to Have the Peace of Christ (chap. 4)

In a series of exhortations, Paul urges the Philippians to have peace with the brethren by living a life-style of unity, prayerful dependence, and holiness (4:13). In 4:4–9, Paul describes the secrets of having the peace of God as well as peace with God. He then rejoices over their gift, but explains that the power of Christ enables him to live above his circumstances (4:10–20). The letter closes with greetings and a benediction (4:21–23).

Outline of Philippians

The Epistle to the Colossians

◆

KEYS TO COLOSSIANS

Key Word: *The Preeminence of Christ*

The resounding theme in Colossians is the preeminence and sufficiency of Christ in all things. The believer is complete in Him alone and lacks nothing because "in Him dwells all the fullness of the Godhead bodily" (2:9).

Key Verses: *Colossians 2:9, 10 and 3:1, 2*

Key Chapter: *Colossians 3*

Chapter 3 links the three themes of Colossians together showing their cause and effect relationship: Because the believer is risen with Christ (3:1–4), he is to put off the old man and put on the new (3:5–17), which will result in holiness in all relationships (3:18–25).

◆

Authorship and Date

Colossians was written by Paul (and Timothy, 1:1) to a Christian community which he had not visited (2:1). Paul had established a resident ministry in Ephesus, 100 miles west of Colossae. For more than two years the influence of his ministry reached "all who dwelt in Asia" (Acts 19:10). Epaphras must have heard Paul in Ephesus and then carried the gospel to Colossae (1:7–8; 4:12–13).

Paul wrote the epistle from prison (4:3, 10, 18), but he did not indicate where he was imprisoned. Caesarea and Ephesus have been suggested, but the most probable place is Rome (Acts 28:30). This would date the epistle in the late 50's or early 60's.

Historical Setting

False teaching had taken root in Colossae. This teaching combined Jewish observances (2:16) and pagan speculation (2:8); it is possible that this resulted in an early form of Gnosticism. This teaching pretended to add to or improve upon the gospel that, indirectly at least, had come from Paul.

Theological Contribution

Paul unmasks the false teaching as "empty deceit . . . of men" (2:8), having the "appearance of wisdom" (2:23), but useless in fact. He declared that the addition of such things dilutes rather than strengthens the faith (2:20).

Survey of Colossians

Supremacy of Christ (chaps. 1—2)

Paul's greeting (1:1, 2) is followed by an unusually extended thanksgiving (1:3–8) and prayer (1:9–14) on behalf of the believers at Colossae. Paul expresses his concern that the Colossians come to a deeper understanding of the person and power of Christ. He is supreme both in creation (1:15–18) and in redemption (1:19–23).

Paul describes his own ministry of proclaiming the mystery of "Christ in you, the hope of glory" (1:27) to the Gentiles and assures his readers that although he has not personally met them, he strongly desires that they become deeply rooted in Christ alone, who is preeminent in the church

Paul's Epistle to the Colossians

FOCUS	Supremacy of Christ			Submission to Christ		
REFERENCE	1:1 ——— 1:15 ———	2:4 ———	3:1 ———	3:5 ———	4:7 ———	4:18
DIVISION	Introduction	Preeminence of Christ	Freedom in Christ	Position of the Believer	Practice of the Believer	Conclusion
TOPIC	Doctrinal			Practical		
	What Christ Did for Us			What Christ Does Through Us		
LOCATION	Rome					
TIME	A.D. 60–61					

(1:24—2:3). This is especially important in view of false teachers who would defraud them through enticing rationalisms (2:4–7), vain philosophy (2:8–10), legalistic rituals (2:11–17), improper mysticism (2:18, 19), and useless asceticism (2:20–23). In each case, Paul contrasts the error with the corresponding truth about Christ.

Submission to Christ (chaps. 3—4)

The believer's union with Christ in His death, resurrection, and exaltation is the foundation upon which his earthly life must be built (3:1–4). Because of his death with Christ, the Christian must regard himself as dead to the old sins and put them aside (3:5–11); because of his resurrection with Christ, the believer must regard himself as alive to Him in righteousness (3:12–17).

Turning from the inward life (3:1–17) to the outward life (3:18—4:6), Paul outlines the transformation that faith in Christ should make in relationships inside and outside the home. This epistle concludes with a statement concerning its bearers (Tychicus and Onesimus), greetings and instructions, and a farewell note (4:7–18).

Outline of Colossians

Part One: The Supremacy of Christ in the Church (1:1—2:23)

The First Epistle to the Thessalonians

Authorship and Date

The vocabulary, style, and thought of the Thessalonian correspondence are genuinely Pauline. Both letters bear his name as author (1 Thess. 1:1; 2 Thess. 1:1) and were most likely written from Corinth (1 Thess. 1:1; 2 Thess. 1:1 in late A.D. 50 or early A.D. 51.

Historical Setting

Paul founded the church at Thessalonica in A.D. 49 or 50 during his second missionary journey (Acts 17:1–9). The church consisted of a few Jewish converts and a larger number

---

KEYS TO FIRST THESSALONIANS

Key Words: *Holiness in Light of Christ's Return*

Throughout this letter is an unmistakable emphasis upon steadfastness in the Lord and a continuing growth in faith and love in view of the return of Christ.

Key Verses: *First Thessalonians 3:12, 13 and 4:16–18*

Key Chapter: *First Thessalonians 4*

Chapter 4 includes the central passage of the epistles on the coming of the Lord when the dead in Christ shall rise first, and those who remain are caught up together with them in the clouds.

---

of former pagans (1 Thess. 1:9; Acts 17:4). Desiring not to handicap the young church, Paul worked at his own job as a tentmaker—and at some sacrifice to himself, he adds (1 Thess. 2:7–12)—twice receiving aid from the ever-faithful Philippians (Phil. 4:16).

Paul's stay in Thessalonica was cut short, however, when the Jews gathered some local troublemakers and an uproar broke out; Paul was escorted out of town, leaving Timothy to patch up the work (Acts 17:1–15). Separated so suddenly from the infant church, Paul describes his feelings as one who had been "orphaned" (Greek text, 1 Thess. 2:17).

Once he was safe in Athens, Paul sent Timothy (who apparently had since rejoined him) back to Thessalonica to strengthen and encourage the believers (1 Thess. 3:2). When Timothy returned to Paul, who had since moved on to Corinth (Acts 18:1–5), he brought news of the love and faith of the Thessalonians. In response to Timothy's encouraging report, Paul wrote the first epistle to Thessalonica. Evidently the Thessalonians were unsettled over the second coming of Christ, because Paul discusses the issue the subsequent letter as well.

Theological Contribution

Paul writes the epistles in the spirit of a true pastor. He is overjoyed with their enthusiastic response to the gospel and longs for the day when they will stand with him in the presence of the Lord Jesus (1 Thess. 2:19–20).

He compares himself to a nursing mother caring for her children (1 Thess. 2:7) and to a father working in behalf of his family (1 Thess. 2:9–12). He gives himself body and soul to the Thessalonians (1 Thess. 2:8) and dares to hope that they will give themselves likewise to God (1 Thess. 5:23).

Special Consideration

On the subject of the Second Coming, Paul assures the Thessalonians what will happen, but not when it will happen. The end, however, will follow widespread rebellion and abandonment of the faith. Paul appeals for them to be level-headed during the time of trouble and warns Christians not to despair when they see the Antichrist pretending to be God (2 Thess. 2:4).

Survey of First Thessalonians

Paul's Personal Reflections on the Thessalonians (chaps. 1—3)

Paul's typical salutation in the first verse combines the customary Greek ("grace") and Hebrew ("peace") greetings of his day and enriches them with Christian content. The opening chapter is a declaration of thanksgiving for the Thessalonians' metamorphosis from heathenism to Christian hope. Faith, love, and hope (1:3) properly characterize the new lives of these believers.

In 2:1–16, Paul reviews his brief ministry in Thessalonica and defends his conduct and motives, apparently to answer

Paul's First Epistle to the Thessalonians

FOCUS	Reflections on the Thessalonians			Instructions to the Thessalonians			
REFERENCE	1:1 ———	2:1 ———	2:17 ———	4:1 ———	4:13 ———	5:1 ———	5:12 ——— 5:28
DIVISION	Commendation for Growth	Founding of the Church	Strengthening of the Church	Direction for Growth	The Dead in Christ	The Day of the Lord	Holy Living
TOPIC	Personal Experience			Practical Exhortation			
	Looking Back			Looking Forward			
LOCATION	Written in Corinth						
TIME	c. A.D. 51						

enemies who are trying to impugn his character and message. He sends Timothy to minister to them and is greatly relieved when Timothy reports the stability of their faith and love (2:17–3:10). Paul therefore closes this historical section with a prayer that their faith may continue to deepen (3:11–13).

Paul's Instructions to the Thessalonians (chaps. 4—5)

The apostle deftly moves into a series of exhortations and reminds them of his previous teaching on sexual and social matters (4:1–12). Now rooted in the Word of God (2:13), the readers must resist the constant pressures of a pagan society.

Paul has taught them about the return of Christ, and they have become distressed over the deaths of some among them. In 4:13–18, Paul comforts them with the assurance that all who die in Christ will be resurrected at His *parousia* ("presence, coming, or advent"). In anticipation of the coming day of the Lord (5:1–11). believers are to "watch and be sober." They must deal with integrity toward one another and to continue growing spiritually (5:12–22). The epistle closes with a wish for their sanctification, three requests, and a benediction (5:23–28).

Outline of First Thessalonians

The Second Epistle to the Thessalonians

◆

KEYS TO SECOND THESSALONIANS

Key Word: *Understanding the Day of the Lord*

The theme of this epistle is an understanding of the day of the Lord and the resulting lifestyle changes.

Key Verses: *Second Thessalonians 2:2, 3 and 3:5, 6*

Key Chapter: *Second Thessalonians 2*

The second chapter is written to correct the fallacious teaching that the day of the Lord has already come upon the Thessalonian church.

◆

Background and general themes of 2 Thessalonians are discussed under 1 Thessalonians (pp. 281–285).

Survey of Second Thessalonians

Paul's Encouragement in Persecution (chap. 1)

After his two-verse salutation, Paul gives thanks for the growing faith and love of the Thessalonians and assures them of their ultimate deliverance from those who are persecuting them (1:3–10). They are encouraged to patiently endure their afflictions, knowing that the Lord Jesus will judge their persecutors. He concludes this section with a prayer for the spiritual welfare of his readers (1:11, 12).

Paul's Explanation of the Day of the Lord (chap. 2)

Because of the severity of their afflictions, the Thessalonians have become susceptible to false teaching (and possibly a fraudulent letter in the name of Paul), claiming that they are

Paul's Second Epistle to the Thessalonians

FOCUS	Encouragement in Persecution			Explanation of the Day of the Lord		Exhortation to the Church	
REFERENCE	1:1 ——— 1:5 ———		1:11 ———	2:1 ———	2:13 ———	3:1 ———	3:6 ——— 3:18
DIVISION	Thanksgiving for Growth	Encouragement in Persecution	Prayer for Blessing	Events Preceding	Comfort of the Believer	Wait Patiently	Withdraw
	Discouraged Believers			Disturbed Believers		Disobedient Believers	
TOPIC	Thanksgiving for Their Life			Instruction of Their Doctrine		Correction of Their Behavior	
LOCATION	Written in Corinth						
TIME	c. A.D. 51						

already in the day of the Lord (2:1, 2). This was particulary disturbing because Paul's previous letter had given them the comforting hope that they were not destined for the wrath of that day (1 Thess. 5:9). Paul therefore assures them that the day of the Lord is yet in the future and will not arrive unannounced (2:3–12). He concludes this section with a word of encouragement and a benedictory prayer of comfort.

Paul's Exhortation to the Church (chap. 3)

Paul requests the Thessalonian church to pray on his behalf and to wait patiently for the Lord (3:1–5). Having thus commended, corrected, and comforted his readers, the tactful apostle closes his letter with a sharp word of command to those who have been using the truth of Christ's return as an excuse for disorderly conduct (3:6–15; cf. 1 Thess. 4:11, 12). The doctrine of the Lord's return requires a balance between waiting and working. It is perspective that should encourage holiness, not idleness. This final section, like the first two, closes on a benedictory note (3:16–18).

Outline of Second Thessalonians

The First Epistle to Timothy

◆

KEYS TO FIRST TIMOTHY

Key Word: *Leadership Manual*

The theme of this epistle is Timothy's organization and oversight of the Asian churches as a faithful minister of God. Paul writes so that Timothy will have effective guidelines for his work during Paul's absence in Macedonia (3:14, 15).

Key Verses: *First Timothy 3:15, 16 and 6:11, 12*

Key Chapter: *First Timothy 3*

Listed in chapter 3 are the qualifications for the leaders of God's church, the elders and deacons. Notably absent are qualities of worldly success or position. Instead, Paul enumerates character qualities demonstrating that true leadership emanates from our walk with God rather than from achievements or vocational success.

◆

Authorship and Date

The authorship and date of the Pastoral Epistles remain an unresolved question in New Testament studies. On the one hand, the epistles bear the name of Paul as author (1 Tim. 1:1; 2 Tim. 1:1; Titus 1:1) and preserve personal references to him (1 Tim. 1:3, 12–16; 2 Tim. 4:9–22; Titus 1:5; 3:12–13). Other considerations, however, pose problems for Paul's authorship of the Pastorals, among them, a marked difference in vocabulary and stlye.

The letters could be dated between Paul's first and second Roman imprisonments, about A.D. 65, or as late as the close of the first century.

Historical Setting

First and Second Timothy differ in historical context. In the first epistle Paul writes from Macedonia to young Timothy (1 Tim. 4:12), who has been left in Ephesus to oversee the congregation (1 Tim. 1:3). The second epistle, also written to Timothy in Ephesus (2 Tim. 1:18), comes from Rome where Paul is undergoing a second (2 Tim. 4:16) and harsher imprisonment (2 Tim. 1:8, 16; 2:9). Paul is alone (except for Luke, 2 Tim. 4:11), and he knows the end of his life will come soon (2 Tim. 4:6).

Theological Contribution

For Paul, the best medicine for false teaching and apostasy is "sound doctrine" (1 Tim. 1:10; 4:3). The gospel is a spiritual inheritance to be received from faithful witnesses and passed on to such (2 Tim. 2:2). It brings about wholeness or health ("sound" in Greek), not only in belief, but also in good deeds.

Special Considerations

The Epistles to Timothy might be considered our earliest manual of church organization. Within them we find guidelines for the selection of church leaders (1 Tim. 3:1–13) and an awareness of the need for standard forms of expressing the faith. Second Timothy presents the first (and only) pronouncement in the New Testament on the Bible as "Scripture" (referring to the Old Testament, 2 Tim. 3:14–17), "inspired" or "breathed into by God."

Survey of First Timothy

Paul's Charge Concerning Doctrine (chap. 1)

After his greetings (1:1, 2), Paul warns Timothy about the growing problem of false doctrines, particularly as they relate to the misuse of the Mosaic Law (1:3–11). The aging apostle then recounts his radical conversion to Christ and subsequent calling to the ministry (1:12–17). Timothy, too, has received a divine calling, and Paul charges him to fulfill it without wavering in doctrine or conduct (1:18–20).

Paul's Charge Concerning Public Worship (chaps. 2—3)

Next Paul addresses the issues of church worship and leadership. Efficacious public prayer should be a part of the role of men in the church (2:1–8). He then turns to the role of women (2:9–15), wherein he emphasizes the importance of the inner quality of godliness.

In 3:1–7, Paul lists several qualifications for overseers or bishops. The word for "overseer" *(episkopos)* is used synonymously with the word for "elder" *(presbuteros)* in the New Testament, because both originally referred to the same office (see Acts 20:17, 28; Titus 1:5, 7). The qualifications for the office of deacon *(diakonos,* "servant") are listed in 3:8–13.

Paul's Charge Concerning False Teachers (chap. 4)

Timothy obviously had difficulties with some of the older men (5:1) who had left the faith. Paul carefully advises on the issues of marriage, food, and exercise. The closing charge exhorts Timothy not to neglect the spiritual gift given to him.

Paul's Charge Concerning Church Discipline (chap. 5)

One of the most difficult pastoral duties for the young minister is to lead in the exercise of church discipline. Commencing with the general advice of treating all members of the church as family (5:1, 2), Paul concentrates on the two special areas of widows and elders, focusing on Timothy's responsibility and providing practical instruction.

Paul's Charge Concerning Pastoral Duties (chap. 6)

In addition, the insidious doctrine was being taught that godliness will eventually result in material blessing. Paul, in no uncertain terms, states "from such withdraw yourself"

Paul's First Epistle to Timothy

FOCUS	Doctrine	Public Worship	False Teachers	Church Discipline	Pastoral Motives
REFERENCE 1:1 ———	2:1 ———	4:1 ———	5:1 ———	6:1 ——— 6:21	
DIVISION	Problem of False Doctrine	Public Worship and Leadership	Preserve True Doctrine	Prescriptions for Widows and Elders	Pastoral Motivations
TOPIC	Warning	Worship	Wisdom	Widows	Wealth
	Dangers of False Doctrine	Directions for Worship	Defense Against False Teachers	Duties Toward Others	Dealings with Riches
LOCATION	Written in Macedonia				
TIME	c. A.D. 62–63				

(6:5). The book closes with an extended charge (6:11–21), which is supplemented by an additional charge that Timothy is to give to the wealthy of this age (6:17–19).

Outline of First Timothy

The Second Epistle to Timothy

◆

KEYS TO SECOND TIMOTHY

Key Word: *Endurance in the Pastoral Ministry*

Paul commissions Timothy to endure faithfully and carry on the work that the condemned apostle must now relinquish, using the Word of God constantly in order to overcome growing obstacles to the spread of the gospel.

Key Verses: *Second Timothy 2:3, 4 and 3:14–17*

Key Chapter: *Second Timothy 2*

The second chapter of Second Timothy ought to be required daily reading for every pastor and full-time Christian worker. Paul lists the keys to an enduring ministry: a reproducing ministry (vv. 1, 2), an enduring successful ministry (vv. 3–13), a studying ministry (vv. 14–18), and a holy ministry (vv. 19–26).

◆

Background and general themes of 2 Timothy are discussed under 1 Timothy (p. 289–293).

Survey of Second Timothy

Persevere in Present Testing (chaps. 1—2)

After his salutation to his "beloved son" (1:2), Paul expresses his thanksgiving for Timothy's "genuine faith" (1:5). He then encourages Timothy to stand firm in the power of the gospel and to overcome any fear in the face of opposition. He must reproduce in the lives of others what he has received in Christ (four generations are mentioned in 2:2). He is responsible to work hard and discipline himself like a teacher, a soldier, a farmer, a workman, a vessel, and a servant, follow-

Paul's Second Epistle to Timothy

FOCUS	Persevere in Present Testings			Endure in Future Testings		
REFERENCE	1:1 ——— 1:6 ———	2:1 ———		3:1 ———	4:1 ———	4:6 ——— 4:22
DIVISION	Thanksgiving for Timothy's Faith	Reminder of Timothy's Responsibility	Characteristics of a Faithful Minister	Approaching Day of Apostasy	Charge to Preach the Word	Approaching Death of Paul
TOPIC	Power of the Gospel		Perseverance of the Gospel	Protector of the Gospel	Proclamation of the Gospel	Requests
	Reminder		Requirements	Resistance		Requests
LOCATION	Roman Prison					
TIME	c. A.D. 67					

ing the example of Paul's perseverance (2:1–13). In his dealings with others, Timothy must not become entangled in
false speculation, foolish quarrels, or youthful lusts, which
would hamper his effectiveness. As he pursues "righteousness, faith, love, peace" (2:22), he must know how to graciously overcome error.

Endure in Future Testing (chaps. 3—4)

Paul anticipates a time of growing apostasy and wickedness
when men and women will be increasingly susceptible to
empty religiosity and false teaching (3:1–9). Arrogance and
godlessness will breed further deception and persecution, but
Timothy must not waver in using the Scripture to combat
doctrinal error and moral evil (3:10–17). The Scriptures are
inspired ("God-breathed") and with them Timothy is
equipped to carry out the ministry to which he was called.

Paul's final exhortation to Timothy (4:1–5) is a classic
summary of the task of the man of God to proclaim the gospel in spite of opposing circumstances. This very personal letter closes with an update of Paul's situation in Rome along
with certain requests (4:6–22). Paul bids Timothy to "come
quickly before winter" (4:9, 21), and bring certain articles,
especially "the parchments" (probably portions of the Old
Testament Scriptures).

Outline of Second Timothy

The Epistle to Titus

◆

KEYS TO TITUS

Key Word: *Conduct Manual for Church Living*

This brief letter focuses on Titus's role and responsibility in the organization and supervision of the churches in Crete. It is written to strengthen and exhort Titus to firmly exercise his authority as an apostolic representative to churches that need to be put in order.

Key Verses: *Titus 1:5 and 3:8*

Key Chapter: *Titus 2*

Summarized in Titus 2 are the key commands to be obeyed which insure godly relationships within the church.

◆

Authorship and Date

The circumstances were the same as those under which the apostle Paul wrote the letters to Timothy. The Pastorals were written during the fourth missionary tour between Paul's two Roman imprisonments. The date would be about A.D. 64–66.

Historical Setting

A number of Jews from Crete were present in Jerusalem at the time of Peter's sermon on the Day of Pentecost (Acts 2:11). Some of them may have believed in Christ and introduced the gospel to others on the island upon their return. According to Titus 1:5, Paul left Titus on Crete to continue establishing churches by appointing "elders in every city."

Theological Contribution

Titus emphasizes sound doctrine (1:9; 2:8, 10) and challenges believers to good works (1:16; 2:14; 3:14). Paul included three doctrinal sections in this letter to emphasize that proper belief gives the basis for proper behavior.

Survey of Titus

Appoint Elders (chap. 1)

The salutation to Titus is actually a compact doctrinal statement, which lifts up "His word" as the source of the truth that reveals the way to eternal life (1:1–4). Paul reminds Titus of his responsibility to organize the churches of Crete by appointing elders (also called overseers; see 1:7) and rehearses the qualifications these spiritual leaders must meet (1:5–9). This is especially important in view of the disturbances that are being caused by false teachers who are upsetting a number of the believers with their Judaic myths and commandments (1:10–16).

Set Things in Order (chaps. 2—3)

Titus is given the charge to "speak the things which are proper for sound doctrine" (2:1), and Paul delineates Titus's role with regard to various groups in the church, including older men, older women, young women, young men, and servants (2:2–10). The knowledge of Christ must effect a transformation in each of these groups so that their testimony will "adorn the doctrine of God" (2:10).

The second doctrinal statement of Titus (2:11–14) gives the basis for the appeals Paul has just made for righteous living. God in His grace redeems believers from being slaves of sin, assuring them the "blessed hope" of the coming of Christ that will eventually be realized.

In chapter 3, Paul moves from conduct in groups (2:1–10) to conduct in general (3:1–11). The behavior of believers as citizens must be different than the behavior of unbelievers

Paul's Epistle to Titus

FOCUS	Appoint Elders		Set Things in Order	
REFERENCE	1:1 ——————— 1:10 ———————		2:1 ——————— 3:1 ——————— 3:15	
DIVISION	Ordain Qualified Elders	Rebuke False Teachers	Speak Sound Doctrine	Maintain Good Works
TOPIC	Protection of Sound Doctrine		Practice of Sound Doctrine	
	Organization	Offenders	Operation	Obedience
LOCATION	Probably Written in Corinth			
TIME	c. A.D. 64			

because of their regeneration and renewal by the Holy Spirit.

The third doctrinal statement in this book (3:4–7) emphasizes the kindness, love, and mercy of God, who saves us "not by works of righteousness which we have done" (3:5). Nevertheless, the need for good deeds as a result of salvation is stressed six times in the three chapters of Titus (1:16; 2:7, 14; 3:1, 8, 14). Paul exhorts Titus to deal firmly with dissenters who would cause factions and controversies (3:9–11) and closes the letter with three instructions, a greeting, and a benediction (3:12–15).

Outline of Titus

The Epistle to Philemon

Authorship, Date, and Historical Setting

The Epistle to Philemon is a companion to the Epistle to the Colossians. Both were written during Paul's imprisonment, probably in Rome (Col. 4:18; Philem. 9). The date for the two letters is the late 50's or early 60's.

Philemon was a resident of Colossae (Philem. 1–2) and a convert of Paul (v. 19). Philemon's house was large enough to serve as the meeting place for the church there (v. 2). He was benevolent to other believers (vv. 5–7), and his son, Ar-

◆

KEYS TO PHILEMON

Key Word: *Forgiveness from Slavery*

Philemon develops the transition from bondage to brotherhood that is brought about by Christian love and forgiveness. Just as Philemon was shown mercy through the grace of Christ, so he must graciously forgive his repentant runaway who has returned as a brother in Christ.

Key Verses: *Philemon 16, 17*

◆

chippus evidently held a position of leadership in the church (see Col. 4:17; Philem. 2). Philemon may have had other slaves in addition to Onesimus, and he was not alone as a slave owner among the Colossian believers (Col. 4:1). Thus this letter and his response would provide guidelines for other master-slave relationships.

Theological Contribution

The Epistle to Philemon is a lesson in the art of Christian relationships. No finer example of "speaking the truth in love" (Eph. 4:15) exists than this beautiful letter. While it was Philemon's legal right in the ancient world to punish or even kill a runaway slave, Paul hoped—indeed expected (v. 19)—that Philemon would receive Onesimus back as a brother in the Lord, not as a slave (v. 16).

Special Consideration

Although Paul never, so far as we know, called for an end to slavery, the Epistle to Philemon laid the ax at the root of that cruel and deformed institution—and to every way of treating individuals as property instead of persons.

Paul's Epistle to Philemon

FOCUS	Prayer of Thanksgiving	Petition for Onesimus	Promise to Philemon
REFERENCE	1 ——————— 8	——————— 17	——————— 25
DIVISION	Commendation of Philemon's Life	Intercession for Onesimus	Confidence in Philemon's Obedience
TOPIC	Praise of Philemon	Plea of Paul	Pledge of Paul
	Character of Philemon	Conversion of Onesimus	Confidence of Paul
LOCATION	Rome		
TIME	c. A.D. 60–61		

Survey of Philemon

Prayer of Thanksgiving for Philemon (vv. 1–7)

Writing this letter as a "prisoner of Christ Jesus," Paul addresses it personally to Philemon, his family, and the church that meets in Philemon's house, with a prayer of thanksgiving for Philemon's faith and love.

Petition of Paul for Onesimus (vv. 8–16)

Basing his appeal on Philemon's character, Paul refuses to command Philemon to pardon and receive Onesimus. Instead, Paul seeks to persuade his friend of his Christian responsibility to forgive even as he was forgiven by Christ. Paul urges Philemon not to punish Onesimus but to receive him "no longer as a slave" but as "a beloved brother" (v. 16).

Promise of Paul to Philemon (vv. 17–25)

Paul places Onesimus's debt on his account, but then reminds Philemon of the greater spiritual debt which Philemon himself owes as a convert to Christ (vv. 17–19).

Paul closes this discreet epistle with a hopeful request (v. 22), greetings from his companions (vv. 23, 24), and a benediction (v. 25). The fact that it was preserved indicates Philemon's favorable response to Paul's pleas.

Outline of Philemon

NINE

GENERAL EPISTLES (LETTERS)

◆

THESE eight epistles exert an influence out of proportion to their length, which is less than ten percent of the New Testament. They supplement the thirteen Pauline Epistles by offering different perspectives on the richness of Christian truth. The term *general epistle* appears in the King James Version titles of James, 1 and 2 Peter, 1 John, and Jude, but it was not used in the oldest manuscripts. These epistles were not addressed to specific churches or individuals, and they came to be known as the general or "catholic" (universal) epistles. The Book of Revelation is the culmination of the New Testament as well as the Bible as a whole, since it completes the story begun in Genesis.

GENERAL EPISTLES (LETTERS)	
BOOK	**SUMMARY**
Hebrews	A presentation of Jesus Christ as High Priest, addressed to Jewish believers
James	Practical instructions for applied Christianity
1 Peter	Encouragement and comfort from Peter to suffering Christians
2 Peter	Peter's warning against false teachers

1 John	John's reminder of Christ's humanity
2 John	John's letter of encouragement
3 John	John's personal note of appreciation
Jude	A strong warning against false teachers
Revelation	An encouraging prophecy of the final days and God's ultimate triumph

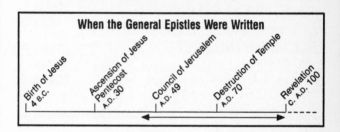

When the General Epistles Were Written

Birth of Jesus 4 B.C. — Ascension of Jesus Pentecost A.D. 30 — Council of Jerusalem A.D. 49 — Destruction of Temple A.D. 70 — Revelation C. A.D. 100

The Epistle to the Hebrews

Authorship and Date

Other than 1 John, the Epistle to the Hebrews is the only letter in the New Testament with no greeting or identification of its author. The two most likely candidates are Apollos and Barnabas: Apollos because he was an eloquent Alexandrian Jew who knew the Scriptures well (Acts 18:24), and Barnabas because he was a Levite (Acts 4:36). The letter could have been written sometime before A.D. 70. The only clue about where Hebrews was written is found in the closing remark, "Those from Italy greet you" (13:24). This may indicate that the author was writing from Italy, presumably Rome.

KEYS TO HEBREWS

Key Word: *The Superiority of Christ*

The basic theme of Hebrews is found in the word *better*, describing the superiority of Christ in His person and work (1:4; 6:9; 7:7, 19, 22; 8:6; 9:23; 10:34; 11:16, 35, 40; 12:24). The words *perfect* and *heavenly* are also prominent. He offers a better revelation, position, priesthood, covenant, sacrifice, and power.

Key Verses: *Hebrews 4:14–16 and 12:1, 2*

Key Chapter: *Hebrews 11*

The hall of fame of the Scriptures is located in Hebrews 11 and records those who willingly took God at His word even when there was nothing to cling to but His promise.

Historical Setting

The repeated use of Old Testament quotations and images in Hebrews suggests that the people who received this book had a Jewish background. The repeated warnings against spiritual unbelief reveal that the readers of this epistle were on the verge of renouncing the Christian faith and returning to their former Jewish ways (2:1–4; 3:7–4:14; 5:12–6:20; 10:19–39; 12:12–29).

Theological Contribution

In a spirit similar to Stephen's defense before the Jewish Sanhedrin (Acts 7), Hebrews sets out to show that Christianity is superior to Judaism because of the person of Jesus Christ, who is the Son of God, the Great High Priest, and the author and finisher of salvation. Christ stands as the peak of revelation, superior to angels (1:1–2:9) and to Moses (3:1–6). He is the Son of God, the reflection of God's own glory and, indeed, the very character and essence of God (1:3). Whatever revelations appeared before Jesus were but shadows or outlines of what was to appear in Him.

Special Consideration

Two passages in Hebrews often trouble Christians. In 6:4–6 and 10:26 the author warns that if a person willingly turns from fellowship with Christ, he can no longer be forgiven. The intent of these verses is to cause Christians to remember the great cost of God's grace and to take their profession of faith seriously, not to cause believers to doubt their salvation. The backbone of this epistle is the finality of Christ for salvation.

Survey of Hebrews

The Superiority of Christ's Person (1:1—4:13)

Instead of the usual salutation, this epistle immediately launches into its theme—the supremacy of Christ even over the Old Testament prophets (1:1-3). Christianity is built upon the highest form of divine disclosure: the personal revelation of God through His incarnate Son. Christ is therefore greater than the prophets, and He is also greater than the angels, the mediators of the Mosiac Law (1:4—2:18; see Acts 7:53; Heb. 2:2). This is seen in His name, His position, His worship by the angels, and His incarnation. The Son of God partook of flesh and blood and was "made like His brethren" in all things (2:17) in order to bring "many sons to glory" (2:10).

Christ is also superior to Moses (3:1–6), for Moses was a servant in the house of God, but Christ is the Son over God's household. Because of these truths, the readers are exhorted to avoid the divine judgment that is visited upon unbelief

(3:7—4:13). Their disbelief had prevented the generation of the Exodus from becoming the generation of the conquest, and the rest that Christ offers is so much greater than what was provided by Joshua.

The Superiority of Christ's Work (4:14—10:18)

The high priesthood of Christ is superior to the Aaronic priesthood (4:14—7:28). Christ was not a Levite, but He qualified for a higher priesthood according to the order of Melchizedek. Levi paid tithes through Abraham to Melchizedek (7:9–10); Melchizedek, unlike Aaron, was unique. He had no predecessors and no successors. He was, therefore, a priest forever, like the Son of God (7:1–3). As a consequence of His being like Melchizedek, Jesus inaugurated a new and better covenant (8:1–13).

The new covenant has made the old covenant obsolete (8:6–13). Unlike the former priests, He has offered Himself as a sinless and voluntary sacrifice once and for all (9:1—10:18).

The parenthetical warning in 5:11—6:20 exhorts the readers to "go on to perfection" by moving beyond the basics of salvation and repentance.

The Superiority of the Christian's Walk of Faith (10:19—13:25)

The author applies what he has been saying about the superiority of Christ by warning his readers of the danger of discarding their faith in Christ (10:19–39). The faith that the readers must maintain is defined in 11:1–3 and illustrated in 11:4–40. Just as Jesus endured great hostility, those who believe in Him will sometimes have to endure divine discipline for the sake of holiness (12:1–29).

The readers are warned not to turn away from Christ during such times, but to place their hope in Him. The character of their lives must be shaped by their dedication to Christ (13:1–19), and this will be manifested in their love of each

The Epistle to the Hebrews

FOCUS	Christ's Person			Christ's Work			The Walk of Faith		
REFERENCE	1:1 ———	1:4 ———	3:1 ———	4:14 ———	8:1 ———	9:1 ———	10:19 ———	12:1 ———	13:1 ———13:25
DIVISION	Christ over Prophets	Christ over Angels	Christ over Moses	Priest-hood	Covenant	Sanctuary and Sacrifice	Assurance of Faith	Endurance of Faith	Exhortation to Love
TOPIC	Majesty of Christ			Ministry of Christ			Ministers for Christ		
	Doctrine						Discipline		
LOCATION	Place of Writing Unknown								
TIME	c. A.D. 64–68								

other through their hospitality, concern, purity, contentment, and obedience. The author concludes this epistle with one of the finest benedictions in Scripture (13:20, 21) and some personal words (13:22–25).

Outline of Hebrews

The Epistle of James

Authorship and Date

The author identifies himself as "James, a servant of God
and the Lord Jesus Christ" (1:1). At least five personalities
named James appear in the New Testament. None has a
stronger claim to being the author of this epistle than James,
the brother of the Lord. Apparently neither a disciple nor an
apostle during Jesus' lifetime, he is first mentioned in Mark
6:3, where he is listed as the first (oldest) of Jesus' four youn-
ger brothers. After the ascension of Jesus, James emerged as a
leader of the church in Jerusalem (Acts 15:13; 1 Cor. 15:7;
Gal. 2:9)—a position he must have occupied for nearly 30
years, until his martyrdom, according to church tradition.

The epistle may have been written after Paul's letters were

◆

KEYS TO JAMES

Key Word: *Faith That Works*

James develops the theme of the characteristics of true faith, using them as a series of tests to help his readers evaluate the quality of their relationship to Christ.

Key Verses: *James 1:19–22 and 2:14–17*

Key Chapter: *James 1*

One of the most difficult areas of the Christian life is that of testings and temptations. James reveals our correct response to both: to testings, count them all joy; to temptations, realize God is not the source.

◆

in circulation, because James' emphasis on works may be intended to offset Paul's emphasis on faith. This would date the epistle around A.D. 60.

Historical Setting

James addressed the epistle "to the twelve tribes which are scattered abroad" (1:1). This implies a readership of Jewish Christians living outside Palestine. Elsewhere in the epistle, however, James refers to hired field labor (5:4), and this locates his audience inside Palestine. In James' day only in Palestine did farmers employ hired rather than slave labor, as was customary elsewhere.

Theological Contribution

The Epistle of James is a sturdy, compact letter on practical religion. For James, the acid test of true religion is in the doing rather than in the hearing, "believing," or speaking. In this respect James echoes clearly the ethical teaching of Jesus, especially as it is recorded in the Sermon on the Mount (Matt. 5—7).

Special Consideration

Some Bible scholars suggest that James and Paul differ in their views on the saving significance of faith and works. Paul states, "A man is justified by faith apart from the deeds of the law" (Rom. 3:28), and James says, "A man is justified by works, and not by faith only" (James 2:19). A closer reading of the two however, reveals that they differ more in their definition of faith than in its essence. James writes to readers who are inclined to interpret faith as mere intellectual acknowledgment (2:19). As a consequence he stresses that a faith which does not affect life is not saving faith; hence, his emphasis on works. Actually, this is quite close to Paul's understanding. For Paul, faith is the entrusting of one's whole life to God through Christ, with the result that one's life becomes renewed with the "fruit of the Spirit" (Gal. 5:22).

Survey of James

The Test of Faith (1:1–18)

After a one-verse salutation to geographically dispersed Hebrew Christians (1:1), James quickly introduces his first subject, outward tests of faith (1:2–12). These trials are designed to produce mature endurance and a sense of dependence upon God. Inward temptations (1:13–18) do not come from the One who bestows "every good gift" (1:17).

The Characteristics of Faith (1:19—5:6)

A righteous response to testing requires that one be "swift to hear, slow to speak, slow to wrath" (1:19), and this broadly summarizes the remainder of the epistle. Quickness of hearing involves an obedient response to God's Word (1:19–27). A genuine faith should produce a change in attitude from partiality to the rich to a love for the poor as well as

The Epistle of James

FOCUS	Test of Faith		Characteristics of Faith	Triumph of Faith		
REFERENCE	1:1 ——————— 1:13 ———————		1:19 ——————— 5:7 ———————	5:13 ———————	5:19 ———————	5:20
DIVISION	Purpose of Tests	Source of Temptation	Outward Demonstration of Inner Faith	Endures Waiting	Prays for Afflicted	Confronts Sin
TOPIC	Development of Faith		Works of Faith	Power of Faith		
	Response of Faith		Reality of Faith	Reassurance of Faith		
LOCATION	Probably Jerusalem					
TIME	c. A.D. 46–60					

the rich (2:1–13). True faith should also result in actions (2:14–26).

Moving from works to words, James shows how only the power of God applied by an active faith can tame the tongue (3:1–12). Just as there are wicked and righteous uses of the tongue, so there are demonic and divine manifestations of wisdom (3:13–18). James contrasts seven characteristics of human wisdom with seven qualities of divine wisdom.

The strong pulls of worldliness (4:1–12) and wealth (4:13—5:6) create conflicts that are harmful to the growth of faith. The world system is at enmity with God, and the pursuit of its pleasures produces covetousness, envy, fighting, and arrogance (4:1–6). The believer's only alternative is submission to God out of a humble and repentant spirit. This will produce a transformed attitude toward others as well (4:7–12). This spirit of submission and humility should be applied to any attempts to accrue wealth (4:13–17), especially because wealth can lead to pride, injustice, and selfishness (5:1–6).

The Triumph of Faith (5:7–20)

James encourages his readers to patiently endure the sufferings of the present life in view of the future prospect of the coming of the Lord (5:7–12) and concludes his epistle with some practical words on prayer and restoration (5:13–20). The prayers of righteous men (e.g., elders in local churches) are efficacious for the healing and restoration of believers. When sin is not dealt with, it can contribute to illness and even death.

Outline of James

The First Epistle of Peter

◆

KEYS TO FIRST PETER

Key Word: *Suffering for the Cause of Christ*

The basic theme of 1 Peter is the proper response to Christian suffering. Knowing that his readers will be facing more persecution than ever before, Peter writes to give a divine perspective so that they will be able to endure without wavering.

Key Verses: *First Peter 1:10–12 and 4:12, 13*

Key Chapter: *First Peter 4*

Central in the New Testament revelation concerning how to handle persecution and suffering caused by one's Christian testimony is 1 Peter 4. Christ's suffering to be our model (4:1, 2), but we also are to rejoice in that we can share in His suffering (4:12–14).

◆

Authorship and Date

First Peter identifies its author as "Peter, an apostle of Jesus Christ" (1:1), but as a former associate of the apostle Paul, and as one who doubtlessly came to the Greek language as a native, Silvanus may have played an important role in bringing this epistle to completion. We might say of 1 Peter that the idea came from Peter, but the design from Silvanus. The reference to "Babylon" (5:13), a common image for civil power opposed to God, indicates that the epistle was written from Rome.

Historical Setting

First Peter is addressed to Christians living in "Pontus, Galatia, Cappadocia, Asia, and Bithynia" (1:1)—places in the northern and western parts of Asia Minor (modern Turkey). The readers appear to have been Gentiles (1:14, 18; 2:10; 4:3), although they probably had not been evangelized by Peter himself (1:12).

Theological Contribution

First Peter was written by one who sensed the triumphant outcome of God's purpose for the world (1:4). The triumph of the future depends in no way on what we have done but on the resurrection of Jesus Christ. Because God has raised Jesus from the dead, God is deserving of praise; for "His abundant mercy has begotten us again to a living hope" (1:3).

Survey of First Peter

The Salvation of the Believer (1:1—2:12)

Addressing his letter to believers in several Roman provinces, Peter briefly describes the saving work of the triune Godhead in his salutation (1:1, 2). He then extols God for the riches of this salvation by looking in three temporal directions (1:3–12). First, Peter anticipates the future realization of the Christian's manifold inheritance (1:3–5). Second, he looks at the present joy that this living hope produces in spite of various trials (1:6–9). Third, he reflects upon the prophets of the past who predicted the gospel of God's grace in Christ (1:10–12).

The proper response to this salvation is the pursuit of sanctification or holiness (1:13–2:10). Peter exhorts his readers to "desire the pure milk of the word, that [they] may grow" (2:2).

The Submission of the Believer (2:13—3:12)

Submission for the Lord's sake to those in governmental (2:13–17) and social (2:18–20) authority will foster a good testimony to outsiders. Before moving on to submission in marital relationships (3:1–7), Peter again picks up the theme of Christian suffering with Christ as the supreme model: He suffered sinlessly, silently, and as a substitute for the salvation of others (2:21–25; cf. Is. 52:13–53:12). Peter summarizes his appeal for Christlike submission and humility in 3:8–12.

The Suffering of the Believer (3:13—5:14)

Peter encourages his readers to be ready to defend their faith in an intelligent and gracious way (3:13–16). Three times he tells them that if they must suffer, it should be for righteousness' sake and not as a result of sinful behavior (3:17; see 2:20; 4:15, 16). The end of this chapter (3:18–22) is an extremely difficult passage to interpret, and several options have been offered. Verses 19 and 20 may mean that Christ, during the period between His death and resurrection, addressed demonic spirits or the spirits of those who were alive before the Flood. Another interpretation is that Christ preached through Noah to his pre-Flood contemporaries.

As believers in Christ, the readers are no longer to pursue the lusts of the flesh as they did formerly, but rather the will of God (4:1–6). In view of hardships, Peter exhorts them to

The First Epistle of Peter

FOCUS	Salvation of the Believer		Submission of the Believer	Suffering of the Believer		
REFERENCE	1:1 ——— 1:13 ——————		2:13 ——————	3:13 ——— 3:18 ——— 4:7 ——— 5:1 ——— 5:14		
DIVISION	Salvation of the Believer	Sanctifica- tion of the Believer	Government, Business, Marriage, and All of Life	Conduct in Suffering	Christ's Example of Suffering	Commands in Suffering	Minister in Suffering
TOPIC	Belief of Christians		Behavior of Christians	Buffeting of Christians		
	Holiness		Harmony	Humility		
LOCATION	Either Rome or Babylon					
TIME	c. A.D. 63–64					

be strong in their mutual love and to exercise their spiritual gifts in the power of God so that they will be built up (4:7–11).

They should not be surprised when they are slandered and reviled for their faith because the sovereign God has a purpose in all things, and the time of judgment will come when His name and all who trust in Him will be vindicated (4:12–19).

In a special word to the elders of the churches in these Roman provinces, Peter urges them to be diligent but gentle shepherds over the flocks that have been divinely placed under their care (5:1–4). The readers as a whole are told to clothe themselves with humility toward one another and toward God who will exalt them at the proper time (5:5–7). They are to resist the adversary in the sure knowledge that their calling to God's eternal glory in Christ will be realized (5:8–11). Peter ends his epistle by stating his theme ("the true grace of God") and conveying greetings and a benediction (5:12–14).

Outline of First Peter

The Second Epistle of Peter

First Peter deals with problems from the outside; Second
Peter deals with problems from the inside. Peter writes to
warn the believers about the false teachers who are peddling
damaging doctrine. He begins by urging them to keep close
watch on their personal lives. The Christian life demands dili-
gence in pursuing moral excellence, knowledge, self-control,
perseverance, godliness, brotherly kindness and selfless love.
Although God may be long-suffering in sending judgment,
ultimately it will come. In view of that fact, believers should
live lives of godliness, blamelessness, and steadfastness.

Authorship, Date, and Historical Setting

Although the epistle claims to come from the apostle Peter
(1:1; 3:1–2), who witnessed the transfiguration of Christ
(1:18) and at the time of writing was nearing his death
(1:14), few scholars believe Peter wrote the letter. Instead,
2 Peter may have been written by anonymous author but at-

◆

KEYS TO SECOND PETER

Key Word: *Guard Against False Teachers*

The basic theme that runs through 2 Peter is the contrast between the knowledge and practice of truth versus falsehood.

Key Verses: *Second Peter 1:20, 21 and 3:9–11*

Key Chapter: *Second Peter 1*

The Scripture clearest in defining the relationship between God and man on the issue of inspiration is contained in 1:19–21. Three distinct principles surface:

(1) that the interpretation of Scriptures is not limited to a favored elect but is open for all who "rightly [divide] the word of truth" (2 Tim. 2:15);
(2) that the divinely inspired prophet did not initiate the Scripture himself; and
(3) that the Holy Spirit (not the emotion or circumstances of the moment) moved holy men.

◆

tributed by someone to the apostle Peter in order to assure a hearing for a message in a time well after Peter's death. Since it makes no mention of its audience, 2 Peter was probably intended for a general readership.

Theological Contribution

Second Peter shifts the emphasis from a hope by which one can live to a hope on which one can count. The epistle speaks to the assurance of salvation in chapter 1 by making the extraordinary claim that Christians are "partakers of the divine nature" (1:4). The second chapter deals with false teachers. The unique contribution of 2 Peter, however, comes in chapter 3. God does not delay "the day of the Lord" coming because He lacks power or concern. Rather, He is patient, "not willing that any should perish but that all should come to repentance" (3:9).

Survey of Second Peter

Cultivation of Christian Character (chap. 1)

Peter's salutation (1:1, 2) is an introduction to the major theme of chapter 1, that is, the true knowledge of Jesus Christ. The readers are reminded of the "great and precious promises" that are theirs because of their calling to faith in Christ (1:3, 4). They have been called away from the corruption of the world to conformity with Christ, and Peter urges them to progress by forging a chain of eight Christian virtues from faith to love (1:5–7). If a believer does not transform profession into practice, he becomes spiritually useless, perverting the purpose for which he was called (1:8–11).

This letter was written not long before Peter's death (1:14) to remind believers of the riches of their position in Christ and their responsibility to hold fast to the truth (1:12–21). The clearest biblical description of the divine-human process of inspiration is found in 1:21: "but holy men of God spoke *as they were* moved by the Holy Spirit."

Condemnation of False Teachers (chap. 2)

Peter's discussion of true prophecy leads him to an extended denunciation of false prophecy in the churches. These false teachers were especially dangerous because they arose within the church and undermined the confidence of believers (2:1–3). Peter's extended description of the characteristics of these false teachers (2:10–22) exposes the futility and corruption of their strategies.

The Second Epistle of Peter

FOCUS	Cultivation of Christian Character		Condemnation of False Teachers			Confidence in Christ's Return	
REFERENCE	1:1 ———	1:15 ———	2:1 ———	2:4 ———	2:10 ———	3:1 ———	3:8 ——— 3:18
DIVISION	Growth in Christ	Grounds of Belief	Danger	Destruction	Deception	Mockery in the Last Days	Day of the Lord
TOPIC	True Prophecy		False Prophets			Prophecy: Day of the Lord	
	Holiness		Heresy			Hope	
LOCATION	Probably Rome						
TIME	c. A.D. 64–66 if by Peter; later if by an anonymous author						

Confidence of Christ's Return (chap. 3)

Scoffers will claim in the last days that God does not powerfully intervene in world affairs, but Peter calls attention to two past and one future divinely induced catastrophic events: the Creation, the Flood, and the dissolution of the present heavens and earth (3:1–7). God's perspective on the passing of time is quite unlike that of men, and the apparent delay in the *parousia* is due to His patience in waiting for more individuals to come to a knowledge of Christ (3:8, 9). When the day of consummation comes, all the matter of this universe will evidently be transformed into energy from which God will fashion a new cosmos (3:10–13).

In light of this coming day of the Lord, Peter exhorts his readers to live lives of holiness, steadfastness, and growth (3:14–18). He mentions the letters of "our beloved brother Paul" and significantly places them on a level with the Old Testament Scriptures (3:15, 16). After a final warning about the danger of false teachers, the epistle closes with an appeal to growth, and a doxology.

Outline of Second Peter

The First Epistle of John

◆

KEYS TO FIRST JOHN

Key Word: *Fellowship with God*

The major theme of 1 John is fellowship with God. John wants his readers to have assurance of the indwelling God through their abiding relationship with Him (2:28; 5:13). Belief in Christ should be manifested in the practice of righteousness and love for the brethren, which in turn produces joy and confidence before God.

Key Verses: *First John 1:3, 4 and 5:11–13*

Key Chapter: *First John 1*

The two central passages for continued fellowship with God are John 15 and 1 John 1. John 15 relates the positive side of fellowship, that is, abiding in Christ. First John 1 unfolds the other side, pointing out that when Christians do not abide in Christ, they must seek forgiveness before fellowship can be restored.

◆

Authorship and Date

Although 1, 2, and 3 John were written by an anonymous author, he wrote affectionately to his readers as "little children" and referred to himself as "the elder" (2 John 1; 3 John 1). He must have been well-known and well-loved by those to whom he wrote.

The inclusion of personal testimony (1 John 1:1–4) indicates that John the elder depended directly on the testimony of the apostle John in writing these documents. The epistles were probably written from Ephesus toward the close of the first century A.D.

Historical Setting

First John has none of the usual features of an epistle: no salutation or identification of author; no greetings; and no references to persons, places, or events. Ironically, although its format is impersonal, like a sermon or treatise, its tone is warm and personal. This suggests that it was written to a broad audience (probably in and around Ephesus) that was very dear to the author.

Theological Contribution

Like the Gospel of John, the epistles of John are built on the foundation blocks of love, truth, sin, world, life, light, and the Holy Spirit. The epistles of John emphasize the great themes of knowing, believing, walking, and abiding. The keystone in the arch of the gospel is that God has appeared in human form (1:1–4). The Incarnation is life (1:2); and this life is available in the Son of God, Jesus Christ (5:11). Fellowship with God is realized by knowing God and abiding in Him: joined to Him in righteousness (2:29), truth (3:19), and especially love (4:7–8).

Special Consideration

Many Christians wonder about John's declaration, "Whoever abides in Him [Jesus Christ] does not sin" (3:6). This does not mean that if someone sins he is not a Christian. Indeed, in these epistles we are told that Christ came to forgive sins; and we are admonished to confess our sins to Him (1:6—2:2; 3:5; 4:10). The statement means that Christ has transferred us from death to life and has caused us to share in the nature of God. Consequently, we are no longer confined to darkness, because Jesus Christ has broken the power of sin in our lives (3:8).

Survey of First John

The Basis of Fellowship (1:1—2:27)

John's prologue (1:1–4) recalls the beginning of apostolic contact with Christ. It relates his desire to transmit this apostolic witness to his readers so that they may share the same fellowship with Jesus Christ, the personification of life. This proclamation is followed by a description of the conditions of fellowship (1:5—2:14).

The readers' sins have been forgiven and they enjoy fellowship with God. As a result, they know "Him *who is* from the beginning" and are strengthened to overcome the temptations of the evil one (2:12–14). The cautions to fellowship are both practical (2:15–17) and doctrinal (2:18–23). The antidote to heretical teachings is abiding in the apostolic truths that they "heard from the beginning," which are authenticated by the anointing they have received (2:24–27).

The Behavior of Fellowship (2:28—5:21)

The basic theme of First John is summarized in 2:28—assurance through abiding in Christ. The next verses introduces the motif of regeneration, and 2:29—3:10 argues that regeneration is manifested in the practice of righteousness. Because we are children of God through faith in Christ, we have a firm hope of being fully conformed to Him when He appears (3:1–3). Our present likeness to Christ places us in a position of incompatiblity with sin, because sin is contrary to the person and work of Christ (3:4–6). When the believer sins, he does not reflect the regenerate new man but Satan, the original sinner (3:7–10). Righteousness is manifested in love (3:10–23). The apostle uses the example of Cain to illustrate what love is not and Christ to illustrate what love is.

The First Epistle of John

FOCUS	Basis of Fellowship		Behavior of Fellowship	
REFERENCE	1:1 ——————— 2:15 ———————	2:28 ———————	5:4 ———————	5:21
DIVISION	Conditions for Fellowship	Cautions to Fellowship	Characteristics of Fellowship	Consequences of Fellowship
TOPIC	Meaning of Fellowship		Manifestations of Fellowship	
	Abiding in God's Light		Abiding in God's Love	
LOCATION	Written in Ephesus			
TIME	c. A.D. 90			

In 3:24 John introduces two important motifs, which are developed in 4:1–16; the indwelling God, and the Spirit as a mark of this indwelling. The Spirit of God confesses the incarnate Christ and confirms apostolic doctrine (4:1–6). The mutual abiding of the believer in God and God in the believer is manifested in love for others, and this love produces a divine and human fellowship that testifies to and reflects the reality of the incarnation (4:7–16). It also anticipates the perfect fellowship to come and creates a readiness to face the One from whom all love is derived (4:17–19).

John joins the concepts he has presented into a circular chain of six links: love, obedience, faith, Christ, witness, prayer. The epilogue (5:18–21) summarizes the conclusions of the epistle in a series of three certainties:

(1) Sin is a threat to fellowship, and it should be regarded as foreign to the believer's position in Christ (cf. Rom 6).
(2) The believer stands with God against the satanic world system.
(3) The incarnation produces true knowledge and communion with Christ.

Outline of First John

The Second Epistle of John

◆

KEYS TO SECOND JOHN

Key Word: *Avoid Fellowship with False Teachers*

The basic theme of this brief letter is steadfastness in the practice and purity of the apostolic doctrine that the readers "have heard from the beginning" (v. 6).

Key Verses: *Second John 9, 10*

◆

Background and general themes of 2 John are discussed under 1 John (pp. 326–331).

Survey of Second John

Abide in God's Commandments (vv. 1–6)

The salutation (vv. 1–3) centers on the concept of abiding in the truth. The apostle commends his readers on their walk

The Second Epistle of John

FOCUS	Abide in God's Commandments			Abide Not with False Teachers	
REFERENCE	1 —— 4 —— 5 —— 7 —— 10 —— 12 —— 13				
DIVISION	Salutation	Walk in Truth	Walk in Love	Doctrine of False Teachers	Avoid the False Teachers	Benediction
TOPIC	Walk in Commandments			Watch for Counterfeits		
	Practice the Truth			Protect the Truth		
LOCATION	Written in Ephesus					
TIME	c. A.D. 90					

in truth in obedience to God's commandment (v. 4), and reminds them that this commandment entails the practice of love for one another (vv. 5, 6).

Abide Not with False Teachers (vv. 7–13)

Moving from the basic test of Christian behavior (love for the brethren) to the basic test of Christian belief (the person of Christ), John admonishes the readers to beware of deceivers "who do not confess Jesus Christ *as* coming in the flesh" (vv. 7–9). In no uncertain terms, the apostle enjoins the readers to deny even the slightest assistance or encouragement to itinerant teachers who promote an erroneous view of Christ (and hence of salvation; vv. 10, 11).

This letter closes with John's explanation of its brevity: he anticipates a future visit during which he will be able to "speak face to face" with his readers (v. 12).

Outline of Second John

The Third Epistle of John

◆

KEYS TO THIRD JOHN

Key Word: *Enjoy Fellowship with the Brethren*

The basic theme of this letter is to enjoy and continue to have fellowship (hospitality) with fellow believers, especially full-time Christian workers. This is contrasted between the truth and servanthood of Gaius and the error and selfishness of Diotrephes.

◆

Background and general themes of 3 John are discussed under 1 John (pp. 326–331).

Survey of Third John

Commendation of Gaius (vv. 1–8)

The "elder" writes to one of his beloved "children" whose godly behavior has given the apostles great joy (vv. 1–4). The apostle urges Gaius to continue supporting traveling teachers in faithfulness, love, and generosity (vv. 5–8).

Condemnation of Diotrephes (vv. 9–14)

Suddenly John describes a man whose actions are diametrically opposed to those of Gaius (vv. 9–11). Diotrephes boldly rejects John's apostolic authority and refuses to receive the itinerant teachers sent out by the apostle. Orthodox in his doctrine, his evil actions indicate a blindness to God.

By contrast, John gives his full recommendation to Demetrius, another emissary and probably the bearer of this letter to Gaius (v. 12). John expresses his hope of a personal visit in the closing remarks (vv. 13, 14), as he does in Second John.

The Third Epistle of John

FOCUS	Commendation of Gaius		Condemnation of Diotrephes	
REFERENCE	1 ———— 2 ———— 5		———— 9 ———— 12 ———— 13 ————14	
DIVISION	Salutation	Godliness of Gaius	Generosity of Gaius	Pride of Diotrephes	Praise for Demetrius	Benediction
TOPIC	Servanthood			Selfishness		
	Duty of Hospitality			Danger of Haughtiness		
LOCATION	Written in Ephesus					
TIME	c. A.D. 90					

Outline of Third John

The Epistle of Jude

◆

KEYS TO JUDE

Key Word: *Contend for the Faith*

This epistle condemns the practices of heretical teachers in the church and counsel the readers to stand firm, grow in their faith, and contend for the truth.

Key Verse: *Jude 3*

◆

Authorship, Date, and Historical Setting

The author of the epistle introduces himself as "Jude, a servant of Jesus Christ, and brother of James" (v. 1). There is no further identification, and the James mentioned is probably the Lord's brother (Gal. 1:19). Jude, therefore, would also be a brother of Jesus (Judas, Mark 6:3; Matt. 13:55), although not an apostle (Jude 17). The emphasis on remembering "the words which were spoken before the apostles" (v. 17) suggests that the epistle was composed some time after the apostles had taught, thus favoring a date near the close of the first century. The epistle of Jude has the character of a tract or brief essay written for a general Christian audience (v. 1).

Theological Contribution

Jude writes as a defender of the faith who is "contending earnestly for the faith which was once for all delivered to the saints" (v. 3). The "ungodly" are not the heathen outside the church; they are the false teachers inside (v. 12). Their association with the faith, however, does not mean they live in the faith: the ungodly have not the Spirit (v. 19), whereas the faithful do (v. 20); the ungodly remain in eternal darkness (v. 13), but the saints have eternal life (v. 21).

Special Consideration

Jude's last word on the problem of corruption in the church is preserved in a memorable benediction. Only God can keep us from error and bring us to Himself (vv. 24–25).

Survey of Jude

Purpose of Jude (vv. 1–4)

Jude addresses his letter to believers who are "called," "sanctified," and "preserved," and wishes for them the threefold blessing of mercy, peace, and love (vv. 1, 2). Grim news about the encroachment of false teachers in the churches has impelled Jude to write this timely word of rebuke and warning (vv. 3, 4).

Description of False Teachers (vv. 5–16)

Jude begins his extended exposé of the apostate teachers by illustrating their ultimate doom with three examples of divine judgment from the Pentateuch (vv. 5–7).

The Epistle of Jude

FOCUS	Purpose	Description of False Teachers			Defense Against False Teachers	Doxology
REFERENCE 1 ——		5 ——	8 ——	14 ——	17 ——	24 —— 25
DIVISION	Introduction	Past Judgment	Present Characteristics	Future Judgment	Duty of Believers	Conclusion
TOPIC		Reason to Contend			How to Contend	
		Anatomy of Apostasy			Antidote for Apostasy	
LOCATION			Unknown			
TIME			c. A.D. 66–80			

Like unreasoning animals, these apostates are ruled by the things they revile, and they are destroyed by the things they practice (vv. 8–10). Even the archangel Michael is more careful in his dealings with superhuman powers than are these arrogant men. He compares these men to three spiritually rebellious men from Genesis (Cain) and Numbers (Balaam and Korah) who incurred the condemnation of God (v. 11). Verses 12 and 13 succinctly summarize their character with five highly descriptive metaphors taken from nature. After affirming the judgment of God upon such ungodly men with a quote from the noncanonical Book of Enoch (vv. 14, 15), Jude catalogs some of their practices (v. 16).

Defense Against False Teachers (vv. 17–23)

This letter has been exposing apostate teachers (vv. 8, 10, 12, 14, 16), but now Jude directly addresses his readers ("But you, beloved, remember" v. 17). He reminds them of the apostolic warning that such men would come (vv. 17–19) and encourages them to protect themselves against the onslaught of apostasy (vv. 20, 21). The readers must become mature in their own faith so that they will be able to rescue those who are enticed or already ensnared by error (vv. 22, 23).

Doxology of Jude (vv. 24, 25)

Jude closes with one of the greatest doxologies in the Bible. It emphasizes the power of Christ to keep those who trust in Him from being overthrown by error.

Outline of Jude

The Book of Revelation

◆

KEYS TO REVELATION

Key Word: *The Revelation of the Coming of Christ*

The purposes for which Revelation was written depend to some extent on how the book as a whole is interpreted.

(1) The *symbolic or idealist view* maintains that Revelation is not a predictive prophecy, but a symbolic portrait of the cosmic conflict of spiritual principles.

(2) The *preterist view* (the Latin word *praeter* means "past") maintains that it is a symbolic description of the Roman persecution of the church, emperor worship, and the divine judgment of Rome.

(3) The *historicist view* approaches Revelation as an allegorical panorama of the history of the (Western) church from the first century to the Second Advent.

(4) The *futurist view* acknowledges the obvious influence that the first-century conflict between Roman power and the church had upon the themes of this book. It also accepts the bulk of Revelation (chaps. 4—22) as an inspired look into the time immediately preceding the Second Advent (the Tribulation, usually seen as seven years; chaps. 6—18), and extending from the return of Christ to the creation of the new cosmos (chaps. 19—22).

Advocates of all four interpretive approaches to Revelation agree that it was written to assure the recipients of the ultimate triumph of Christ over all who rise up against Him and His saints. The readers were facing dark times of persecution, and even worse times would follow. Therefore they needed to be encouraged to persevere by standing firm in Christ in view of God's plan for the righteous and the wicked.

Key Verses: *Revelation 1:19 and 19:11*

Key Chapters: *Revelation 19—22*

When the end of history is fully understood, its impact radically affects the present. In Revelation 19—22 the plans of God for the last days and for all of eternity are recorded in explicit terms.

◆

Authorship and Date

The author identifies himself as John (1:4, 9; 21:2; 22:8), a prophet (1:1–4; 22:6–7). He was familiar enough with his readers to call himself their "brother and companion in tribulation" (1:9). He indicates that he was exiled to the island of Patmos (1:9) off the west coast of Asia Minor (modern Turkey), and that on the "Lord's Day" (Sunday) he was caught up "in the Spirit" (1:10) and saw the visions recorded in his book. The book was probably written during the latter years of the reign of the Roman Emperor Domitian (A.D. 81–96).

Theological Contribution

The grand theme of the Book of Revelation is that of two warring powers, God and Satan, and of God's ultimate victory. It would be a mistake to consider the two powers as equal in might. God is stronger than Satan, and Satan continues his scheming plots only because God permits him to do so.

Special Contributions

One of the unique characteristics of Revelation is its use of four, twelve, and seven. Among the examples, we find four living creatures, four horsemen, and four angels; twelve elders, twelve gates to the city of God, seven churches, seven seals, seven bowls. In apocalyptic literature these numbers represent completeness and perfection. Conversely, $3^1/_2$ is a number frequently associated with Satan (11:2; 13:5; 42 months or $3^1/_2$ years); this number symbolizes a fracturing and diminishing of God's unity. With this in mind, the 144,000 elect in chapter 7 should not be taken literally, but rather (12,000 times 12) stands for totality. This means that no martyr will fail to see God's reward. The number of the beast, 666 (13:18), probably refers to Nero, or more specifically to the idea that Nero would return alive to lead the armies of Satan against God.

Survey of Revelation

"The Things Which You Have Seen" (chap. 1)

Revelation contains a prologue (1:1–3) before the usual salutation (1:4–8). The Revelation was received by Christ from the Father and communicated by an angel to John. This is the only biblical book that specifically promises a blessing to those who read it (1:3), but it also promises a curse to those who add to or detract from it (22:18, 19). The salutation and closing benediction show that it was originally written as an epistle to seven Asian churches. A rich theological portrait of the triune God (1:4–8) is followed by an overwhelming theophany (visible manifestation of God) in 1:9–20.

"The Things Which Are" (chaps. 2—3)

The message to the seven churches refer back to an aspect of John's vision of Christ and contain a command, a commendation and/or condemnation, a correction, and a challenge.

"The Things Which Take Place After This" (chaps. 4—22)

John is translated into heaven where he is given a vision of the divine majesty. In it, the Father ("*One* sat on the throne") and the Son (Lion/Lamb) are worshiped by the twenty-four elders, the four living creatures, and the angelic host because of who they are and what they have done (creation and redemption; chaps. 4—5).

Three cycles of seven judgments in chapters 6—16 consist of seven seals, seven trumpets, and seven bowls. The seven seals (6:1—8:5) include war, the famine and death that are associated with war, and persecution. The prophetic insert between the sixth and seventh seals (chap. 7) describes the protective sealing of 144,000 "Children of Israel," 12,000 from every tribe. It also looks ahead to the multitudes from every part of the earth who come "out of the great tribulation." The catastrophic events in most of the trumpet judgments are called "woes" (8:2—11:19).

The prophetic interlude between the sixth and seventh trumpets (10:1—11:14) adds more details about the nature of the tribulation period and mentions a fourth set of seven judgments (the "seven thunders"), which would have extended it if they had not been withdrawn. Two unnamed witnesses minister during three-and-a-half years of the Tribulation (forty-two months or 1,260 days). At the end of their ministry they are overcome by the beast, but their resurrection and ascension confound their enemies.

In chapter 12 a woman gives birth to a male child, who is caught up to God. The woman flees into the wilderness and is pursued by a dragon, who is cast down to earth.

Chapter 13 gives a graphic description of the beast and his false prophet, both empowered by the dragon. The first beast is given political, economic, and religious authority and is

The Revelation of Jesus Christ

FOCUS	"Things Which You Have Seen"	"Things Which Are"	"Things Which Will Take Place"			
REFERENCE	1:1 ——	2:1 ——	4:1 —— 6:1 —— 19:7 —— 20:1 —— 21:1 —— 22:21			
DIVISION	The Lord Jesus Christ	Seven Churches	The Judge	Tribulation	Second Coming	Millennium	Eternal State
TOPIC	Vision of Christ		Vision of Consummation			
	Theophany	Talks	Tribulations	Tribulations	Trumpets	Together
LOCATION	Written on the Island of Patmos					
TIME	c. A.D. 81–96					

worshiped as the ruler of the earth. Chapter 14 contains a series of visions including the 144,000 at the end of the tribulation, the fate of those who follow the beast, and the outpouring of the wrath of God.

The seven bowl judgments of chapter 16 are prefaced by a heavenly vision of the power, holiness, and glory of God in chapter 15. Chapters 17 and 18 anticipate the final downfall of Babylon, the great harlot sitting upon a scarlet-colored beast.

The marriage banquet of the Lamb is ready and the King of Kings, Lord of Lords leads the armies of heaven into battle against the beast and his false prophet. They are cast into a lake of fire (19).

In chapter 20 the dragon—Satan—is bound for a thousand years. He is cast into a bottomless pit. During this one thousand-year period Christ reigns over the earth with His resurrected saints, but by the end of this millennium, many have been born who refuse to submit their hearts to Christ. Satan is released and a final battle ensues. This is followed by the judgment at the great white throne.

A new universe is created, this time unspoiled by sin, death, pain, or sorrow. The new Jerusalem, described in 21:9—22:5, will continually be filled with light, but the greatest thing of all is that believers will be in the presence of God and "they shall see His face."

Revelation concludes with an epilogue (22:6-21), which reassures the readers that Christ is coming quickly.

Outline of Revelation

Part Three: "The Things Which Will Take Place After This" (4:1—22:21)

PART THREE

◆

THE APOCRYPHA

THE Old Testament Apocrypha (from the Greek term meaning ("hidden books" pronounced uh POK ri fuh) are a group of books written during a time of turmoil in the history of the Jewish people, from about 200 B.C. to about A.D. 100. (The books known as the New Testament Apocrypha were written during the second and third centuries A.D., long after the death of the apostles and other eyewitnesses to the life and ministry of Jesus. None of these books were included in the New Testament because they were judged as unworthy and not authoritative by officials of the early church. The New Testament Apocrypha are not dealt with in this handbook.)

The books of the Old Testament Apocrypha were written during the period from about 150 B.C. to about A.D. 100, when the Jewish people were in rebellion against the repression of foreign military rulers. These books were excluded from the Jewish Old Testament but included in the Greek (Eastern Orthodox) and Latin Vulgate (Roman Catholic) Old Testaments. The fact that the Apocrypha were excluded from the Jewish canon explains why they are not included in most Protestant editions of the Bible. Evangelical Protestants consider the Apocrypha to be worthy of study, but not authoritative as canonical Scripture.

BOOKS OF THE APOCRYPHA/DEUTEROCANON

BOOK	SUMMARY
Tobit	God's mercy to a Jewish family in exile
Judith	A Jewish heroine defeats the Assyrian general Holofernes
Additions to Esther	Explicit references to divine intervention lacking in the canonical text
Wisdom of Solomon	The deliverance of Wisdom personified
Ecclesiasticus (Sirach)	Exhortations to righteous living
Baruch	Prayers of Jeremiah's scribe
Letter of Jeremiah	Exhortations to the exiles to avoid idolatry
Prayer of Azariah and the Song of the Three Jews	God's deliverance of Daniel's friends in the fiery furnace
Susanna	A chaste woman vindicated from her lecherous accusers
Bel and the Dragon	The impotence of the Babylonian deities
1 Maccabees	Historical narrative of the Maccabean revolt

2 Maccabees	Divine intervention in the events leading to Jewish independence
1 Esdras	Attempts to rebuild the Jewish temple
Prayer of Manasseh	Repentance of the wicked king of Judah
Psalm 151	The Song of David, the shepherd hero
3 Maccabees	God's deliverance of the Jews in Egypt
2 Esdras	An apocalypse concerning the last things
4 Maccabees	A philosophical treatise on martyrdom

Historical Background

After the fall of Jerusalem to Babylon in 587 B.C., control over the Holy Land passed from the Babylonians (586–539 B.C.) and Persians (539–332 B.C.) to the Hellenistic dynasties of the Ptolemies in Egypt (332–198 B.C.) and the Seleucids in Antioch, Syria (198–164 B.C.). The series of events that led to the writing of the Old Testament apocryphal books began in 167 B.C., when the Jews revolted against the king of Syria, Antiochus IV Epiphanes. A pious Jewish priest, Mattathias, and his sons led the rebellion. Mattathias refused to obey Antiochus's command that the Jews worship his gods and offer a pagan sacrifice. Mattathias killed the Syrian official as well as a fellow Jew who was offering the sacrifice.

Guerrilla warfare against the Syrians followed, until the Jews established control of Palestine. Early in the revolt one of the sons of Mattathias, Judas Maccabeus (Maccabeus means "hammer"), cleansed the Temple in Jerusalem from the pollution of the Syrian sacrifices. This day has been celebrated annually by the Jews since that time in the festival known as Chanukah (or Hanukkah), the Feast of Dedication (John 10:22).

From 142 to 63 B.C. the Jews were led in their rebellion against foreign oppression by the family of Mattathias, known as the Hasmoneans. Simon Asamonaios was the grandfather of Mattathias, and his name was applied to all the members of this great family. In spite of the respect given to the Hasmoneans in the early years of their influence, civil strife again plagued the Jews. The Syrians continued to fight for power over the land of Israel. Judas Maccabeus finally made an agreement with Rome that the Romans would come to the aid of the Jews if they should need assistance in their struggle. About a century later some of the Jews did appeal to Rome for help. Pompey, a powerful Roman general, brought order to Jerusalem and made Judea part of a Roman province.

In 37 B.C. the land of Israel, called Palestine, was placed under the rule of a Roman official, Herod the Great (37–4 B.C.). Herod was actually a Roman vassal and was hated by most of the Jews. In spite of this hostility, Herod managed to launch an ambitious building program in Palestine. He created the magnificent port city of Caesarea on the Mediterra-

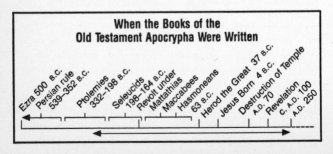

When the Books of the Old Testament Apocrypha Were Written

Ezra 500 B.C. / Persian rule 539–352 B.C. / Ptolemies 332–198 B.C. / Seleucids 198–164 B.C. / Revolt under Mattathias / Maccabees / Hasmoneans 63 B.C. / Herod the Great 37 B.C. / Jesus Born 4 B.C. / Destruction of Temple A.D. 70 / Revelation c. A.D. 100 / A.D. 250

nean Sea and improved the Temple in Jerusalem. The western wall still stands today in Jerusalem as evidence of Herod's skill as a builder.

After Herod's death (4 B.C.), his sons divided Palestine into four regions, ruling the land with varying degrees of success. In A.D. 66 the Jews again grew angry over the foreign domination of their land. Under the encouragement of radical freedom fighters known as Zealots, the Jews started a disastrous war with the Romans. This led to the destruction of Jerusalem and the Temple in A.D. 70 and the end of the Jewish nation.

The Book of Tobit

Concise Outline

Survey of Tobit

Tobit is a Jew taken into captivity to Nineveh and a strict observer of the law of Moses. One night he is blinded by droppings from a swallow that fall into his eyes (1:1—3:6). Tobit sends out his son Tobias, accompanied by the angel Raphael, to collect his inheritance in Media and to marry his relative Sarah in Ecbatana (3:1—6:7). Tobias journeys to do his father's bidding, defeating the demon Asmodeus (the name of a Persian deity) who has been plaguing Sarah (6:2—9:6). The story ends happily when Tobias returns to his parents. Tobit is healed from his blindness, and he sings a hymn of praise to God (10:1—14:15).

Authorship, Setting, Theological Contribution

The Book of Tobit was written in Hebrew or Aramaic around 200–170 B.C. by a Jew who probably lived in Egypt.

The setting of the book is eighth century Nineveh, the capital of Assyria, although the story is clearly a fictional one.

Tobit was written to show the place of prayer, almsgiving, and fasting, the "Three Pillars of Judaism," in the lives of the faithful. It teaches that God breaks into human history, using His angels to rescue people.

The Book of Judith

Concise Outline

Survey of Judith

Nebuchadnezzar, king of Assyria decides to extend his rule by conquering Media. He asks for help from the nations to his west in Persia, Syria, Samaria, and Egypt. These western nations refuse aid, whereupon the enraged Nebuchadnezzar sends his general Holofernes to conquer them (1:1—3:10). The Israelites in Judea, facing imminent destruction by Holofernes, repent before God (4:1—15). Holofernes captures the Ammonite king Achior, who warns him against attacking the divinely protected Israel. Angered, Holofernes delivers Achior to the inhabitants of Bethulia ("Virginity") in preparation for the seizure and sacking of the city (5:1—6:21). The people, led by Uzziah, pray to God for help, asking Him to help them within five days or they will surrender (7:1—32). The pious widow Judith protests Uzziah's decision and determines to defeat Holofernes singlehandedly (8:1—36). She prays for God's assistance (9:1—14). She enters Holofernes' camp on pretense, agrees to sleep with Holofernes, and is summoned to his tent by his eunuch Bagoas (10:1—12:30). Once alone with the drunk Holofernes, she cuts off his head with his own sword. She takes the news to the Jews in Bethulia, who then rout the leaderless Assyrian army (13:1—15:14).

Authorship, Date, and Setting

Judith was probably written around 150–100 B.C. by a Palestinian Jew who was inspired by the Maccabean revolt. The story is set in the sixth century B.C. because of the mention made of the ruler during the Jewish Exile, Nebuchadnezzar. Its setting is not strictly historical however, since Nebuchadnezzar, the king of Babylon, is represented as being the king of the earlier Assyrian empire.

Theological Contribution

Judith emphasized the importance of faithfulness to the law of Moses and the power of God in the lives of His people. Her constant prayers and fasting show the influence of Pharisaism, a Jewish sect that emerged during the Maccabean period.

Special Consideration

Judith parallels the story of the female judge Deborah and the heroine Jael, who beheads the Canaanite general Sisera (Judg. 4:1–24).

Additions to Esther

Concise Outline

Survey of Additions to Esther

Addition A, inserted before 1:1 of the canonical Esther, consists of Mordecai's dream of the two dragons (himself and his nemesis Haman). Mordecai exposes the plot of two officials close to Haman. In Addition B, inserted after 3:13, Artaxerxes, goaded by Haman, orders the extermination of the Jews. In Addition C, inserted after 4:17, Mordecai and Esther pray to God for deliverance from Artaxerxes' edict. In Addition D, replacing 5:1–2, Esther seeks the favor of the king. In Addition E, occurring after 8:12, Artaxerxes revokes his edict against the Jews. In Addition F, inserted after 10:4, Mordecai's dream of Addition A is interpreted.

Authorship and Date

The Additions to Esther were written in Greek by a Jew living in Alexandria, Egypt, in the first century B.C. The fifth century A.D. translator Jerome recognized that they were not in the original Hebrew text and placed them at the end of the book in the Latin Vulgate.

The Book of the Wisdom of Solomon

Concise Outline

Survey of the Wisdom of Solomon

The Wisdom of Solomon is organized into various topics for convenient use by those who study the book. The first section (1:1—6:11), like the Book of Job, treats the issue of why the good suffer and the wicked prosper. Those of the materialist philosophy do not believe in the afterlife; they mock and oppress the righteous with impunity. The answer to this question is the affirmation of immortality and of the future judgment. At the judgment the just will be resurrected to eternal life and the wicked to eternal punishment.

The second section (6:12—9:18) deals with Wisdom personified, her attributes and work in creation, and the need for wisdom in practical and political affairs. It recalls Proverbs 8.

The third section (10:1—19:21) deals with the actions of God among His people. It is similar to Stephen's speech in Acts 7:2–53 (compare Rom. 1:18–32).

Authorship and Date

The Wisdom of Solomon was composed in Greek by a Jew living in Alexandria, Egypt, which was a center of Greek culture. A number of scholars believe that it was written by two different authors, but the evidence is inconclusive. A possible date of composition is between 50 B.C. and 1 B.C. Some scholars believe that it was written in 40 A.D. by the Apollos of Acts 18:24–28.

Historical Setting

The Wisdom of Solomon was named after the great wise man of Israel, King Solomon, who reigned from 970 to 931 B.C. Allusions in the text show the writer's concern about the materialism, oppression, idolatry, and immoral behavior that were to be found in Alexandrian Egypt.

Theological Contribution

The whole book assumes that as a creative Spirit, God is actively involved in human affairs. The human soul is immortal and there will be judgment and a resurrection of the just and unjust to reward and punishment. Wisdom comes from God and is necessary for the creation and preservation of this world. Immortality awaits those who live by this wisdom. Idolatry is foolish and leads to punishment.

Special Considerations

The personification of Wisdom in the book was immensely influential in the doctrine of Christ in the New Testament and the early church theologians. The description of Wisdom as "a pure emanation of the glory of the Almighty . . . a reflection of eternal light . . . an image of his goodness" (7:25–26, NRSV), anticipates the prologue to the Book of Hebrews. Wisdom is identified with the creative Word (9:1–2) who was present with God at creation (9:9), anticipating the prologue to the Gospel of John. Verse 9:17, "Who has learned your counsel, unless you have given wisdom and sent your holy spirit from on high?" (NRSV) anticipates the Christian doctrine of the Trinity. Verse 18:15, "Your all-powerful word leaped from heaven, from the royal throne, into the midst of the land that was doomed, a stern warrior" (NRSV) was taken by the early church as a reference to the Incarnation. The depiction of the Lord's "whole armor" (5:15–20, NRSV) is to be compared with Ephesians 6:13–17.

The Book of Ecclesiasticus, or the Wisdom of Jesus, Son of Sirach

Concise Outline

Survey of Ecclesiasticus

The Book of Ecclesiasticus is a masterpiece of wisdom literature, organized into teachable units. Many subjects are contained in this work, including faith in God as Creator and Sustainer of life, love of wisdom and ethical conduct, friendship, virtue and good deeds, sin and redemption, proper behavior in eating and drinking, work and commerce, study and teaching, poverty and wealth, health and sickness, and the happy family life. The section on the famous men of Israel is similar to Hebrews 11. It places emphasis on religious figures and prophets rather than the kings of Israel. The book concludes with ben Sira's autobiographical remarks and a prayer.

Authorship and Date

Ecclesiasticus was written in Hebrew by Jesus ben ("the son of") Eleazar ben Sira (Sirach in Greek), a Jew living in Jerusalem around 180 B.C. A prologue and epilogue were written in 132 B.C. by his grandson, who also translated the book into Greek.

Historical Setting

Ben Sira was a wise man, scribe, and diplomat who lived in a time of relative tranquility in Jewish history. He was an adherent of the Sadducees, a sect of Judaism which denied the existence of an afterlife or of angels, but a later version of Ecclesiasticus was edited to reflect the views of the Pharisees, who did hold to such beliefs.

Theological Contribution

The author of Ecclesiasticus upholds Israel's traditions as a channel through which God's Word—Wisdom—is communicated.

Special Considerations

Much of ben Sira's teachings on the giving of alms, prayer, fasting, and forgiveness of one's neighbor reflect the Sermon on the Mount. Compare also 11:18–19 to the story of the rich fool in Luke 12:16–21.

Wisdom is identified with the Law or Torah, existing with God before the Creation. Chapter 24 parallels Job 28, Proverbs 8, and the later Wisdom of Solomon 6—9. Wisdom was present at Creation, dwelt in Israel, and overflows with knowledge. Wisdom is not just head knowledge, but includes the fear of the Lord and righteous conduct. The perspectives on wisdom and on the harnessing of the tongue are echoed by the Book of James.

The Book of Baruch

Concise Outline

Survey of Baruch

The introduction to the book sets the historical setting (1:1–14). The person of Baruch confesses to God Israel's sin which resulted in exile, and prays for Israel's restoration (1:15–3:8). Then follows a poem on Wisdom (3:9–4:4). The book concludes with words of encouragement to the exiles (4:15–5–9).

Authorship and Date

This book is a collection of materials written during the period from 160 B.C. to 60 B.C. Some scholars believe Baruch was reworked many times and put into its final form after the destruction of the Temple in A.D. 70.

Historical Setting

The Book of Baruch is set in the period of the prophet Jeremiah and his secretary Baruch around 581 B.C. According to the opening verse, Baruch was in exile in Babylon, although in the canonical Jeremiah Baruch accompanied Jeremiah to Egypt. The book actually speaks to Jews who were living during the period of the Hasmoneans (142–63 B.C.).

Theological Contribution

Jerusalem had fallen into the hands of the enemy, but this book declares that God will not forget His people. The Jewish people are to accept suffering and exile, expecting that God will punish Israel's enemies.

Special Consideration

Baruch 1:15—2:26 is dependent on Daniel 9:1–19. Baruch 3:9—4:4 is dependent on Job 28 and Proverbs 8. Wisdom is praised as being worth more than gold. The lines "[God] found the whole way to knowledge, and gave [Wisdom] to his servant Jacob and to Israel, whom he loved. Afterward she appeared on earth and lived with humankind" (3:36–37, NRSV) was taken by the early church to be a reference to the Incarnation.

The Letter of Jeremiah

Concise Outline

Survey of the Letter of Jeremiah

The Letter of Jeremiah consists of an introduction followed by ten warnings against idolatry. Idols cannot speak (6:8–16), are useless (6:17–23), helpless (6:24–29), have no power of deliverance (6:30–40a), are held in contempt even by the Babylonians (6:40b–44), are but made of wood (6:45–52), cannot establish justice (6:53–56), are easily plundered (6:57–59), are powerless before the elements of nature commanded by God (6:60–65), have no effect on us (6:66–69), and have no more use than a scarecrow, bush, or dead body (6:70–73).

Authorship and Date

The Letter of Jeremiah was written in Hebrew by a Jew living in Babylon around 300 B.C. It was later translated into Greek around 150 B.C.

Historical Setting

From Jeremiah 29:1–28 we know that the prophet Jeremiah did write a letter to the exiles in Babylon after 597 B.C. However, the Letter of Jeremiah was written when Babylon was no longer at the height of power, although there were still traces of its former splendor.

Theological Contribution

As in Jeremiah 10:1–16 and Isaiah 44:9–20, the writer explains clearly that wooden idols are useless and are not to be worshiped instead of Almighty God.

Special Consideration

Compare 6:12, where the author reminds the people that the idols of Babylon "cannot save themselves from rust and corrosion" (NRSV) to Matthew 6:19.

The Prayer of Azariah and the Song of the Three Jews

Concise Outline

Survey of the Prayer of Azariah and the Song of the Three Jews

The author expands the famous story in Daniel 3 about Shadrach, Meshach, and Abednego—the three young Hebrews who were thrown into the fiery furnace by the king of Babylon in the sixth century B.C. Azariah (Abednego) begins to pray while the three young Hebrews are in the fire (vv. 1–22). King Nebuchadnezzar orders the furnace to be stoked further (vv. 23–27). Unharmed, all three begin to sing as they stand in the flames (vv. 28–68).

Authorship, Date, and Historical Setting

It probably was written in Hebrew about 170–165 B.C. by a pious Jew. However, scholars believe that this addition was probably composed on occasion of the persecutions of Antiochus IV Epiphanes on the eve of the Maccabean Revolt.

Theological Contribution

The Prayer of Azariah consists of a confession of the sins of the Jewish people and a petition for deliverance. The Song of the Three Jews is a summons to all the forces of nature and "all people on earth" (v. 60, NRSV) to "Bless the Lord . . . sing praise to him and highly exalt him forever" (NRSV).

Special Consideration

The Song of the Three Jews comes from various passages of the Book of Psalms, especially Psalms 148 and 136.

Susanna

A Concise Outline of Susanna

Survey of Susanna

The story is about a beautiful, virtuous married woman named Susanna, who is falsely accused by two respected elders of the community after she escapes their attempt at rape (vv. 1–27). Susanna is brought to court by the elders on a charge of adultery. She is condemned and sentenced to death (vv. 28–41). She prays to God for vindication. Daniel reopens the case by raising a contradiction in the elders' testimony and proves that the two elders lied. The elders are executed while Susanna returns to her husband Joakim (vv. 42–64).

Authorship and Date

Susanna was written in Hebrew around 95–80 B.C. The author was a Pharisee in Maccabean Israel who was critical of the legal system dominated by the Sadducees.

Historical Setting

The story is set in Babylon amidst the Jewish exiles there in the sixth century B.C. Daniel is still a young man. However, this story challenges the normal method of taking evidence in Jewish courts during the first century B.C.

Theological Contribution

The Book of Susanna emphasizes that God will establish justice, even when it is perverted by religious leaders.

Special Consideration

The Book of Susanna is reminiscent of the story of Joseph and Potiphar's wife (Gen. 39:6–23) and the story of David, Bathsheba, and the prophet Nathan (2 Sam. 11:1—12:25).

Bel and the Dragon

Concise Outline

Survey of Bel and the Dragon

Daniel demonstrates that there is no God other than the Lord God of the Hebrews and that Bel, the supposed god of Babylon, does not exist (vv. 1–22). In this book Daniel also kills a dragon in a clever way (vv. 23–27). The Babylonians are enraged at Daniel and convince the king to have Daniel put in the lion's den for six days. Daniel is miraculously fed by the prophet Habbakuk. The king frees Daniel and praises the one Lord God (vv. 28–42).

Authorship, Date, and Historical Setting

Bel and the Dragon was written by a Jew in Palestine around 150–50 B.C. The story is set late in Daniel's life, when the Persian Cyrus ruled over Babylon after conquering the country in 539 B.C.

Theological Contribution

The author uses Babylonian mythology to declare that the God of the Hebrews can outwit the tricks of the priests of Babylon through the faith of the prophet Daniel. This is the author's way of showing that pagan gods are worshiped because the priests deceive the people and influence the political rulers. Only God is worthy of our praise, because He is a living God.

Special Consideration

The story of Bel is reminiscent of Daniel 3, where the King of Babylon requires worship of the golden statue. The story of Daniel in the lion's den under the Persian ruler Cyrus is reminiscent of Daniel 6. Cyrus's repentance and the Babylonian god Bel are mentioned in Isaiah 45—46. The prophet Habakkuk is introduced into the story for dramatic emphasis.

The First Book of Maccabees

Concise Outline

Authorship and Date

The author was probably a Sadducean Jew living in Jerusalem who supported the Maccabean revolt and the importance of the law of Moses and the Temple of Jerusalem. Some scholars suggest that one of the members of the family of the Maccabees wrote the book, around 90–70 B.C.

Survey of the First Book of Maccabees and Its Historical Setting

The First Book of Maccabees is a history of the struggle of the Jews in Judea under the leadership of one family, the Hasmoneans, from about 175 to 134 B.C. Most of the action took place in and around Jerusalem. The revolt began during the reign of Antiochus IV Epiphanes, the Hellenistic king in Syria, led by the high priest Mattathias from Modein in 167 B.C. (1:1—2:70).

After Mattathias's death in 166 B.C., his third son Judas Maccabeus became the family's most famous leader from 166–160 B.C. During Judas's reign his older brother Eleazer was killed in the battle of Bethzur in 163 B.C. (3:1—9:22).

When Judas died in the battle of Berea, Mattathias' fifth son Jonathan Maccabeus ruled from 160–142 B.C. His oldest brother John was killed by treachery in 159 B.C. Jonathan attempted to form alliances with Rome and Sparta against Syria (9:23—12:53).

When Jonathan died by the treachery of the Syrian general Trypho, Mattathias's second son Simon ruled from 142–134 B.C. The Syrian king permitted Simon to coin his own money, equivalent to a recognition of the independence of Israel. Simon also died by treachery and was succeeded by his son, John Hyrcanus, who ruled from 134–104 B.C. (13:1—16:24).

Theological Contribution

The First Book of Maccabees is striking for not mentioning God. Instead, it uses the name "Heaven."

Special Consideration

The First Book of Maccabees includes a number of valuable authentic documents of the period described in the narrative. Many of the events of the book were retold by the Jewish historian Josephus in the first century A.D.

The Second Book of Maccabees

Concise Outline

Survey of the Second Book of Maccabees

The first part of the book (1:1–2:32) consists of two letters. One of the letters (1:1–10) was from Jews in Jerusalem to Jews in Egypt, telling them how to observe the Jewish holiday of Chanukah (or Hanukkah) which celebrates the cleansing of the Temple under Judas Maccabeus in 164 B.C. The other letter (1:10–2:18) was sent by the same group of Jews in Jerusalem to Aristobulus, a Jewish teacher in Egypt, encouraging him to celebrate the Temple festival.

The second section of the Second Book of Maccabees (3:1–5:27) describes the actions of the good priest Onias and the wicked priest Menelaus, who comes to power by supporting the Syrian king. This is followed by a moving section on the martyrdoms of the elderly scribe Eleazar and the seven brothers and her mother (6:1–7:42). The final section describes the revolt of Judas Maccabeus (8:1–15:39), which is parallel to 1 Maccabees 3:1–7:50. A good description of the celebration of Chanukah (Hanukkah) appears in 10:1–9.

Authorship, Date, and Historical Setting

The Second Book of Maccabees was written in Greek by a Jew of the Pharisaic sect in Alexandria, Egypt, around 110–50 B.C. It is a summary of a five-book history of the Maccabees written by the Jew Jason of Cyrene (see 2:23). In a sense, the Second Book of Maccabees serves as a prelude and a parallel to the First Book of Maccabees.

Theological Contribution

The Second Book of Maccabees has references to God's deliverance that are lacking in the First Book of Maccabees. At several points God miraculously intervenes in the course of events. The theme of the book is that faithful obedience to the Law brings success by God's standards.

Special Considerations

The entire book is important because of its teaching that the world was created "out of nothing" (7:28). There is a clear statement of belief in the resurrection of the dead and in the value of martyrdom (6:1–7:42).

The First Book of Esdras

Concise Outline

Survey of the First Book of Esdras

Included in the First Book of Esdras is a description of the building of the Temple by the returned exiles in Jerusalem and the problems encountered in its reconstruction.

Authorship and Date

The First Book of Esdras was probably written abut 150 B.C., by a zealous Jew in Alexandria, Egypt, who held to the Jewish worship tradition and encouraged others to do the same.

Historical Setting

The First Book of Esdras begins with the Passover celebrated by Josiah, the king of Judah (640–609 B.C.). After Josiah's death in the battle of Megiddo the story continues with the events leading up to the fall of Jerusalem and the deportation of the Jews to Babylon (587 B.C.). Cyrus, the great king of the Medes who freed the Jews from bondage in Babylon in 539 B.C., is also described.

Theological Contribution

The purpose of the First Book of Esdras was to promote the value of worship of the Lord among Jews.

The Prayer of Manasseh

Concise Outline

1. Invocation and Praise to God 1–7
2. Confession of sins 8–12
3. Request for Forgiveness 13
4. Concluding Thanksgiving 14–15

Survey of the Prayer of Manasseh

The outline of the prayer follows a typical outline for a worship service: invocation and praise to God (vv. 1–7), confession of sins (vv. 8–12), a request for forgiveness (v. 13), and a concluding thanksgiving (vv. 14–15).

Authorship, Date, and Setting

The Prayer of Manasseh was written by a pious Jew in Greek between 150 B.C. and 1 B.C.

Manasseh (reigned 687–642 B.C.) was one of the most wicked kings in the history of the southern kingdom of Judah. He burned his sons as offerings (2 Chr. 33:6) and practiced magic. After a humiliating defeat in battle, Manasseh repented of his sin, and God forgave him (2 Chr. 33:10–13). The Prayer of Manasseh supplies the text of the prayer lacking from this account.

Psalm 151

Psalm 151 is a short psalm that is included in the Eastern Orthodox Bible. It originally consisted of two psalms which were written in Hebrew around 150 B.C. by a Jew living in Palestine. These were combined and shortened into the one psalm that we have. Psalm 151 is based on 1 Samuel 16–17. It describes how David, even though the youngest among his brothers, slew the Philistine Goliath by God's help.

The Third Book of Maccabees

Concise Outline

Survey of the Third Book of Maccabees

Ptolemy, upon defeating Antiochus II and seizing control over Israel, attempts to sacrifice in the Temple of Jerusalem but is rebuffed by the high priest Simon (1:1–2:24). Enraged, he orders that the Jews in Egypt be rounded up in the arena to be trampled by elephants (2:25–5:51). The Jewish Priest Eleazer prays to God for deliverance, whereupon two angels drive the elephants away and Ptolemy acknowledges the God of Israel (6:1–7:23).

Authorship, Setting, and Theological Contribution

The Second Book of Maccabees was written by a Jew living in Alexandria, Egypt, during the first century B.C.

The Third Book of Maccabees is set during the rule of Ptolemy IV Philopator, who struggled for control of Palestine with king Antiochus III of Syria at the battle of Raphia, Palestine, in 217 B.C. The book is not strict history, but weaves together actual historical events with legends relating to the Jews in Egypt.

The Third Book of Maccabees stresses God's deliverance of His chosen people Israel from its enemies.

Special Consideration

The story of a pagan king who persecutes the Jewish people and then converts is also found in the Book of Esther and in Daniel 3—4.

The Second Book of Esdras

Concise Outline

Survey of the Second Book of Esdras

The original Hebrew text consists of a series of seven visions to Salatiel, identified with Ezra. The first four visions (3:1—5:20) deal with the providence of God and the fate of the righteous and the wicked. The fifth eagle vision (11:1—12:39) recounts the political history of Rome, with the eagle's wings representing the various Roman emperors. The sixth vision (13:1–58) depicts the Messiah as a man rising from the sea. The seventh vision (14:1–48) recounts how

God divinely re-inspired the Old Testaments writings lost during the Babylonian exile to the prophet Ezra, while also inspiring an additional 70 secret writings (including 2 Esdras).

Authorship and Date

The main portion of the Second Book of Esdras, chapters 3—14, was written in Hebrew during the same period as the Book of Revelation in the New Testament, around A.D. 100, by a Palestinian Jew. Some scholars believe that the eagle vision, the vision of the Messiah, and the vision of Ezra and the Holy Scriptures were written by different authors from the visions of chapters 3—10.

Historical Setting

Salatiel (Shealtiel), the prophet figure of chapters 3—13, was a Jewish exile in Babylon active around 556 B.C. (His son Zerubbabel attempted to restore the Temple of Jerusalem in 515 B.C.) Ezra, on the other hand, who appears in chapters 1—2 and 14, was active in restoring the Temple a century later, in 444 B.C. The actual author of the Second Book of Esdras was disillusioned over the destruction of the Temple of Jerusalem in A.D. 70.

Theological Contribution

The author was puzzled by the apparent evil in a world where God was supposed to be in control. This gloomy book is tied together with a thread of hope. Deliverance for God's people is assured. God is ultimately in control of history, and His Word (in written form) will never disappear.

Special Considerations

Chapters 1—2 were written in Greek by a Christian author around A.D. 150. Its author reflects early Christian views of the end times and refers to several New Testament books.

Chapter 7 gives valuable information on the views of the period on the conscious "intermediate state" of the righteous and the wicked after death and before the resurrection (vv. 36–105).

The Fourth Book of Maccabees

The Fourth Book of Maccabees is a philosophical treatise on martyrdom. It draws on the Greek Stoic philosophy on the need for reason to control the emotions. It was written in the late first century B.C. or early first century A.D. by a Jew living in Alexandria, Egypt, or possibly Antioch, Syria. It gives a clear defense of the doctrine of immortality. It elaborates on the martyrdoms of Eleazer (5:1–7:23), the seven brothers (8:1–14:10), and their mother (14:11–18:24), for refusing to obey the order of Antiochus IV Epiphanes to sacrifice to Greek idols in 167 B.C. It is based on the account of 2 Maccabees 6:1–7:42.

For Further Reading About the Apocrypha

Dentan, Robert C. *The Apocrypha, Bridge of the Testaments.* Greenwich, CT: Seabury Press, 1954.

Goodspeed, Edgar J. *The Story of the Apocrypha.* Chicago: U. of Chicago Press, 1939.

The Holy Bible. New Revised Standard Version with Apocrypha. Nashville: Thomas Nelson, 1990.

Metzger, Bruce M. *An Introduction to the Apocrypha.* New York: Oxford University Press, 1957.

Metzger, Bruce M., and Roland E. Murphy, eds. *The New Oxford Annotated Bible.* New Revised Standard Edition. New York: Oxford University Press, 1991.

Nichelsburg, George W. E. *Jewish Literature Between the Bible and the Mishnah.* Philadelphia: Fortress Press, 1981.

SURVEYING THE BIBLE

Nelson's Quick-Reference Bible Handbook is an ideal resource for an individual or a study group that wants to survey the entire Bible. As leader of such a group, your task is to organize the study, making reading assignments from this book and the Bible, present the appropriate material, and lead the group in its study and discussion. The following practical suggestions should help you in your important role as group study leader.

Preparing for the Study

Before you can lead a group in a survey of the Bible, you should make sure you are well prepared for this important task. For best results, complete the following activities several weeks before the study is scheduled to begin.

1. Preview *Nelson's Quick-Reference Bible Handbook* by checking the contents page and then scanning the material in

quick-read fashion. Note the major divisions of the book as well as the articles and outlines of individual books. This preview should show you how this book is organized and give you a general idea of its contents.

2. Read the book again, slowly and deliberately this time, paying special attention to the articles on individual books in the Bible. Notice that each article includes the following points about a Bible book: (1) authorship and date, (2) historical setting, (3) theological contribution, (4) special considerations, (5) survey (with chart), and (6) outline.

As you read, underline significant information and write notes to yourself about each Bible book in the margins of your book. These will help you review each Bible book quickly when you begin teaching.

3. Check out two or three additional books on the Bible and its message from your local church library or public library. Take time to study these books as part of your general preparation for leading your group.

Pay special attention to these books to such matters as inspiration of the Bible, preservation of the ancient texts of the Bible, the original languages in which the Bible was written, and translation of the Bible into different languages across the centuries. Some supplementary reading on these topics should prepare you thoroughly for this important study.

4. Using large sheets of heavy poster board and a black felt-tip pen, make three posters that list and summarize the 66 individual Bible books under the appropriate major divisions of the Bible to which they belong and another that does the same for the books of the Apocrypha.

- Poster #1 includes the Old Testament Books of the Law, Books of History, and Books of Poetry and Wisdom.
- Poster #2 includes the Old Testament Books of the Major and Minor Prophets and the New Testament Gospels and Acts.

- Poster #3 shows the Epistles of the Apostle Paul and the General Epistles.
- Poster #4 includes the Books of the Apocrypha/ Deuterocanon.

Study these posters carefully and make sure you have the contents of the Bible's major division well in mind before the first session of your study group. Place the posters in a prominent place in your classroom, and refer to them again and again throughout this survey of the Bible.

In addition to making the important preliminary preparations for this study outlined above, you must also decide on a suitable schedule for completing this overview of the Bible. As you think about a schedule for your study group, remember that it is virtually impossible to cover the entire Bible as outlined in this book in just a few study sessions. You will need at least 13 sessions of one to two hours each in order to cover the material adequately and keep the members of your group interested and involved.

On the other hand, don't drag the study on endlessly for two or three years until it becomes boring and burdensome to the group. For the best results, try to finish the study in no more than 52 sessions of one to two hours each. This approach will allow you to cover the entire Bible in a year if your study group meets once a week.

Following are four suggested plans for surveying the Bible with a group. These schedules range from 13 sessions to 52 sessions in length. Choose the plan that meets the unique needs of your group and the time your class members have available to devote to this survey.

No matter which plan you select, make sure the members of your study group are informed about the precise schedule at the beginning of your study. Note specific dates for each session and distribute copies of the schedule. Announce ahead of time the reading assignments which members should complete from their books in preparation for specific sessions. These actions will help keep them excited about this important study from the very first session right on through to the concluding meeting several months later.

1. Schedule for a 13-session Study Plan

Session 1: Introducing The Books of the Law
Session 2: Books of History (Joshua through 2 Samuel)
Session 3: Books of History (1 Kings through Esther)
Session 4: Books of Poetry and Wisdom
Session 5: Books of the Major Prophets
Session 6: Books of the Minor Prophets
Session 7: Books of the Apocrypha
Session 8: Jesus and the Gospels (Matthew, Mark)
Session 9: Jesus and the Gospels (Luke, John)
Session 10: The Book of Acts
Session 11: Paul and His Letters (Romans through Ephesians)
Session 12: Paul and His Letters (Philippians through Philemon)
Session 13: The General Epistles

2. Alternate Schedule for a 13-session Study Plan (Without the Books of the Apocrypha)

Session 1: Introduction
Session 2: In the Beginning (Genesis 1–11)
Session 3: The Age of the Patriarchs (Genesis 12–50)
Session 4: The Exodus (Exodus through Deuteronomy)
Session 5: Occupation of the Land of Canaan (Joshua)
Session 6: The Rule of the Judges (Judges)

3. *Schedule for a 52-session Study Plan*

4. *Schedule for a 26-session Study Plan*

Session 1: Introduction; The Bible and Its Major Divisions
Session 2: Books of the Law (Genesis; Exodus)
Session 3: Law (Leviticus; Numbers; Deuteronomy)
Session 4: Books of History (Joshua; Judges; Ruth)
Session 5: History (1 and 2 Samuel; 1 and 2 Kings; 1 and 2 Chronicles)
Session 6: History (Ezra; Nehemiah; Esther)
Session 7: Books of Poetry and Wisdom (Job; Psalms)
Session 8: Poetry and Wisdom (Proverbs; Ecclesiastes; Song of Solomon)
Session 9: Books of the Major Prophets (Isaiah)
Session 10: Major Prophets (Jeremiah; Lamentations)
Session 11: Major Prophets (Ezekiel; Daniel)
Session 12: Books of the Minor Prophets (Hosea; Joel; Amos)
Session 13: Minor Prophets (Obadiah; Jonah; Micah; Nahum)
Session 14: Minor Prophets (Habakkuk; Zephaniah; Haggai; Zechariah; Malachi)
Session 15: Introduction, The Apocrypha; Tobit—Baruch
Session 16: Letter of Jeremiah—4 Maccabees
Session 17: Introduction to the New Testament; Introduction, Jesus and the Gospels
Session 18: The Synoptic Gospels (Matthew; Mark; Luke)
Session 19: The Fourth Gospel (John)
Session 20: Acts
Session 21: The Epistles of Paul (Romans; 1 and 2 Corinthians)
Session 22: Paul's Epistles (Galatians; Ephesians)
Session 23: Paul's Epistles (Philippians; Colossians; 1 and 2 Thessalonians)
Session 24: Paul's Epistles (1 and 2 Timothy; Titus; Philemon)

Session 25: The General Epistles (Hebrews; James; 1 and
2 Peter; 1, 2, and 3 John; Jude)
Session 26: General Epistles (Revelation); Review and Conclusion

Involving Members of the Study Group

One key to effective group Bible study is involvement of
the entire class in the learning experience. This is particularly
true of a Bible survey project such as this that will last for
several months. You must have high group interaction and
member involvement to keep the people interested and coming back week after week. Following are some practical suggestions for generating this level of involvement among
members of your group.

1. Use this book, *Nelson's Quick-Reference Bible Handbook,* as
a textbook for the class. Make sure every member of the
group has a copy of the book. Make specific reading assignments in the book to support each class session. Each week
ask discussion questions that are drawn directly from the
reading assignment. This will motivate members of the group
to read the assignment and be prepared to contribute their
insights and ideas.

2. Make periodic special assignments to members of the
study group and ask them to share their findings with the
entire class. This survey of the entire Bible, particularly if you
select the 26-week or the 52-week study plan, offers numerous opportunities for members to prepare such special reports. Major Bible personalities such as Abraham, David,
Moses, Jeremiah, the apostle Paul, or Barnabas are ideal subjects for such reports. So are individual books of the Bible and
major biblical events.

3. Use the teaching posters that show books of the Bible
and the Bible's major divisions to help class members get a

visual image of the Bible as a whole and the overall organization of the Scriptures.

By the end of the study, all members of the study group should be able to place the Bible's 66 individual books (and those of the Apocrypha, if you choose to include its books) with the appropriate major sections of the Scripture to which they belong. They should also have a general idea of the theme and contents of each individual book. If you achieve this worthy goal with your class, you will have succeeded in your role as study group leader.

Nelson's Quick-Reference™ Series

Nelson's Quick-Reference™ Bible Concordance
Gives you easy access to over 40,000 key Bible references that are most often sought. Save time and avoid the tedium that goes with wading through long lists of references less sought after. Keyed to the New King James Version, but useful with any.
400 pages / 0-8407-6907-5 / available now

Nelson's Quick-Reference™ Bible Dictionary
More like a "mini-encyclopedia" than a standard dictionary, this compact reference offers an A-Z way to discover fascinating details about the Bible—its characters, history, setting, and doctrines.
784 pages / 0-8407-6906-7 / available now

Nelson's Quick-Reference™ Bible Questions and Answers
Learning is fun, lively, and exciting with the over 6,000 questions and answers covering the whole Bible. Variety keeps interest high—short answer, true/false, multiple choice, fill in the blank, and sentence completion.
384 pages / 0-8407-6905-9 / available now

Nelson's Quick-Reference™ Introduction to the Bible
Introduces the Bible as a whole and describes all its parts from an historical and evangelical theological perspective. Explore the fascinating variety in Scripture—story and song, poetry and prophecy, and more. Discover its divinely revealed answers to the most important questions of life.
approx 400 pages / 0-8407-3206-6 / August, 1993

Nelson's Quick-Reference™ Bible People and Places
From Aaron to Zurishaddain, and from Dan to Beersheba, quickly identify each person and place in the Bible—and many

key events. One list, arranged from A to Z, gives brief descriptions and Scripture references, and tells what the names mean, how to say them, and which refer to the same person or place. Variant spellings make this guide useful with any translation.
approx 400 pages / 0-8407-6912-1 / August, 1993

Nelson's Quick-Reference™ Bible Maps and Charts
Make any Bible a study Bible with this unique collection of maps, book charts, and other visuals that present clear information about Bible people, events, and teachings in ways that heighten your interest, retention, and understanding in Bible study. Seeing it helps you believe it!
approx 300 pages / 0-8407-6908-3 / April, 1994